This book should be returned to any branch of the
~~~~~~~~~~~~~~~~ the date

BACK TO THE FUTURE OF SOCIALISM

Also by Peter Hain

Ad and Wal: Values, duty, sacrifice in apartheid South Africa (2014)

Outside In (2012)

Mandela (2010)

Sing the Beloved Country: The struggle for the new South Africa (1996)

Ayes to the Left (1995)

The Peking Connection (1995)

A Putney Plot? (1987)

Proportional Misrepresentation (1986)

Political Strikes (1986)

Political Trials (1984/1985)

The Democratic Alternative (1983)

Neighbourhood Participation (1980)

Debate of the Decade (ed) (1980)

Policing the Police, volume 2 (ed) (1978)

Policing the Police, volume 1 (ed) (1977)

Mistaken Identity (1976)

Community Politics (ed) (1976)

Radical Regeneration (1975)

Don't Play with Apartheid (1971)

BACK TO THE FUTURE
OF SOCIALISM

Peter Hain

First published in Great Britain in 2015 by

Policy Press
University of Bristol
1-9 Old Park Hill
Bristol BS2 8BB
UK
t: +44 (0)117 954 5940
e: pp-info@bristol.ac.uk
www.policypress.co.uk

North American office:
Policy Press
c/o The University of Chicago Press
1427 East 60th Street
Chicago, IL 60637, USA
t: +1 773 702 7700
f: +1 773-702-9756
e: sales@press.uchicago.edu
www.press.uchicago.edu

© Peter Hain 2015

British Library Cataloguing in Publication Data
A catalogue record for this book is available from the British Library

Library of Congress Cataloging-in-Publication Data
A catalog record for this book has been requested

ISBN 978 1 44732 166 8 hardcover
ISBN 978 1 44732 170 5 ePub
ISBN 978 1 44732 169 9 Kindle

Cover by Soapbox Design.
Front cover image: Getty.
Printed and bound in Great Britain by TJ International, Padstow.
Policy Press uses environmentally responsible print partners.

Contents

What counts in life is not the mere fact
that we have lived. It is what difference we
have made to the lives of others.

Nelson Mandela

Preface

C.P. Snow wrote that political memory lasts about a fortnight. Wrong. Some phrases live on in political life. Anthony Crosland's special adviser from 1972 to 1977, David Lipsey, is the self-proclaimed originator of three: 'the party's over' (1975), 'the winter of discontent' (1978–79), and 'New Labour' (1992).

In his autobiography, *In the Corridors of Power*, David wrote about an idea for a book he had in the 1980s: 'I should perhaps at some point have settled down to write a new *Future of Socialism*. But I had to earn a living and, besides, I had no confidence that I was up to it.'

I know how he felt.

Which is why I am grateful to Roger Berry, Richard Corbett, John Denham, Arnie Graf, Charles Grant, Richard Grayson, Geoff Hodgson, Madeleine Jennings, Andre Karihaloo, Fiona Millar, Greg Power, Nick Tott, Marcus Roberts, Dorothy Smith, Jack Stanley, David Taylor, Derek Vaughan and Matt Ward for their input and assistance; and to Elizabeth Haywood for her incisive comments, corrections and unswerving love. My thanks, too, to Alison Shaw and Sonny Leon for so enthusiastically publishing the book.

I am grateful also to my South Wales Neath constituents who have given me such steadfast loyalty over a quarter of a century – especially my close friend and first agent, Howard Davies, and his successors, Lyn Harper and Cari Morgans. Part of the thinking behind this book has sprung from my life and grassroots involvement in the towns and valley villages of the Neath constituency.

But this book could not have been written without my good friend Phil Wyatt, who has a rare ability: he is an economist who can write readable prose. Since retiring as Research Director at the GMB Union, for some years now he has fed me drafts for articles and speeches – with the same self-effacing modesty he has insisted upon for this book. I am both fortunate and very grateful to him, and so I decided to honour his father in the following way:

On 20 December 1940 the *London Gazette* listed some 3,600 members of Britain's armed services whose names had been 'brought to notice in recognition of distinguished services in connection with operations in the field, March–June 1940'. Heading the list was Vice Admiral Sir Bertram Ramsay who had led Operation Dynamo, the rescue of the British Expeditionary Force from Dunkirk. For organising what Winston Churchill called 'a miracle of deliverance' Ramsay was mentioned in despatches.

Also on the list was Company Quarter Master Sergeant Philip Ernest Wyatt of the Royal Engineers. In the chaotic retreat to Dunkirk, his unit was ordered to render their column of vehicles of no use to the enemy, which they did. Then came a countermanding order. But despite the confusion they made it to the beaches. This was his second mention in despatches for distinguished service with the BEF in France.

Thanks to the bravery of others, including my father-in-law Lieutenant Commander Douglas Haywood who served on one of the Dunkirk rescue ships, Sergeant Wyatt returned to Ramsgate on 31 May 1940, one of 68,000 allied evacuees who made it back to Britain that day. He left the army, with the rank of Captain, in 1945 after 20 years' service, with a long service and good conduct medal and an army pension. He died aged 74 on Friday 13 June 1980.

Peter Hain
Ynysygerwn, Neath
November 2014

INTRODUCTION

Back to the future of socialism

The Labour Party is a democratic socialist party. It says so in its rule book and on the back of every membership card. Democratic socialism is what the party believes in. But if you ask anyone what that means today, expect an uncertain response. The people's flag may be deepest red but for the 1994–2010 New Labour period it flew from a pale grey masthead. What was therefore once distinct about the Labour Party became a matter of doubt, with even the party itself unsure what it stood for.

The uncertainty crept in well before the 2008 banking crisis exposed the limitations of New Labour's light-touch, low-tax approach to economic management. Dealing with the credit crunch required a rapid change of stance. Labour bailed out bust banks to save the financial system from collapse and took strong fiscal and monetary steps to fight recession and get the economy growing again.

But although these measures worked, they meant big increases in government borrowing and national debt, providing the pretext for leading supporters of neoliberal economics who share an ideology of small government to implement severe public spending cuts and shrink the size of the state.

In Britain – as across the world, notably continental Europe – the left struggled to offer a coherent response, instead slipstreaming the centre-right parties in their call for huge cuts. But that just meant heading down the same austerity road at a slower pace, when (as Keynes showed in the 1930s) getting the economy back on the growth path was always a surer way to sort out the public finances.

Even before the global banking crisis, governments of the democratic left were equally hesitant in responding to, and surviving in, the new world order that followed the end of the Cold War and the development of a global economy. In Britain, New Labour took office in 1997 on a landslide vote of hope but departed in 2010 on a humiliating vote of distrust without ever really changing the basis of the system we inherited. Despite the cataclysmic failure of neoliberalism which the 2008 global banking crisis represented, it hardly incited a resurgence of democratic socialism.

That may be because of a lack of self-confidence by those preaching the democratic socialist message. Some tacked to the neoliberal wind. Others were stuck mouthing old slogans as society moved on, around and past them. Ideologies always need to be interpreted anew to fit contemporary circumstances because society itself is always changing, especially during times of economic upheaval. Political parties have continually to translate their basic beliefs into updated practical policies, spelling out what they stand for and where their priorities lie. Sometimes they make a poor fist of it, as most centre-left parties have done over the past decade or so. This causes their fundamental motivation to be called into question by voters in general, and not just the ones who dismiss party promises as tall stories conjured up by politicians who write their speeches using fictionaries, not dictionaries. And by members who feel their party has drifted away from their values and hopes.

The spirit and soul of the Labour Party

A milestone in the Labour Party's history is in 2018, its centenary. A hundred years earlier the First World War had transformed Britain. The Edwardian era was on its way out, and people demanded something better – including homes fit for heroes. They needed to know what each party could offer once peace came.

In response the Labour Party adopted in 1918 a new constitution and a fresh policy programme for postwar reconstruction. Entitled *Labour and the new social order*, it clarified what objectives the party would pursue and whose interests it would promote, ostensibly removing any ambiguity about what Labour stood for or whose side it was on. But Sidney Webb, the leading Fabian who helped write both the constitution and the policy programme, attached more significance to what had really inspired them. He declared that 'the programme of the Labour Party is, and will probably remain, less important ... than the spirit underlying the programme, that spirit which gives any party its soul'.[1]

This book is about the spirit that gives the Labour Party its soul, the core values and fundamental democratic socialist purposes that Labour exists to promote and which attract and unite Labour supporters. The reason for writing it stems from the same concern that prompted Anthony Crosland's classic text, *The Future of Socialism*, in 1956: that during a long period in office Labour had somehow lost its soul and had yet to rediscover it.

Loss of national office always comes as a shock to leaders and followers alike, Crosland summing up the reaction to the fall of the 1945–51 Labour government: 'No one who has observed the Party since 1951, furiously searching for its lost soul, can have failed to sense a mood of deep bewilderment,' he wrote. [2] That ongoing confusion among Labour supporters after 1951 was echoed half a century later in Roy Hattersley's frank indictment of the 2010 defeat: 'The party not only failed to set out a clear and coherent idea of what it proposed to do. It was not even sure about the purpose of its existence.'[3]

Crosland's response to 1951 was to develop his 'revisionist' theory of socialism, what today we call democratic socialism or 'social democracy'. By freeing Labour from past fixations that social change had rendered redundant, and by offering fresh objectives to replace those which had already been achieved or whose relevance had faded over time, Crosland showed how socialism made sense in modern society.

By giving traditional Labour values a contemporary appeal he gave the party a controversial fresh focus, reviving its spirit and restoring its impatience for progress. Crosland's approach – essentially one in which the state sought to spread the benefits of economic growth within the capitalist framework, and without challenging it – provided much of the basis for Labour's policy programme both in opposition and in government from the late 1950s, including its New Labour period from 1994 until the global economic crisis of 2008.

Labour's response to numbing defeat in May 2010 was to elect a new leader who insisted on a fundamental rethink, not simply of policy but of the party's deeper purpose. Ed Miliband believed that the sheer scale of the defeat raised fundamental questions about what Labour stood for, even what socialism offered, and he launched an immediate review to take stock of the party's situation.

Part of this was the Refounding Labour project which he asked me to chair and which reported in 2011. It was as frank an analysis of itself as the party had ever published, and began by acknowledging that since 1997 thousands of councillors, over 200,000 members and 5 million voters had been lost. Our activist base had been severely depleted and disillusionment in the membership was widespread. The world had changed since 1951 but the dilemma facing the Labour Party had returned. Voters and members alike were uncertain what Labour stood for, unsure whose side it was on, and unconvinced about where it was heading. While navigators are never lost, they sometimes become temporarily uncertain of their position. If Labour had not lost its soul it certainly seemed bereft of reference points from which to chart its course.

That was not just a reaction to our general election defeat. The signs had surfaced well before Labour lost power after 13 years – by far its longest ever period in office. Six months after taking over from Tony Blair, Gordon Brown was told candidly by his pollster Deborah Mattinson in December 2007 how voters viewed his new government: 'They do not know what it stands for and there is no sense of the direction it is heading in.'[4]

Whether Labour had indeed been losing its soul was examined by Eric Shaw in his 2007 review of the fundamental purposes and core values that the party stood for during its 'New Labour' period. He assessed New Labour's record against the standard set by *Labour's Aims*. That was Hugh Gaitskell's proposed revision in 1960 of Clause IV of the 1918 party constitution and he encapsulated Tony Crosland's restatement of Labour values.

Gaitskell proposed the Labour Party stood for

> social justice, for a society in which the claims of those in
> hardship or distress come first; where the wealth produced

4

by all is fairly shared among all; where differences in rewards depend not upon birth or inheritance but on the effort, skill and creative energy contributed to the common good; and where equal opportunities exist for all to live a full and varied life.

He downplayed the pursuit of material wealth, rejecting selfishness and competitive rivalry in favour of fellowship, cooperation and service.[5]

Shaw concluded that New Labour had displayed a firm commitment to social justice by putting the claims of those in hardship or distress first and alleviating poverty among society's most vulnerable members, promoting opportunities for all and boosting public services. To this extent he found that Labour's soul remained intact. But he also found that 'the values of competition, individual self-assertion and "entrepreneurialism", and not "fellowship, co-operation and service" are those that New Labour extols … To this extent Labour has lost its soul.'

Back to the Future of Socialism argues that New Labour fell short of the standard set by Tony Crosland in 1956 for building what he called a socialist society. It attempts to dispel doubts felt inside and outside the Labour Party about what it stands for and where it is heading. By reappraising Crosland's original criteria and setting them in a current context it redefines Labour's future up to 2020 and beyond.

It argues that the kind of capitalism we face today is a more integrated, more unstable and more unfair system than Crosland's generation ever anticipated: productive but prone to paralysis, dynamic but discriminatory. It is one whose self-destructive tendencies require far more radical responses than the neoliberal economic orthodoxy that followed the banking crisis could ever provide. Responses that pose acute challenges to a Labour Party intent on getting the economy growing again, and keeping it on the growth path, while putting the public finances back in order.

This book agrees with Thomas Piketty that since the 1980s capitalism has reverted to type and revealed an inbuilt tendency to generate shocking degrees of inequality in wealth and income, but one which democracy can control by placing the general interest ahead of private interests. He demonstrated that 60 per cent of the increase in US national income after 1977 went to just 1 per cent of earners, the top 10th of that 1 per cent did better still and the top 100th of the 1 per cent did best of all.[6] But unlike Piketty, whose unconvincing answer to slow growth and increasing inequality is a global wealth tax and an 80 per cent top rate of income tax, *Back to the Future of Socialism* provides a practical political alternative.

By developing a fresh perspective on the purpose and role of government in what conventional wisdom determines must be an era of austerity, the book explores how Labour must change, both by adopting a new policy programme and by becoming a different type of political party, in order to win and implement that vision. It is a vision of a pro-European party committed to progressive internationalism that tackles all the big challenges to humankind, above all climate change. It confronts the neoliberalism of recent decades – an ideology favouring market forces wherever possible and tolerating state regulation only where absolutely necessary. Although that same ideology caused the banking crisis, it has clung on nevertheless, as if somehow it were not the very root of the problem all along.

Back to the Future of Socialism takes on the fundamental choice facing democratic politics today: between the right's insistence on minimalist government and the left's belief in active government; between the right's insistence on a free market free-for-all, and the left's belief in harnessing markets for the common good.

Echoed by a predominantly compliant media, the right's bullishness has been breath-taking. Having in 2007 publicly backed Labour's spending plans with a pledge to maintain them until beyond the 2010 election, Conservative leader David Cameron suddenly switched after the crisis to announce in October 2009: 'It is more government that got us into this mess.'

He made no mention of irresponsible bankers, still less of the failure of politicians to control them. The entire global banking crash was apparently nothing to do with Big Finance: it was all the fault of Big Government. The cause was too much public spending – not too little public regulation. In November 2013 Cameron as Prime Minister went even further, pledging at the Lord Mayor's Banquet to build 'a leaner, more efficient state. We need to do more with less. Not just now but permanently'. He announced that if they were still in power the Tories would maintain and deepen their already significant cuts until at least 2020. Obviously no one on the left seriously advocates a 'fatter' more 'inefficient' state, but his case went to the heart of the fundamental argument about our future.

Undoubtedly, governments across the world gradually allowed the financial system over a 30-year period to get out of control and become a law unto itself. But the real culprit was an obsession with keeping government at bay, with making non-interventionism, rather than interventionism, the watchword. Takeovers and mergers led to banks so big they couldn't be allowed by government to fail. Bankers bent rules to lend ever more riskily without anything like enough capital cover, until it all unravelled to catastrophic effect. This new, integrated, almost impenetrably complex structure of global finance was a world away from Crosland's day. In truth – at the very least in terms of finance – governments were too small and too passive, *not* too big and too active.

Back to the Future of Socialism explains why and offers a perspective aimed at reinvigorating the left's self-confidence and self-belief. But – except perhaps on the fundamental question of the economy – it is not intended as a mini-manifesto covering every policy area. Rather, it is an *argument*, a broad ideological case that democratic socialism not neoliberalism retains its compelling primacy, remains the calling for our age, and provides the way forward as people seek answers to the challenges both they and our societies face.

CHAPTER 1

The Crosland agenda

Even at the height of New Labour's ascendancy in 1998, Tony Crosland's writing still carried significance. As the Labour historian Ben Pimlott wrote then: 'To describe yourself as a "Crosland socialist" still carries meaning ... For if much of the Crosland canon seems dated, there remains a core which has increased in relevance with the passage of time.'[1]

In 2013 David Sainsbury, though very much a New Labourite, argued: 'the recent Labour government suffered from not having a credible, alternative political economy to neoliberalism ... no one had produced a new progressive political economy since Tony Crosland wrote *The Future of Socialism* in 1956.'[2] Sainsbury argued that New Labour settled for 'neoliberalism plus an enhanced welfare state' and by implication owed little to Crosland – although, like many others, Sainsbury oversimplified his message, reducing Crosland's view of social justice to one word, equality, which he dismissed as not being useful in practical politics.[3]

So how important was Tony Crosland to understanding Labour's soul, and what if anything has he got to offer that can help Labour's future and Britain's future?

Crosland's most important ministerial achievements were probably in the 1960s. He championed both comprehensive secondary education over a bitterly divisive system of '11-plus' selection, and a binary system of higher education which, alongside traditional universities, featured over 30 polytechnics offering professional vocational education and academic education.

Perhaps more pertinent to Labour's future – and key to an alternative to contemporary austerity, the central thrust of this book – was his opposition within two separate Labour Cabinets to what he saw as two fatal misjudgements that undermined Labour's mission by curtailing economic growth. First, in the mid-1960s, what he believed were futile efforts by Harold Wilson, George Brown and Jim Callaghan to shore up sterling and stave off devaluation by deflating the economy through tax rises, a temporary surcharge on imports, and public spending cuts – rendering Labour's 4 per cent annual economic growth target unattainable.

Crosland insisted that Britain faced a chronic balance of payments deficit, with imports far in excess of exports, and he was emphatic that this could not be corrected at the prevailing exchange rate, because there was a fundamental lack of UK competitiveness. But Jim Callaghan, Labour's Chancellor of the Exchequer, ignored Crosland's challenge to Treasury orthodoxy and tried to defend the exchange rate with a series of deflationary measures including tax increases in July 1965. A year later that desperate, flailing policy culminated – as Crosland had feared – in a £500 million package of further tax rises and spending cuts plus a six-month wage and price freeze in July 1966 which completely removed the ground from under Labour's National Plan for growth. Eventually the still deteriorating balance of payments forced the government to accept the inevitable, and devalue the pound in November 1967, vindicating Crosland's original assessment.

Nine years later, this time with Jim Callaghan as Prime Minister, and again from within the Cabinet, Crosland argued in November 1976 that the public spending cuts proposed by Labour's Chancellor Denis Healey as part of the Treasury's plan for a loan from the International Monetary Fund (IMF) were excessive and would entail needless sacrifice. He called instead for a much smaller package of cuts, passionately insisting that government borrowing would fall if the economy were allowed to grow rather than be held back by an overly tight fiscal squeeze. Again, Crosland was vindicated because, nearly three years later, that squeeze propelled Labour out of office after strikes against cuts in the infamous 'winter of discontent'.

The Crosland thesis

But Crosland's most lasting significance to the Labour Party stems from *The Future of Socialism*, his influential 1956 restatement of what the party then stood for. He began by pointing out that, despite severe postwar austerity, the degree of social change brought in by the 1945–51 Labour government had exceeded even the most optimistic expectations of 1930s Labour radicals like G.D.H. Cole, Douglas Jay and Evan Durbin. The world had changed. Keynes with his potent economic management, and Beveridge with his welfare system to underpin it, had helped foster a social revolution. Labour's beliefs needed to be brought up to date and to take account of Britain's new circumstances and her brighter economic prospects.

Tony Crosland argued that many of Labour's traditional aims had already been achieved. As his political adviser David Lipsey recorded:

> he believed that capitalism had changed radically. It had evolved from the crude exploitative beast of Victorian times to the shareholder capitalism of the 1950s, where civilised companies worked in civilised ways. It would be interesting to have his take on the new and rawer capitalism which emerged between the election of Margaret Thatcher and the financial crash of 2008.[4]

Primary poverty had largely been eliminated due to the 'Beveridge revolution' and Labour's creation of the welfare state; full employment had been established with the adoption of Keynesian fiscal and monetary policies; living standards were rising rapidly as the economy grew; and failing private utilities had been taken into public ownership.

Some Labour aims had lost their former appeal, like the Old Left's threats to abolish private property, when taxation could deliver a fairer distribution of income from capital. Other traditional Labour policies had been superseded by more effective means (for example, trade unions could provide protection at work without some notional system of workers' control intrinsic to G.D.H. Cole's self-governing guilds, which in Crosland's view had been rendered impractical by economies of large-scale production and technical complexity).

For Crosland, the roots of democratic socialist belief lay not in narrow commitments like 'public ownership of the means of production' (as in Clause IV of the 1918 Labour Party constitution) but in something far wider, something summed up in Clause V: 'the Political Social and Economic emancipation of the People and more particularly of those who depend directly upon their own exertions by hand or brain for the means of life'. Socialism for him was essentially libertarian (but not in the modern right-wing, laissez-faire sense, rather in the socialist sense). It was about freedom.

Crosland argued that Labour's fundamental purpose embraced a wide set of moral values which he labelled the five basic socialist aspirations:

- a protest against poverty;
- a concern for social welfare and the interests of the disadvantaged in particular;
- a belief in greater equality and a classless society;
- support for cooperation and fraternity over competition and self-interest; and
- a protest against capitalism's tendency towards mass unemployment.

He saw economic growth as the key to realising all five aims and the state as pivotal in fostering that growth and delivering the requisite social policies, using collective power to promote and protect both individual rights and the common good.

This was nearly 20 years before the Club of Rome published their controversial book *Limits to Growth* arguing that economic growth could not continue forever as the world would run out of natural resources, especially oil. It was well before talk of climate change or a green revolution and Crosland could not have foreseen the environmental challenges we now face. When he served as Secretary of State for the Environment from 1974 to 1976 his priorities were housing and taking development land into public ownership, not decarbonising the energy sector and green jobs.

Most important to his mid-1950s thesis, Crosland expected poverty and unemployment to be conquered, thanks to economic growth and Keynesian full employment policies pursued by governments of either major party. In 1956 – and a year before Harold Macmillan claimed that 'most of our people have never had it so good' – Tony Crosland coined the phrase 'prosperity is here to stay', such was his confidence in Britain's prospects for full employment and rapid growth.

However, while he saw scope for further state action to improve social welfare, promote cooperation (especially at work) and achieve greater equality, Crosland also saw limits to what could be achieved by 'Keynes-plus-modified-capitalism'. He recognised explicitly that new social problems were now emerging, like mental illness and child neglect, which were unrelated to material poverty and which warranted an even higher priority than greater equality. At the same time he was also confident that popular support for the full employment welfare state had obliged the Conservative Party to learn to live with the new social framework: the Tories, he believed, had been forced to accommodate the post-Second World War settlement.

However, when a new edition of *The Future of Socialism* appeared in 1964 Crosland acknowledged that he had been too optimistic about growth in the Anglo-Saxon economies, especially Britain and America, which had failed to realise their growth potential and been outpaced by Japan and West Germany. Thirty years after Crosland first wrote, and a decade after Margaret Thatcher took office, Bryan Gould argued that Crosland's 'comfortable certainties seem not so much misplaced as laughable'. Britain's economic experience in the 1970s and 1980s showed that the

> Croslandite faith that we had discovered the secret of sustainable growth was misplaced. The British economy, notwithstanding the short-term benefits of North Sea oil, is no nearer to resolving the endemic problems of inflation, trade deficits and declining competitiveness that were already becoming apparent when Crosland was writing ... Inequality and poverty have both increased. The advance of the public sector has been not only halted but reversed. The Welfare State has been weakened and

undermined ... capitalist ethics of ... laissez-faire are rampant. The trade unions have been emasculated and sidelined ... Most significant, the unemployment that Crosland so confidently regarded as a thing of the past, has not only re-emerged in greater dimensions than before; it has subsisted for a decade, and reversed all the advances in the condition of labour that Crosland had identified as a consequence of full employment.

Gould added that Crosland's prism was a domestic one and took no account of Britain's place in the world economy. But by the late 1980s all that had changed with the internationalisation of capital, including, at a European level, UK membership of a much expanded European Community.[5] Reasonable points these may have been, but Gould's comprehensive dismissal of Crosland's analysis is less convincing in the light of Labour's subsequent success between 1997 and 2008 in cutting child and pensioner poverty, achieving year-on-year growth, renewing much of Britain's public infrastructure and raising UK employment to record levels.

Meanwhile Marxist critics like Ralph Miliband asserted that this only added to the reasons why Crosland's analysis was untenable. They denounced what historian John Gray has summarised as 'Crosland's vision of a domesticated and pacified capitalism'.[6]

Ralph Miliband dismissed leaders of social democracy like Crosland as incapable of delivering anything more than marginal change due to the tendency to compromise that is the essence of parliamentary politics. 'They are the willing managers of capitalism and so steeped in its system of thought that they find no moral difficulty in this role. Not only do these leaders not believe in radical and structural change: they are in fact actively opposed to it.'[7] However, since Miliband also dismissed the creation of the National Health Service and social insurance as 'ransom' rather than radicalism,[8] it is difficult to gauge what he would have regarded as radical change: he was strong on critical analysis but weak on practical prescription.[9]

Ralph Miliband also underestimated parliamentary democracy's ability to deliver fundamental change. He was blind to the refusal of working-class Labour supporters to back revolutionary change and even their reluctance to back non-violent direct action except – perhaps – for tightly specified purposes, like the 1971–72 Upper Clyde Shipbuilders sit-in and the 1969–70 anti-apartheid Stop the Seventy Tour campaign to prevent a visit by South Africa's cricket team.

Above all, Miliband ignored the ability of West European market economies, tempered by varying degrees of state action, to deliver economic growth, compared with the much poorer performance of centrally planned East European countries which were *less than 20 per cent* as productive. Markets are essential, as the comparison in the table between Eastern block countries and social democratic states in Europe demonstrates.[10]

Table 1: An East–West comparison in GDP per capita before the fall of the Iron Curtain

East block Soviet-style economy	GDP per capita ($)	Matched West block social democracy	GDP per capita ($)	Percentage gap
Russia	2,340	Finland	19,300	88%
Hungary	3,350	Austria	23,510	86%
Czech Republic	2,710	Germany	23,560	88%
Poland	2,260	Sweden	24,740	91%

Source: J. Bradford DeLong, 'Lecture notes for economics 2', 29 January 2014, University of California at Berkeley.

However, Crosland's confidence that economic growth would deliver most of what the Labour Party stood for allowed the other aspects of his thinking to slip out of view. It is the commitment to greater equality that has proved most distinctive and most enduring about Crosland's view of Labour's purpose. Looking back, he wrote in 1974:

> Socialism, in our view, was basically about equality. By equality, we meant more than a meritocratic society of equal opportunities in which the greatest rewards would go to those with the most fortunate genetic endowments and family background; we adopted the

'strong' definition of equality – what Rawls subsequently called the 'democratic' as opposed to 'liberal' conception. We also meant more than a simple (not that it has proved simple in practice) redistribution of income. We wanted a wider social equality embracing also the distribution of property, the educational system, social-class relationships, power and privilege in industry – indeed all that was enshrined in the age-old socialist dream of a more 'classless society'.[11]

Commenting on that, Lipsey adds:

At the same time, his egalitarianism was never intended to lead to the authoritarianism typical of eastern European communist states ... he abhorred communism even more than he abhorred the inequalities of contemporary Britain. Indeed he went so far as to reject even traditional Fabianism ... and its addiction to bureaucratic remedies for society's ills ... Crosland believed in the highest sustainable level of public expenditure. However he was not in favour of public expenditure per se. Rather he favoured public expenditure so constructed as to do most to help the poor and least to benefit the middle and upper classes. This, for him, was what Labour governments were chiefly for.[12]

This point was illustrated in February 2012 by a brief exchange between David Miliband and Labour's former deputy leader Roy Hattersley which focused attention momentarily on what the Labour Party should stand for today, and which also showed how attempts by staunch Crosland supporters to distil the essence of his views have oversimplified them and thereby distorted today's debate about where Labour's true purpose lies.

David Miliband had labelled as 'Reassurance Labour' an article by Roy Hattersley and Dr Kevin Hickson of Liverpool University welcoming the election of David's brother, Ed Miliband, their 'candidate of conviction', as Labour leader.[13] They argued that Labour should base its policies clearly on genuine social democratic values, 'particularly the pursuit of greater equality and the freedom which it provides', and that the party should accept that the state has a crucial role to play in putting social democracy into practice.

They saw consistency between Ed Miliband's stance – that Labour could win power through a clear commitment to social democratic ideals – and Hugh Gaitskell's approach, which combined practical answers to current problems with a clear ideological commitment to equality. Although at the time Gaitskell was seen by the left inside and outside the party as a Labour right-winger, his vision encapsulated the restatement of Labour values provided by Tony Crosland.

The thrust of David Miliband's criticism was that Hattersley and Hickson had overlooked the limitations of an unreformed state, that equality should take into account issues like merit, reward and responsibility, and that Labour must make a convincing case for economic growth.[14]

In their respective ripostes both Hattersley and Hickson argued that Labour should have a single overall aim: 'its ideological objective should be a more equal society … and state power is essential to its achievement', according to Hattersley;[15] 'the fundamental purpose of a Labour government is to achieve greater equality … the state is the only thing which can get us out the economic mess', according to Hickson.[16]

But, although Ed Miliband continuously pointed to widening inequality, the Hattersley/David Miliband debate about Labour's principles and purposes became subsumed within the more immediate question of how a Labour government could get the economy growing again and how the public finances could be managed in the years beyond.

For today the 'age of abundance' that Crosland forecast in the 1950s – and that Britain seemed briefly to experience under Labour between 2000 and 2008 – has been replaced by 'an age of austerity'. An age of squeezed living standards and public spending cuts. An age which challenges Labour to spell out the future of democratic socialism for Britain in conditions far removed from those which anyone expected before the global financial crisis plunged the economy into recession. And an age which requires an alternative to the suffocating and disastrous grip of neoliberal orthodoxy.

CHAPTER 2

New Labour, Crosland and the crisis

Despite huge misgivings about his suitability for the job, virtually all of Gordon Brown's parliamentary colleagues, myself included, nominated him to succeed Tony Blair as Labour Party leader and Prime Minister in June 2007 because his position was unassailable – largely due to the evident success of New Labour's economic policies under his Chancellorship since 1997.

Britain appeared to have turned into a 'Goldilocks economy', one which had broken free from the cycle of boom and bust and which grew inexorably at a steady pace, with low inflation, low interest rates and record employment levels. One which could afford to cut poverty, expand the welfare state and improve living standards. One, in fact, rather like that envisaged by Tony Crosland.

Yet Labour had lost nearly 1,000 council seats in the English and Scottish local elections of 2006–07 and four seats in the 2007 Welsh Assembly elections. If the UK economy was doing so well why was it bearing such poor political fruit? Presumably past Labour supporters were sharing in the gains from growth, so why were they giving up on the party in such numbers? It was a quandary that the elections for a new Labour leadership team never adequately addressed as the party basked in the transition from Blair to Brown.

In his final budget as Chancellor in March 2007 Gordon Brown planned to meet his 'golden rule' – to borrow only to invest over the economic cycle – by slowing the annual rise in public spending over the next three years to just 2 per cent. This was half that achieved since April 1999 when New Labour broke free from the Tory spending ceilings that they had promised to abide by during their first two years in office, but still higher than that delivered by the Tories between 1979 and 1997.

Ten years of steady economic growth had pushed total UK employment to record heights, with 3 million net extra jobs, despite the number of manufacturing jobs falling from 4.5 million in 1997 to only 3 million in 2007. Consumer spending had been growing strongly for years, albeit against a backdrop of increasing household debt. House prices had boomed, making many lucky homeowners feel better off. The pound sterling had risen above the $2 mark for the first time since 1992, making travel budgets stretch a lot further on foreign holidays, adding to the sense of well-being. One week before becoming Prime Minister Gordon Brown congratulated Britain's financial services sector for being at 'the beginning of a new golden age for the City of London'.

Investor confidence was high, partly because Britain's national debt was low. As a proportion of national income it had fallen under Labour from 42 per cent in 1997 to 38 per cent in 2007 – below that of France, Germany, the US, Italy or Japan. Over the period 2000 to 2007 the UK overall budget deficit as a proportion of GDP was only 1.7 per cent, lower than that for Germany (2.3 per cent), the US (2.5 per cent), France (2.8 per cent), or Italy (3.0 per cent).[1] Indeed, the UK's annual budget deficit was well within the 3 per cent limit set by the European Union's Stability and Growth Pact.

Contrary to the subsequent amnesic trashing of Labour's record by both the Tories and the Liberal Democrats, no one was particularly bothered about the level of government spending or public sector borrowing. The consensus was that the UK economy was in fine shape and the future looked bright.

Then came the crisis

That's how things looked in June 2007 just as the international economy felt the first tremors from a series of financial shockwaves. The ensuing global banking crisis caused the world's financial system to seize up almost completely, threatened a world depression as bad as in the 1930s, and destabilised the public finances of nation states big and small.

It started in the US when investment bank Bear Stearns confirmed that two of its hedge funds were in difficulty due to a downgrading of their mortgage-based bonds as borrowers fell behind on their mortgage repayments. In August 2007 BNP Paribas of France suspended three of its funds dealing in mortgage debt. Signs of financial distress began to surface elsewhere, in Germany at IKB Deutsche Industriebank and Commerzbank, in Switzerland at Credit Suisse, and in the UK at Northern Rock in September 2007.

Evidence mounted that banks had been lending recklessly for years, manipulating risky gambles into what looked like safe bets and masking their financial affairs behind obscure off-balance-sheet devices. All that had left them overly reliant on debt capital borrowed from other financial institutions and with too thin a safety margin of equity capital from shareholders to act as a cushion against losses.

Interbank lending began to dry up as banks held onto their cash in an atmosphere of uncertainty in which no one knew who held which dodgy assets, who was exposed to how much risk and who could be relied on to repay their debts. Central banks around the world pumped cash into their banking systems, to boost liquidity and maintain the flow of credit on which business activity depends.

By October 2007 banks all over the world were admitting to huge financial losses linked to mortgage-backed securities. In the US initial reports of losses by the big banks amounting to $20 billion were quickly revised up to $45 billion. Equally shocking losses were reported by the Royal Bank of Scotland in the UK, Nomura in Japan, Deutsche Bank in Germany and Credit Suisse in Switzerland.

Some banks sought safety by agreeing to be taken over by bigger rivals, like Bear Stearns in the US. Others frantically sought massive injections of fresh capital – sometimes as investments by billionaires or by foreign state-owned sovereign wealth funds, sometimes as bailouts by their own governments, but hardly ever by abandoning bonus payments or cancelling dividend payments and using the money saved to strengthen their balance sheets.

The crisis came to a head in September 2008 with the collapse of American bank Lehman Brothers, closely followed by a $180 billion bailout by the US taxpayer of insurance company AIG. It had guaranteed billions of dollars' worth of securities held by the big banks, banks which faced crippling losses if AIG collapsed.

Across the world nation states found extraordinary resources to bolster their banking systems. By 2010 the British government had supported UK banks by buying bank shares, providing loans and offering guarantees which together totalled £512 billion – five times the annual cost of the NHS.[2]

By 2012 the gross cost to the taxpayers of direct support to the financial sector had reached phenomenal levels: in the UK 6.7 per cent of GDP (or £100 billion), in the US 4.8 per cent, in Belgium 7.4 per cent, in Germany 12.8 per cent, in the Netherlands 14.6 per cent and in Ireland fully 40.5 per cent.[3]

But even this gargantuan support did not work. Desperate attempts to calm panicking financial markets, first by central banks pumping cash into their banking systems and cutting short-term interest rates, then by governments steering huge sums of taxpayers' money into recapitalising bank balance sheets, could not stop a collapse of confidence. Economies sunk into recession as firms and families cut back on their spending. Business investment and consumer spending fell, tax revenues collapsed and government borrowing soared. Global output and world trade began falling faster even than during the start of the 1930s Great Depression.

The economic growth about which Tony Crosland had been so confident, and upon which his concept of a civilised society depended, first stalled, then went into reverse as the British economy slid into recession and UK national income fell back to its 2006 level. Real living standards began to drop as short-time working and redundancies spread throughout the UK economy.

The financial crisis had suddenly rendered invalid the optimistic assumptions which underlay Crosland's vision for Britain's future: no economic growth, no full employment, and no booming tax revenues with which to pay for improving public services. Instead, higher welfare bills as jobs were lost, and massive pressure on the public finances.

Labour's response

Whatever his other shortcomings as Prime Minister, this was Gordon Brown's finest hour. Indeed, without his intuitive understanding of the problem and his deep knowledge of political and economic history, it is doubtful if Britain – even the world – would have emerged without a deep recession becoming a grim depression.

Under Brown, Labour understood that it was a failure of governments to act that had turned a downturn into depression in the 1930s, and accordingly, to stop a slide into slump in 2008–09, it took strong fiscal action.

The government doubled public investment from £27 billion in 2006–07 to £50 billion in 2009–10, the highest for over 30 years, by bringing forward spending from future years. It also introduced a £25 billion fiscal stimulus in 2009 when the economy was at its weakest, and allowed the 'automatic stabilisers' to operate – permitting welfare spending to rise as unemployment went up and accepting higher government borrowing as tax revenue tailed off – to offset the collapse in private sector spending. There was no other way of preventing a catastrophic action replay of the 1930s.

After 2011, when recovery should have been well under way, Labour planned a three-year public spending standstill, a pause before spending could grow again. Within that standstill there could have been scope for current spending to rise, albeit only slowly in order to keep the budget deficit in check, as public investment fell back from its peak.

Labour planned to halve government borrowing by 2014, a cut of £75 billion, and bring the budget back into balance by 2018, by when the economy would be safely returned to its long-term growth path. The economic crisis brought on by irresponsible bank lending would have cost the UK economy a decade of damage and years of fiscal frustration. But Britain would have got through it. Because of Labour's 2009 stimulus the economy began to recover, nearing a 2 per cent annual growth rate by the second quarter of 2010. Employment rose and, with interest rates cut to a historic low and inflation also low, Britain was inching back into business.

Other governments took action on a similar scale to stimulate their economies. In January 2009 the German government adopted a two-year €50 billion stimulus package and in February 2009 the American Congress approved a $787 billion stimulus to kick-start growth.

All this was delivered by the extra government borrowing subsequently attacked as venal by the Conservatives and their neoliberal acolytes. Yet, as the IMF acknowledged in 2010, the worldwide increase in government budget deficits following the global credit crunch had staved off an economic calamity. Without it the world economy would have plunged into freefall. This was testimony to the validity of Keynesian economics and the vigour of Gordon Brown and Alistair Darling's leadership, especially at the G20 summits in November 2008 and April 2009.[4] As Gordon Brown remarked of agreement on the $1 trillion plan for ending the global financial crisis: 'The G20 had averted a second global depression.'[5]

But the two of them were out of office by the time of the G20 Toronto Declaration in June 2010 which switched the priority away from promoting economic recovery and towards faster 'fiscal consolidation' (the technocratic term for cuts). The advanced economies agreed to at least halve public sector deficits by 2013 and to stabilise or cut national debt to national income ratios by 2016. Labour warned that such a timetable risked choking off recovery before it had taken firm hold – which is precisely what happened.

In Britain, after Labour had left office in May 2010, the Tory/Lib Dem coalition abruptly changed course and implemented what can only be described as a savage cuts programme. Apparently believing Keynes was wrong and they were right, they harshly reined back capital investment and public spending. Crosland would have been aghast.

The UK's initial recovery of 2010 petered out under the onslaught of Tory Chancellor George Osborne's severe fiscal squeeze. By the end of 2013 UK output had still not recovered to its 2008 level. It was 15 per cent below where its pre-2007 growth trend would have taken it, a colossal annual loss of national income of some £225 billion.

Urgent international government action, led by Labour, had stopped the world's financial system from seizing up and prevented global depression. But it had three other important consequences.

First, it meant that nation states transformed a *financial* crisis into a *fiscal* one, a crisis of banking finance into a crisis for government finance. Country after country tackled its private sector banking crisis by turning it into a public sector budget headache. Bailing out the banks had cost taxpayers dear. It had prevented economic collapse but could not stop recession plunging the public finances deeply into the red all over the world.

Second, the high government borrowing required to plug the gap between sinking tax revenue and rising public expenditure added to existing national debt, causing it to soar. This combination of high borrowing and rising debt called into question the ability of governments to deal with economic shocks as severe as the 2008 crisis for the foreseeable future. The concern was that governments might find it difficult or impossible to borrow on the financial markets – as the Irish government experienced from 2010 to 2013 – for fear that they might default and fail to repay any loans. Yet this was the very moment when such borrowing was vital to protect society: as if a natural disaster had occurred.

Third, it opened the door to bogus accusations that the economic crisis had been caused by extravagant government spending leading to excessive public borrowing.

Labour's economic record 1997–2010

The Big Deceit of British politics was New Labour 'overspending': the claim that a Labour 'big state' obsession had left the country with the mountainous levels of national debt, budget deficit and public borrowing which the new Tory/Lib Dem government inherited after the 2010 election. For that Big Deceit not only completely traduced Labour's economic record; more important it set the terms for a ruthless right-wing agenda taking Britain backwards to a society of minimal public services, widening inequality, deepening social division and economic decline.

Such was the ferocity of the cuts programme adopted by the Tory/ Lib Dem government that, as a proportion of its national income, Britain was set to go back to pre-1948 levels of total government spending on goods and services. Several generations of broadly cross-party public investment in better education, better health, better public transport, environmental protection and support for economic and industrial transformation, were all to be trashed in favour of a 'leaner state'.

The pretext for justifying this – the deepest, quickest public spending cuts ever in Britain – was an Orwellian re-write of the history of thirteen years of Labour's economic management to persuade voters that there was no serious, credible alternative.

The truth was very different. New Labour took office in 1997 so determined to establish a solid reputation for economic trust and competence that it even committed to standing by the Tories' public expenditure plans for the next two years, introduced tough new rules for government spending and borrowing, and made the Bank of England independent with a mandate to set interest rates, free from ministers with electoral rather than economic cycles uppermost in mind.

The origins of New Labour's mantra, 'no return to boom and bust', lay in the Tory boom of the late 1980s followed by the Tory recession in the early 1990s – and indeed the up and down record of first expansion then contraction which followed the Second World War under both parties. But for Tony Blair and Gordon Brown the roots of this mantra went even deeper: to the experience of the Labour government of 1974–79.

They were rightly preoccupied with banishing the memory of Labour's politically suicidal 1978–79 'winter of discontent' that made it easy for opponents to label Labour as incompetent. But even before that were Labour's 1974–75 days which had worried Tony Crosland when its spending ambitions triumphed over economic reality. Labour dug itself into a hole on public spending and borrowing which it spent the next four years trying to climb out of. In 1974–75 Labour allowed public spending to rise by 35 per cent in cash terms, or over 13 per cent in real terms.[6] 'The first months of the new Government were characterised by our spending money which in the event we did not have,' according to Joel Barnett, Labour's then Chief Secretary to the Treasury. The result – albeit also driven by a leap in global commodity and oil prices – was roaring inflation and economic instability. Industrial relations sank to a new low in 1979 just as trade union membership reached a record peak and trade union power met its high noon. Soon the party was swept out of office by Margaret Thatcher.

When 1997 came New Labour's leadership was entirely correct that fiscal discipline had to be its constant hymn, especially in the context of an economy which was growing and had been since the 1992 'Black Wednesday' debacle, when sterling crashed out of the European exchange rate mechanism. It had to demonstrate that the party could be prudent with the fruits of that growth. And its initial restraint on public spending soon proved productive. By first cutting the public sector deficit and then turning it into a surplus for three years, Labour cut national debt as a share of national income from over 42 per cent inherited from the Conservatives in 1996–97 to less than 30 per cent in 2001–02; though it rose to 36 per cent by 2007–08, that was still well below Tory debt levels.[7]

This helped to establish a stable economic foundation and delivered a decade of record investment in the public services as they were repaired from the dismal Tory inheritance of patients dying on trolleys in hospital corridors, sinking education standards and the worst railways in Western Europe.

By June 2007 New Labour had delivered a historically unprecedented decade of steady economic growth, low inflation and low interest rates which had taken UK employment to record heights. UK GDP per head grew faster than for any other member of the Group of Seven leading developed economies. Britain's national debt as a share of national income was lower than that of France, Germany, the US, Italy or Japan, having fallen by 6 per cent since 1997 (worth some £90 billion today). Lower government debt meant New Labour saved the taxpayer about £3 billion in annual interest payments: it did indeed 'fix the roof when the sun was shining'.

The low yields on UK government bonds before, during and after the credit crunch under Labour bore eloquent testimony to the fact that the international markets had full confidence in its policies; and that they were not clamouring for the right-wing, neoliberal dogma subsequently visited upon Britain.

Before the global financial crisis, government borrowing was some £15 billion lower in today's money than in the Tories' last year in office in 1996–97. Between 1997 and 2007 annual Labour borrowing averaged only one third of annual borrowing by the Thatcher and John Major governments of 1979–97: proof of purposeful prudence and certainly not the 'financial negligence and extravagance' with which the party was subsequently charged.

IMF figures showed that the UK's 2007 public sector deficit, at 2.7 per cent of GDP, was also low: the same as that of France and the US. The deficit also had been significantly cut from the one Labour inherited.

In those salad days before the financial crisis, the economic outlook seemed positive. The FTSE 100 share price index had hit a six-year high, reflecting optimism about the UK's economic prospects under Labour, and bank credit default swap spreads – the cost of insuring bank loans against the risk that borrowers might fail to repay – had fallen to a historic low, a sign of confidence in Britain's future in financial markets. Ministers began to believe that Britain had finally broken free from the cycle of 'boom and bust'. So desperate was he to identify with Labour's success that David Cameron in September 2007 even pledged to match Labour's spending plans for three further years up to 2010.

Not all Labour's spending was efficient of course – some of it was indeed 'wasted', for instance on failed IT projects, a curse for modern government worldwide. Not every million was perfectly targeted. On a government spending total of nearly £700 billion that is hardly surprising – global corporations squander some of their money too and suffer from similar if not greater imperfections. But Labour's increased public investment was absolutely essential to put right the public services and infrastructure that the Tories had shattered over 18 long years in office.

Spending was in fact lower than in France, Germany, the Netherlands, Norway and Sweden, and was never 'out of control'. If it had been, the Tories would surely never have accepted Labour's spending plans.

But then came the international banking crisis, the global credit crunch and the worst recession in Britain for 80 years. The idea that this was caused by Labour's public investment in Britain is risible. The proposition that by building new hospitals and new schools, by recruiting tens of thousands of extra nurses, doctors, teachers and police officers in Britain, Labour caused the subprime mortgage defaults in the US that ricocheted throughout the world's financial institutions is preposterous. It wasn't Labour's public spending that triggered Britain's or the world's economic crisis. It was global interdependency of reckless banking that in 2008 caused an economic meltdown in Britain and right across the globe.

By agreeing to boost public spending and borrowing to offset the catastrophic collapse in private sector spending, the G20 governments took on record annual budget deficits. But these were deficits which stopped a slide into slump and laid the basis for recovery from the biggest shock to hit the world economy in peacetime since the 1930s Great Depression.

Contrary to right-wing free market mantras and Tory/Lib Dem history rewrites, lower public spending and borrowing would have been no guarantee against the tsunami wave that struck the world economy in the form of the financial crisis of 2008–09. Ireland, Iceland and Spain had all run budget surpluses in 2007. They all had national debt lower as a share of national income than the UK. But they were still engulfed.

However the new Tory-led government that took office in May 2010 embarked upon a massive and immediate tax and public spending squeeze. By rushing to reduce the public sector deficit it succeeded in turning a fragile but real recovery under Labour in 2010 into a faltering, flatlining one under the Tory/Lib Dem coalition. That mistake had been made before. In the US in 1936 President Roosevelt, under pressure to balance the American budget, cut back prematurely on his 'New Deal' which, after the Great Depression, had caused the US economy to grow quickly for four years, slashing unemployment. Roosevelt hoped to balance his budget within two years. Instead the US recovery went into reverse as the economy slipped back into recession and unemployment rose again sharply. Full employment was not achieved until the 1940s spending boom generated by the Second World War, more than a decade after the financial crisis that had triggered the 1930s slump.

The Tory/Lib Dem Big Deceit was that the UK budget deficit was caused by Labour's 'reckless spending and borrowing', the cuts therefore all Labour's fault. In fact irresponsible bankers caused the crisis. Before the banking crisis all the key economic indices in Britain were positive – low government debt, deficit and borrowing – lower than under the Tories, and lower than most comparable countries at the time.

Labour's failure was not one of macro-economics or unsound public finances. Like most of the Western world it had been far too lax on financial regulation, which allowed consumer spending to grow strongly, backed by rising household debt. Recklessly irresponsible bank borrowing and lending was allowed to become a law unto itself, untroubled by a weak and flawed system of financial regulation. Market forces were given free rein, and they ran amok, as the herd instinct took financial institutions like lemmings right over the edge.

Yet in his memoir published in 2010, Tony Blair seemed to be in denial when he revealed that his New Labour stance was more aligned with neoliberals than Crosland. 'I profoundly disagree with important parts of the statist, so-called Keynesian response to the economic crisis,' he confessed, adding: 'the market did not fail. One part of one sector did … The role of government is to stabilise and then get out of the way as quickly as is economically sensible.'[8]

The casino side of banking still poses a deadly threat to economic stability, with bankers facing the same temptation to take reckless risks in the belief that the taxpayer will step in to save them when things go wrong again. As they surely will, because free market systems are inherently unstable and financial markets are prone to periodic failure – something that Tony Crosland discounted, though he would have approved of Labour's response to the banking crisis and deplored the scorched earth austerity policies that afterwards became so fashionable.

How New Labour measured up

Despite the dramatic deterioration in the economic situation triggered by the 2007–08 global financial crisis, Labour still left office in 2010 with a respectable record on the five key criteria important to Crosland.

First, cutting *poverty*. Although this never featured on the pledge cards that New Labour issued to party members ahead of the 1997 general election, in office substantial progress was made, most notably among the 400 million people who were helped out of desperate poverty by tripling Britain's overseas aid.

At home relative poverty – the proportion of individuals in households with incomes less than 60 per cent of the contemporary median before housing costs – fell from 19.6 per cent in 1997 to 17.0 per cent by 2009–10, according to research by the Institute for Fiscal Studies. Child poverty fell by 1.1 million, some 600,000 short of Labour's target. Pensioner poverty fell to its lowest level since 1984 in 2009–10 as Labour took a million pensioners out of poverty.

What drove down child and pensioner poverty was extra spending on benefits and tax credits – an £18 billion annual increase in spending on benefits for families with children and an annual £11 billion increase on benefits for pensioners by 2010–11.[9] Working tax credit relieved in-work poverty for 2 million families. Nevertheless Labour left office in 2010 with nearly 3 million children, more than 6 million adults of working age, and 2 million pensioners still in poverty.

On Crosland's second criterion, *social welfare*, New Labour delivered a decade of record investment and reform in public services, building a formidable infrastructure of state support for citizens, especially the disadvantaged.

NHS waiting times and waiting lists were cut by setting European Union standards for health spending, which provided 70,000 more nurses and 40,000 more doctors in England alone, with over a hundred new hospitals and 650 one-stop primary care centres. Targets that once were only aspirations, such as higher survival rates for cancer and heart disease, were reached, helping to make the exceptional the rule. Labour left office with the NHS enjoying record public support. Even so, 17 million people in Britain were still living with a long-term health condition such as a heart condition or asthma.

New Labour's record of strong economic growth meant that, overall – and quite contrary to subsequent Tory mythology – welfare benefits took up a *shrinking* share of national income before the financial crisis. As a share of national income, benefits peaked at 12.69 per cent at the bottom of recession in 1993–94, fell to 10.87 per cent by 1999–2000 as the economy grew (saving some £25 billion per year in today's money), and stood at 11.38 per cent in 2007–08 as the credit crunch began. They then rose to 13.77 per cent of GDP in 2009–10 as recession gripped the economy and still stood at 13.46 per cent under the Tory/Lib Dems in 2011–12.[10]

Education, supposedly New Labour's top priority, saw its share of public spending hardly change. Nevertheless investment in schools meant over 40,000 more teachers and 115,000 more teaching assistants, cutting class sizes and improving educational standards in primary schools in particular. Some 3,000 new Sure Start children's centres provided wrap-around childcare, helping parents, usually mothers, to return to paid work, and focusing support on the most vulnerable.

To promote a safer society Labour provided 15,000 more police officers and 16,000 new police community support officers, helping to cut crime by fully a third since 1997.

On Tony Crosland's third criterion, *equality*, Britain in the 1950s was a class-conscious society, and so when he wrote about inequality he began by addressing class and that meant first and foremost incomes. Unhappily, income inequality increased during Labour's 1997–2010 term in office, ending higher than in any year since the 1950s. Yet the rise was smaller than that under the Tories during the 1980s and would have been even higher had it not been for tax and benefit reforms.

Small wonder that New Labour remained reticent about its record on redistribution. The worse it got, the less New Labour seemed to care. Yes, at the bottom millions more people were lifted out of poverty, but at the top the rich raced ahead as middle Britain trailed behind. Over the past 30 years incomes among those at the very top have powered in front of everyone else as the share of national income going to profits has risen. This seems to be true of most English-speaking countries, though not of continental European countries or Japan.

The credit boom may have masked the fact that middle income households everywhere have been under pressure, since it allowed them to spend more than they earned. But when the credit balloon burst, it exposed Britain's squeezed middle more than ever before and called into question whether their offspring could expect to enjoy the same standard of living achieved by their parents.

Other aspects of inequality not covered by Crosland (or not really an issue when he wrote) included the gender pay gap – which persisted. New Labour's 2003 'Big Conversation' policy consultation failed even to mention equal pay audits in companies. Instead it expressed concern about the small number of women on the boards of FTSE 100 companies. On the other hand there was a very substantial shift in popular culture on equal opportunities, Labour leading the way with many more women Members of Parliament and ministers than ever before in Britain. Positive action was taken on age discrimination and on promoting gay rights, including civil partnerships. But geographical inequality, notably the division between London and the South East and the rest of the UK, remained entrenched. So too did racial inequality – the latter again in spite of very significant Labour leadership on tougher anti-racist legislation, tackling institutionalised racism, and more black and ethnic minority MPs and ministers than ever before.

Crosland would have been surprised by the extent of Britain's ethnic diversity today, less so by the strength of nationalism. Though he wrote the first edition of his book just after the 1955 general election, when (scarcely believable) most MPs elected in Scotland were Tories and no Nationalists won seats in Wales or Scotland, he lived to see both 11 Scots Nats and three Plaid Cymru candidates win seats at Westminster in October 1974 and Labour embrace devolution. New Labour took bold steps to devolve power by establishing the Scottish Parliament and the National Assembly for Wales in 1999.

On his fourth criterion, *fraternity and cooperation*, Crosland recognised that, under the right conditions, either working for a common purpose or for personal gain can each provide effective incentives, and together they can be good for economic growth and living standards. But he was unsure where the right balance lay.

New Labour was not alone in fostering the wrong balance between the competitive instinct and the urge to cooperate in groups lying at the base of human society. Trust and cooperation are fundamental to specialisation and exchange in modern societies: the dividing up of tasks between members of society so that we all become specialists to some degree, more productive as we develop expertise in our chosen tasks, more dependent on mutual cooperation by each trading what we produce for what someone else does, and more trusting that someone else can be relied on to do properly what we need but can't or don't want to do ourselves.

However, trust broke down in 2008 after bankers' competitive instincts overrode reason, leading to an unquestioning acceptance of risks. Massive irresponsible lending went unhindered by minimalist government regulation. Instead it was encouraged by the banks' (correct) expectation of being bailed out by the state if things went wrong.

New Labour's faith in market forces over state action also led to a short-sighted reliance on the Private Finance Initiative (PFI) and on outsourcing the supply of public services. Labour went for immediate benefits – like new hospitals – at the cost of being locked into 20 to 30 year PFI contractual commitments to pay massive capital charges that made the PFI option more expensive in the long term than if the project had been funded through conventional means. New Labour found itself dependent on PFI because it was not prepared to borrow to invest. It argued that PFI transferred risk to the private sector, even though ultimately the risk remained with the public sector because, if a PFI hospital contract went badly wrong, the public sector would have to bail it out to avoid a hospital closure, with all sorts of potential collateral damage, as the case of Lewisham Hospital showed. The high cost of PFI debt charges left the NHS only able to operate from a third to a half of the number of services and staff it would have done had such schemes been financed conventionally.[11] By importing a culture of competition into hospitals in England and privatising prisons, New Labour opened the door to David

Cameron's 'any alternative provider' approach to public services and the privatisation of police cells.

New Labour celebrated winners, not contestants. It associated itself with champions, not finalists; with the fortunate few, not the middling many. There were no leading roles for also-rans in New Labour's cast of characters. As the GMB General Secretary John Edmonds commented in 2002, 'The New Labour Big Tent contained an exclusive VIP area to which only a fortunate few from big business or the shangri-la of middle England had access.'[12]

However, there was one area where New Labour went a long way to deliver Crosland's ideas. That was in cooperation at the workplace. Crosland felt that, while working in Britain had become less of a competitive rat race, more should be done to improve equality of opportunity and to raise the status of workers. In particular he contrasted class resentment and trench warfare attitudes in British employment relations with more harmonious patterns abroad, notably in Sweden.

Unions provide a vital voice for people at work, a place where millions spend a large part of their lives. They are a bulwark against unfair treatment of employees by employers, which is widespread in the UK: confirmed by the number of harassment and unfair treatment cases reported by the Advisory, Conciliation and Arbitration Service (ACAS) and the Citizens Advice Bureaux, and the day-to-day workplace experience of union stewards.

New Labour helped by improving employment protection, including a right to be accompanied at disciplinary or grievance hearings and more protection against unfair dismissal. It introduced stronger union recognition rights and a national minimum wage. It provided new rights to maternity and paternity leave and new protection against discrimination. It provided statutory recognition for union learning representatives to promote extra skills amongst workers and a union modernisation fund.

Although New Labour opted out of the European Union's Charter of Fundamental Rights it did bring into UK law many rights at work agreed at EU level. These included rights to four weeks of annual leave, equal rights for part-time workers, parental leave rights, information and consultation rights, and a law to ban age discrimination. Under union pressure New Labour also took action to enable companies to be prosecuted for corporate manslaughter and help people who had lost out on occupational pensions, both issues I felt strongly about and helped deliver as a Cabinet minister.[13]

Although welcomed by unions, these reforms sometimes fell short of their more radical workplace demands. For example, protection against unfair dismissal only took effect after one year's employment instead of from day one. And industrial action ballots remained a legal minefield.

Nevertheless, all New Labour's improvements should have opened the door to more cooperation in the workplace. But unions in general spurned the opportunity to recruit new members and forge fresh relationships with employers. Instead of embracing change, they reminisced about the closed shop, while the union share of the workforce sank to new lows.

On the fifth and final of Crosland's criteria, full employment and living standards, there were real positives. By the peak of the boom in 2008 total UK employment had risen by 4 million since the bottom of the previous recession in 1993. The UK's flexible labour market had helped it to hit the three employment targets for the working age population of member states in 2010 set by the European Council in Lisbon in 2000: an overall employment rate of 70 per cent, a female employment rate of 60 per cent plus, and an employment rate for older workers (aged 55–64) of 50 per cent. In every single quarter between 1998 and 2008 the employment rate for British-born adults was above 73 per cent, the highest sustained rate in our economic history.

Average living standards grew over the entire life of the 1997–2010 Labour government. However, research for the independent Commission on Living Standards by the Resolution Foundation called into question how far the economic growth Crosland so relied upon meant higher living standards, especially for people on the lower rungs of the income ladder. It found that, despite GDP growth of 11 per cent over the period 2003–08, wages in the bottom half of the income distribution stagnated.

In the US, the UK, Germany and Canada, median wages were stagnant or falling over long periods of economic growth before the

2008 global recession, suggesting a possible 'decoupling' of growth from gain. It may no longer be safe to assume that living standards of people on low-to-middle incomes will rise when economic growth returns.[14] Yet these are people who used to look to Labour for support – which is why an alternative agenda to that of New Labour is required.

Summary

The 2008 banking crisis exposed the limitations of light-touch financial regulation. This left voters questioning New Labour's hard-won reputation for economic competence, and wondering whether there was any alternative to the right's cuts agenda.

There was: and indeed, there still is.

The global financial crisis marked a watershed in New Labour's performance in office. Until 2008 its record ranked well against most of Crosland's criteria for building a socialist society, notably in promoting economic growth for over ten years (the longest sustained period in British economic history), maintaining full employment, cutting poverty, repairing holes in the social safety net and reaching out to 'the least, the last and the lost'.[15]

Sadly, however, New Labour never looked likely to meet some others of Crosland's criteria, in particular encouraging greater equality, promoting fraternity and cooperation, and translating economic growth into higher real living standards for people on low and middle incomes. It displayed deliberate lack of interest in greater equality if that meant taking on the rich and powerful, and appeared not to have noticed that economic growth had stopped delivering the goods to the people whose side Labour was supposed to be on.

CHAPTER 3

Finance and the new capitalism

Throughout his ten years as Chancellor, Gordon Brown's consistent mantra was that New Labour's economic policies had abolished 'boom and bust' and were building 'a platform of stability'.

Sadly, however, that platform proved to have been a polyfilla villa erected on flimsy foundations when the global financial crisis hit in 2008. It was a crisis which confirmed that, since Tony Crosland's death in 1977, capitalism had evolved in ways which he could not have anticipated and would not have welcomed, and which undermined the ability of governments to build stable societies and growing economies. A crisis that shattered the post-1980s neoliberal myth about a financial system with supposedly self-stabilising properties. A crisis that above all else demanded fundamental reform of the financial system: a scale of reform moreover which simply was not attempted, even after all the government promises to ensure the worst global collapse for at least 80 years could never be repeated.

The financial elite

In his January 1961 farewell address, President Eisenhower warned America against two dangers. First, the acquisition of unwarranted influence over government decisions by a 'military-industrial complex'. Second, the risk of public policy becoming captive to a 'scientific-technological elite'.

What no one in the Anglo-Saxon economies foresaw was the emergence of a financial elite, a charmed circle with easy access to the corridors of power gained by instilling the belief that whatever went down well with the big banks and financial institutions on

Wall Street and in the City of London was good for the US and the UK.[1] The rise of such a financial elite in Britain and America was held in check by regulation dating from the 1930s, until the 1980s.

That was when deregulation began under Ronald Reagan and Margaret Thatcher, lifting restrictions separating commercial and investment banking, when traditional retail banks became exposed to the 'profit at any price' culture of the international investment banks, and when the seeds of *securitisation* and *financial engineering* were sown.

Securitisation allows banks to raise capital quickly by selling certificates that entitle the buyer to a share in future streams of cash, say from 25 years of monthly mortgage repayments, and to use that capital to make fresh loans. What such 'mortgage-backed securities' are worth today depends on the value of the flow of future payments.

Financial engineering means restructuring the way a bank is financed to increase its rate of return on shareholders' capital, such as by increasing the proportion of total finance raised by borrowing and reducing the proportion raised from shareholders by selling new shares or by ploughing back profits. The lower the proportion of the bank's capital coming from shareholders, the higher the rate of return on that shareholders' capital that a given amount of profit represents. It also includes practices such as 'hiding' borrowing off the balance sheet through 'structured investment vehicles', to obscure just how dependent on borrowed funds an institution is, and how slim is the margin of funds from shareholders.

These sophisticated, complex and opaque manoeuvres allowed banks to expand quickly. They made banking more profitable but they also made it much more risky. Events were to show that it was not just individual banks that became exposed to increased risk but whole financial systems. Entire economies faced ruin if even one major bank got into trouble because of domino effects – one bank failing could trigger a series of failures until the whole financial system seized up. But that only became plain in the autumn of 2008. Until then supposedly super-clever analysts, quick-thinking traders and self-confident directors at the big banks and in Mayfair hedge funds had increasingly free rein to do daring deals, make handsome profits and pocket big bonuses.

They came to constitute a financial elite – located country by country but globally interconnected – which has not hesitated to hold governments hostage by undertaking ever more precarious lending in the pursuit of profits and bonuses. They bet that if things went wrong and the banks faced failure and defaulted on their debt obligations, governments would have no option but to save their economic system from collapse by bailing out troubled banks. This was a financial elite that included hedge funds which, though they did not enjoy the same state protection as the banks, and several collapsed by taking the wrong bet, also contributed to the risk-taking culture. A financial elite which, in the case of Ireland, lied to and laughed at ministers and state officials as they struggled to prevent national bankruptcy while rescuing Ireland's insolvent banks. A financial elite which in 2007–08 provoked the worst ever banking crisis in global history (including the Great Depression), according to Ben Bernanke, the then Chairman of the Federal Reserve, America's central bank.

That crisis took governments, central banks and financial markets by surprise since they all subscribed to the 'Great Moderation', the term first used by economists James Stock and Mark Watson in 2002, but popularised by Ben Bernanke in 2004, to describe the less volatile US business cycle since the 1980s. This was the view – repeated by Gordon Brown – that 'boom and bust' had been largely beaten, primarily by relying on monetary policy rules enforced by independent central banks. Mild ups and downs might still occur in the business cycle. But severe fluctuations in GDP were regarded as things of the past. It may be hard to comprehend now, but when in January 2003 the President of the American Economic Association Professor Robert Lucas declared the problem of depression prevention 'solved, for all practical purposes',[2] he was reflecting the conventional wisdom of most governments right across the world, from George W. Bush's administration to New Labour, from Frankfurt to Shanghai.

A new era

Things had looked pretty encouraging 50 years earlier too. Tony Crosland argued in the 1950s that capitalism had become less malign since the 1930s because Keynes' full employment policies and Beveridge's welfare state were combining to deliver economic and social stability, promoting the necessary investment and faster economic growth for a more just, more equal society. These, after all, were what Thomas Piketty calls 'the optimistic decades following World War II', when the world economy was growing faster than it had ever done and when wealth inequality in Britain was in the fifth decade of what would prove to be seven consecutive decades of decline.[3]

Britain's growth rate in the 1950s and 1960s largely justified Crosland's confidence. It outstripped that of the depressed 1920s and early 1930s as the country moved from austerity to prosperity, replacing ration cards with credit cards. Between 1948 and 1958 the UK economy grew at an average annual rate of 2.5 per cent and employment rose by 1.25 million, including an extra million in manufacturing industry. Britain's pre-war labour surplus became a post-war labour shortage, with systematic overtime replacing the systematic short-time working of the interwar period.[4]

Another hopeful sign was that the period from the late 1940s to the early 1970s was one of comparative calm in financial markets, with no banking crises in any of the world's three financial centres of London, New York or Paris. This stood in marked contrast to the years from 1800 to 1945 when serial banking crises had been the norm in the UK, the US and France.[5] Depending on definitions the UK had banking crises in 1810, 1815–17, 1819, 1825–26, 1837–39, 1847–48, 1857, 1866, 1878 and 1890 but not again until the secondary banking crisis of 1974.[6]

The US experienced 11 banking crises in the 19th century and a further three in the first three decades of the 20th. After the 1929–33 crisis President Roosevelt introduced federal deposit insurance in 1934. This, according to Milton Friedman, proved to be the structural change most conducive to monetary stability since the American Civil War. It led to a dramatic drop in bank failures and up to 1960 had prevented any further financial crises in the US.[7]

In a post-war world that looked relatively free from financial crises, and in a UK committed to economic and social stability, Crosland was optimistic about Britain's growth prospects. His horizons stretched much further than what he labelled 'Keynes–plus–modified–

capitalism-plus-Welfare-State'. He wanted a more classless society, greater equality and less social distress and physical squalor, none of which 1950s capitalism could be depended upon to deliver without significant government intervention.

Crosland believed that, since the 1930s, changes in public attitudes towards full employment and social welfare, the increased economic role of the state, and a shift in the balance of power from management to labour had led to a new social framework which the Conservatives would not dare to challenge. They might seek to modify it in favour of the better off, but would be deterred from trying to destroy the essential fabric of the postwar world by the certainty of defeat at the polls. On that, at least, a consensus would prevail between the two major parties.

Except for Edward Heath's short 'Selsdon Man' neoliberal episode between 1969 and 1972, this proved an accurate picture of the British political scene until the advent of Margaret Thatcher in 1979. When New Labour embraced much of her neoliberal approach by echoing Tory calls for deregulation of banking and finance, Tory laws on trade union rights and Tory schemes for private financing of public sector projects, a different kind of consensus emerged.

This was a New Labour compromise which made market forces the model for public sector reform and revered financial fat cats – provided three conditions held: the economy kept growing, public services kept expanding, and the workforce stayed fully employed – even if the living standards of those on the middle and lower rungs of the income ladder either grew far slower than those at the top, or barely grew at all.

David Cameron in his initial 'heir to Blair' period as Tory Party leader from 2005 embraced this new kind of consensus with his pledge about 'sharing the proceeds of growth'. But the big increase in Labour government borrowing prompted by the global financial crisis provided too tempting a political target. In 2010 the Tory/ Liberal Democrat coalition reverted to the Treasury View of the 1930s with an unprecedented fiscal squeeze aimed at achieving a balanced budget, a squeeze which killed off the recovery that was under way in 2010 under Labour's growth strategy and trapped the UK in a no growth/slow growth equilibrium for three years.

Escaping from this trap would not have been difficult. President Obama showed how with his 2009 stimulus that got the US economy growing again and saw the American budget deficit fall year after year. However, growth remains vulnerable to interruption from financial crisis unless and until the Anglo-Saxon economies reform their banking systems, because the financial calm that faced Crosland in the 1950s proved to have been short-lived. Deregulation turned the City of London from a supposedly dormant volcano in the 1960s into a rumbling active one in the 1970s and 1980s, and a huge threat to the whole economy when financial crisis erupted in 2008. In the absence of fundamental financial reform, it could explode again in the future at any time.

How finance capitalism changed

In the 1950s and 1960s the finance sector was small relative to the real economy. But today the value of financial deals far outweighs real economic activities. Deregulation that began in the 1970s and leapt ahead in the 1980s completely changed the financial landscape.

Instead of channelling savers' funds into financing real investment, banks created a complex network of interconnected deals among themselves through the massive growth of financial securities, that is to say certificates sold by financial institutions that are valuable because they entitle the buyer to a future flow of income, but which carry the risk of that income drying up if the source suddenly can't pay. The result was a web in which an initial crisis in a single market, like the US 'subprime' housing market in 2006–07, could trigger a global chain reaction. A web in which the routine payment system on which we all rely could be threatened by the gambling casino that investment banking had become. A web in which most people's confidence that their savings were safe depended on government guarantees rather than bankers' assurances or the apparent state of bank balance sheets.

In this new nirvana finance grew bigger, more complex, more risky, more profitable and fabulously well rewarded at the top. The big bonuses were real, but much of the profit that they were based upon proved illusory. Several years of apparent success were bought at the price of enormous financial failure once the bubble burst and the fallout was dumped upon taxpayers at terrible cost.

How the financial elites developed such sway over public policy is explained by official figures suggesting that growth and profitability in the UK finance sector outpaced the rest of the economy, especially after financial markets were liberalised from the 1980s onwards. Whereas in 1964 the total assets of the UK banking system were valued at 34 per cent of the country's total output, by 2007 that figure had risen to an extraordinary 500 per cent, driven by a huge rise in the value of loans and other transactions *among* the banks and building societies rather than *between* them, on the one hand, and households and companies, on the other.[8]

From 1914 to 1970 the growth rate of value added by the UK financial sector was *less* than that of the economy as a whole. But it accelerated after 1970 and grew far faster than the whole economy between 1971 and 2008. UK banks' annual return on equity capital roughly trebled after 1970, rising from about 7 per cent to over 20 per cent. Similar rates of return were enjoyed by major international banks doing business in the US and Europe, roughly double the returns in the non-financial sector.[9]

The rise of risk

However the financial elite's claim to be driving institutions that were faster growing and more profitable than the rest of the economy has been disputed. Former executive director for financial stability and now chief economist at the Bank of England, Andrew Haldane, has shown with his colleagues how these financial profits, like their contribution to GDP, were exaggerated by the mismeasurement of risk and may have been more mirage than miracle. *Reported* returns on equity rose but *risk-adjusted* returns did not.

Haldane et al found that almost all of the rise in the rate of return on equity capital of the major UK banks in the 2000s was due to *higher leverage*. Leverage describes how a bank is financed: where the capital comes from with which it makes loans to customers, buys assets like property or invests in commercial ventures. The degree of leverage is shown by a bank's debt to equity ratio: the proportion of borrowed funds (debt capital on which interest *must* be paid annually and which must eventually be repaid) relative to funds subscribed by shareholders (equity capital on which dividends *might* be paid, depending on how profitable the bank is). The higher a bank's leverage the greater the likelihood of operating profit being eaten up in interest payments on borrowed capital, leaving little for shareholders as dividends or to boost the bank's reserves as ploughed back profits. Higher leverage was a double-edged sword. It allowed banks to report higher rates of return on equity without necessarily having improved their overall rate of return on assets. But it also raised the risk of higher interest payments wiping out any chance of dividends if profits dipped.

Bank balance sheet leverage rose hugely from about four times equity capital in 1900 to about 25 times in 2000. Allowing for accounting adjustments due to off-balance sheet assets which obscured the truth about banks' financial state and made risky investments look like safe bets, Haldane estimates leverage among the major global banks in the world was on average more than 50 times equity at the peak of the boom in 2008, a sharp rise since 2000. This meant that banks were running on wafer-thin margins, with less than 2 per cent of their total financing from equity capital to absorb any sudden shock.

Supposedly safe banks thus had a perilously narrow safety margin of equity with which to absorb any losses should the value of their assets suddenly sink: if, for instance, the market value of financial securities they held were to collapse or if doubt about a bank's viability were to force it to raise cash by disposing of assets in a fire sale at rock-bottom prices. Exactly this happened in the American 'subprime' mortgage market in 2007 after banks had made loans to low-income homebuyers who could not possibly repay them. Many such borrowers handed back the keys to their properties and stopped making mortgage repayments when US house prices began falling in 2006.

A bank whose liabilities exceed the value of its assets is insolvent and cannot pay all its debts if it is wound up. Insolvent businesses cannot continue operating legally and must cease trading at once, as happened to the bust American bank Lehman Brothers on 15

September 2008, triggering the worldwide banking crisis which had such calamitous consequences globally.

Most if not all of the world's leading banks faced insolvency in 2008. One way or another they urgently needed to rebuild their balance sheets with massive injections of equity capital, if not from their existing shareholders or new investors, then ultimately from taxpayers.

Pass the parcel

Financial engineering – ratcheting up leverage on the liabilities side of the balance sheets where the bank's sources of capital are shown – was only one reason why banks faced acute difficulties in 2008. The other was what had been happening to the assets side of those balance sheets. Here they faced double trouble: a sudden loss of access to cash in the short-term wholesale money market, threatening their liquidity, and financial assets which suddenly lost value on a grand scale, threatening their solvency.

Firstly, banks had become more reliant on short-term wholesale funding by reducing the share of highly liquid assets in their total, like holdings of government securities that could quickly be turned into cash if needed, from about 30 per cent to less than 2 per cent in 2009. Some banks became especially dependent on short-term wholesale funding to roll over existing debt as it came up for repayment, replacing one source of funds by another. This increased their liquidity risk, that is to say the risk of being unable to raise cash quickly in order to satisfy depositors demanding their money back in a sudden surge of withdrawals.

That is precisely what happened to Northern Rock building society in August 2007. Its access to the short-term wholesale money market suddenly dried up at a time when institutional lenders declined to renew their loans to the bank as they became due. Individual retail depositors then feared that they might lose their life savings when they heard that Northern Rock had sought help from the Bank of England to overcome a cash crisis. The result was a classic run on a bank, with long queues of anxious customers wanting their money back. But the roots of Northern Rock's problem lay in its dependence on short-term loans from other financial institutions through the wholesale money market. These institutions were all lending to each other in a merry-go-round which rattled happily along, making piles of money for bankers, until there was a default – provoking collateral damage, and in turn a wholesale crisis when cash and credit dried up.

Secondly, since the 1990s banks had built up their holdings of financial securities, especially mortgage-backed securities: bonds sold by banks to institutional investors and to private individuals looking for somewhere safe to place their funds that would yield a reasonable return. The bond buyer receives an entitlement to be paid which the bond issuer may not be able to pay if the flow of monthly mortgage repayments from the pool of homebuyers dries up. In similar vein, hedge funds collect cash from wealthy individuals and use it to buy higher risk financial securities – like *collateralised debt obligations* or CDOs – which promise higher rates of return from cash flows generated by a range of assets like repayments from credit card loans or car loans.

Originally the growth of securitisation had been about banks raising funds from pension funds and insurance companies by selling them mortgage-backed securities, hoping in the process to offload the risk of borrowers defaulting on their repayments. But soon the big banks also began buying each other's securities, intertwining their fates, with serious implications for the risk to the system as a whole.

In the US to begin with, then elsewhere, the summer of 2007 saw rising rates of default by people who had taken out mortgage loans to buy homes or top up mortgages to finance home improvements, buy a new car or pay for a holiday. Increasing default rates called into question the value of *all* such bonds on the market because the underlying cash flows were now in doubt. So the value of all higher risk or 'subprime' mortgage debt dropped, inflicting big losses on banks that had bought each other's mortgage securities and creating uncertainty about the real value of the assets on everyone's balance sheet.

In the second half of 2007 and in 2008 estimates of the size of those financial losses by the world's major banks grew, while guesses at the remaining value of their assets shrank. The reason? Mounting evidence that banks had been recklessly irresponsible in their lending for years. They had taken higher and higher risks on the loans that they made in a blind pursuit of profit and bonuses, while sidestepping even the much more relaxed system of government regulation.

But the conventional regulated banks, like the unregulated so-called 'shadow' banks, had obscured their financial affairs behind intricate off-balance-sheet accounting techniques, making risky financial investments seem like safe bets. Yet neither bank auditors nor credit rating agencies nor the Financial Services Authority nor the Bank of England had sounded a warning signal.

The banks had financed a mortgage lending boom, including to 'subprime' borrowers whose chances of meeting their repayment obligations were suspect, causing property prices to balloon. Then they had played pass the parcel with the risk of being left holding the baby should homeowners default, effectively shifting their share of the blame. They did this in two ways.

Either they sold off their mortgage loans, including the dubious ones, as mortgage-backed securities or bonds to pension funds and insurance companies, somehow persuading credit rating agencies to give high-risk securities their triple A seal of approval. This raised money to do future deals and kept the mortgage boom going. Or they bought protection against the risk by buying *credit default swaps* – insurance contracts which compensate banks buying bonds for any losses if a particular bond defaults – from myopic insurance companies, transferring the risk to someone else in the financial circus. In theory this shared the risk around, making it more manageable in the event of default. In fact it made the entire financial system more exposed because, behind the complexity surrounding financial securities, banks were buying each other's bonds, increasing their interconnectedness and thereby raising the risk of entire system failure if any big bank got into trouble. In several cases the very same institution that had apparently laid off the risk by selling it on to third parties (who themselves sold it on to others) found the risk back in its lap because another part of its operation had bought the risk further down the chain from one of those third parties. Financiers were not only fooling the world, they were fooling themselves.

Originally, banks bought credit default swaps as a hedge against the risk of non-payment on a bond, paying periodic premiums to the insurance company that had sold them the swap. Soon, however, the use of swaps for *hedging* was dwarfed by their use for *gambling* – placing bets on whether a bond would default. Alan Blinder has shown the scale of this slide into casino banking in the US. The value of credit default swaps outstanding in the US at the end of 2001 was $919 billion. By the end of 2007 it had passed a staggering $62,000 billion, and in 2008 about 80 per cent of credit default swaps were pure financial bets rather than hedges. The underlying mortgage risk had been magnified by trillions of dollars of credit default swaps.[10]

In this incestuous process, no one knew who held which assets and who was exposed to how much risk. Banks could not even be sure what lay at the end of the chain attached to any, or all, of their own loans. Was it a pot of gold or a ticking time bomb? So everyone was suspect when the property bubble burst and mortgage payers began to default on their repayments. Interbank lending started to dry up. It stayed stuck even after sudden cuts in interest rates and injections of huge amounts of fresh money into their economies by central banks in the US, the UK and elsewhere in Europe. The global credit crunch had arrived.

Governments to the rescue

The major banks have now become so big, so complex and so interconnected that the failure of any one of them could threaten the entire economic system by causing the flow of credit to seize up, businesses to go bust as they become unable to pay their bills, and trade to come to a stop; even cash transactions could collapse as bank cash machines close and banks hold onto what little liquidity they possess.

To try to prevent such a disastrous collapse of confidence and to calm panicking financial markets in 2008–09, governments made desperate attempts to save the world's financial system from total breakdown. They launched massive bailout plans to rebuild bank balance sheets with fresh capital. Later some central banks even began buying banks' 'bad' assets, replacing loans and securities whose value was in doubt with cash on the assets side of bank balance sheets.

Capitalism had proved to be inherently and precariously unstable, and more powerfully so than Crosland could ever have envisaged or almost anyone had believed possible before 2008. The number of banking crises somewhere in the world had fallen from 30 in 1995 to 10 in 2000 and zero in 2006,[11] encouraging complacency about the solidity of world financial systems. Yet those very systems fell apart in the 2007–08 global credit crunch, throwing the entire financial system into a crisis condition; in the view of Paul Volcker, Alan Greenspan and Ben Bernanke, former chairs of the Federal Reserve, the US central bank, it was poised to plunge the world economy into an even worse slump than the Great Depression of the 1930s.

The focus of failure lay in the financial institutions, in the boardrooms and the trading desks of the big banks on Wall Street, in Canary Wharf and in Frankfurt's financial district. But it was in the Oval Office at the White House, the Cabinet Room at 10 Downing Street and the Bundeskanzleramt in Berlin, in meeting rooms off the corridors of power in the Treasury buildings along Pennsylvania Avenue, Whitehall and Wilhelmstrasse, and in the headquarters of the US, UK and European central banks in Washington DC, London and Frankfurt where the key decisions were made that saved the financial system from itself. It was Congressional, Parliamentary and Bundestag approval for state intervention on a massive scale that saved the banking system from going bust and pulled economies back from the brink of a disaster that neoliberal theory and the efficient markets hypothesis said could not occur.

The scale of these state rescue packages almost beggars belief. Labour initially agreed a comprehensive plan to bail out Britain's failed banks in October 2008. It included a commitment to spend up to £50 billion buying bank shares to boost their capital, without which citizens would have had their savings and bank balances cleaned out, salaries would not have been paid, and businesses would have been bankrupted on a truly catastrophic scale. Those cash outlays buying bank shares soon rose by December 2009, with £76 billion used to buy shares in Royal Bank of Scotland and Lloyds Banking Group alone.

By February 2013 the IMF estimated that state support to the UK financial sector amounted to about £100 billion.[12] In June 2013 the Parliamentary Commission on Banking Standards reported that bailing out Britain's banks had cost UK taxpayers cash outlays peaking at £133 billion. The colossal cost of these cash outlays was financed by huge levels of government borrowing which subsequently became the Conservative mantra for condemning Labour as financially profligate. But without such state action and the much vilified hike in government borrowing, the meltdown would have been terminal.

Nevertheless these cash outlays formed only a small part of the total picture of state support for the financial system, because government guarantees meant that total taxpayer support to the banks could be very much higher. In 2009 such guarantees plus capital injections, purchases of assets and lending by HM Treasury totalled almost 71 per cent of GDP (over £1,000 billion). Liquidity and other support provided by the Bank of England added a further 19 per cent of GDP (about £275 billion).[13] By July 2012 the potential cost to the UK taxpayer of saving Britain's banks had reached £1,162 billion, or fully *ten times the annual cost of the National Health Service*.[14]

On top of these explicit guarantees and cash outlays there are the *implicit* subsidies to UK banks and building societies from the understanding that government will always step in to save the financial system if any of the big banks are about to go bust. It is worth just identifying how monumental these subsidies are. The average annual implicity subsidy for the top five UK banks between 2007 and 2009 was over £50 billion, about the same as UK banks' annual profits prior to the crisis. These estimates exclude the value of the subsidy due to the government guarantee of banks' retail deposits.[15] IMF staff estimated[16] that the largest globally active banks alone benefited from implicit subsidies in 2012 worth up to $590 billion worldwide and up to £70 billion in the UK – gigantic subsidies which also make it doubly difficult for potential new entrants to contest the UK banking market.

The result was spiralling debt – and not simply in the UK as if Labour's stewardship was somehow alone at fault: the 'Big Deceit' mantra of the Tory/Lib Dems. US net debt rose from 48 per cent of GDP in 2007 to 88 per cent by 2012, and eurozone net debt from 52 per cent to 72 per cent.[17]

However, even these enormous amounts do not complete the picture. Allowing for all direct cash support, implicit subsidies, guarantees and contingent liabilities provided to the financial system by central banks and governments in the US, the UK and elsewhere in Europe, plus the backing provided to sovereign governments by international bodies like the IMF, the grand total cost of bailing out the banks and other financial institutions was estimated in 2010 to total a staggering $65 trillion, or roughly 250 per cent of North American plus European GDP.[18]

The financial system of Europe and America has shown itself to be prone to collapse. Small wonder that people fear that an unreformed financial system would lead next time to a crisis in which governments could no longer afford the fiscal and monetary measures needed to bail out a bust banking system, or even lead to governments defaulting on their debt. Either way the entire economy would collapse into a second Great Depression.

It is not as if the risk is low or that financial crises in market economies are rare events. Although banking crises initially became less frequent after 1945, of 66 countries studied by Carmen Reinhart and Kenneth Rogoff all bar one experienced at least one post-war banking crisis prior to the 2008 global credit crunch.[19] Relative financial stability during the immediate post-war period, with only 38 banking or currency crises between 1945 and 1971, was followed by a return to instability with 139 crises between 1973 and 1997, which is why Martin Wolf concluded that 'the age of financial liberalisation was, in short, an age of crises'.[20]

Serious crises requiring government intervention to protect the financial system began to reappear in the 1970s and 1980s on both sides of the Atlantic. The UK experienced four between 1970 and 2007: in the 1974–76 secondary banking crisis when the Bank of England intervened with a 'lifeboat' support operation, press-ganging the bigger banks to lend £1.2 billion to some 30 smaller ones caught short in the wholesale money markets; in 1984 when Johnson Matthey Bankers was rescued from failure by a bailout organised by the Bank of England to prevent a wider banking crisis; in 1991 when Bank of Credit and Commerce International was forced to close by the Bank of England in a fraud scandal; and in 1995 when

Barings Bank collapsed after losing £827 million due to disastrous, unauthorised, speculative trading by one employee based in Singapore, and fundamental management failures.

The US also went through financial crises requiring state intervention to prevent serious system–wide repercussions. In 1984 a $4.5 billion federal rescue package saved Continental Illinois Bank from failure. Between 1980 and the mid–1990s it cost the American taxpayer $160 billion to close nearly 750 failed savings and loan associations. In 1998 the imminent collapse of the hedge fund Long Term Capital Management threatened catastrophic losses throughout the financial system and was only avoided by the Federal Reserve instigating a $3.6 billion bailout for 14 private sector banks.

It was the failure of a similar attempt to find a $33 billion private sector solution to the collapse of Lehman Brothers on Sunday, 14 September 2008, and the refusal of the American government to rescue the bank, that triggered the 2008 global financial crisis. Yet Lehman was an intrinsic part of the modern banking spider's web and its collapse could not be contained. *Within hours* of that refusal the American government had to intervene to save several other banks. *Within days* it had to commit hundreds of billions of taxpayer dollars to save the whole financial system or see the global economy collapse. *Within weeks* both the American and British governments had adopted similar strategies for recapitalising their banks, transforming a private sector crisis fed by reckless risks to achieve soaring bonuses into a huge public sector liability. In turn this led to accusations from the right of extravagant state spending and excessive government borrowing.

The sequence of events and the contagion which followed and escalated into a global panic is worth recalling:

- Lehman Brothers filed for bankruptcy protection at 1.45 am on Monday, 15 September 2008.
- By 4.00 pm on Tuesday, 16 September the American Federal Reserve felt obliged to bail out the insurance giant AIG with an $85 billion loan, increased in November 2008 to £150 billion and eventually reaching $182 billion, for fear of the crippling losses for the banks that AIG's demise would mean. This was the

'backdoor bailout' of Wall Street banks. If AIG had been allowed to fail this would also have forced European banks to write off some $150 billion in assets.[21]

- Only two days later on Thursday, 18 September US Treasury Secretary Henry Paulson and Federal Reserve Chairman Ben Bernanke were presenting Congressional leaders with a vision of imminent economic apocalypse and the possible breakdown of civil order. They begged Congress immediately to back a Troubled Assets Relief Program (TARP) authorising the US Treasury to spend hundreds of billions of dollars rescuing the banks by buying their dubious assets. They confirmed their request for $700 billion on Saturday, 20 September.

- On 29 September, Congress voted down the TARP proposal, causing the S&P 500 index of leading shares to fall by about 9 per cent the following day. Congress approved an amended TARP plan on 3 October and President Bush signed the Emergency Economic Stabilization Act the same day. Even before Congress had voted its approval Chairman Bernanke had persuaded Secretary Paulson to use the funds to inject capital directly into banks by buying their shares instead of by buying their toxic assets, because this would save time and urgent effective action was needed.

- On 8 October, Gordon Brown and Alistair Darling announced a £500 billion ($850 billion) UK bank rescue plan involving government loans and guarantees plus a £50 billion capital injection scheme to recapitalise Britain's banks (most of which went into buying share stakes in Lloyds and Royal Bank of Scotland), surpassing the scale of the American rescue plan.

- On 12 October, US Treasury Secretary Paulson revealed his U-turn and confirmed that TARP funds would be used to inject capital directly into banks rather than to purchase troubled assets. On 13 October, Paulson obliged the heads of the nine biggest banks in the US to accept $125 billion as the US government bought nonvoting preference shares. The US government eventually invested $205 billion in nearly 700 banks under this scheme.[22]

The urgency and the scale of these events show how absurd is the neoliberal idea of a 'self-stabilising' Anglo Saxon financial system and how vital state intervention is when the failure of a single financial institution – one bank or one insurance company – can threaten to bring down the entire house of cards, and with it people's savings, their jobs, their pensions and their pay.

The costs of recession

Urgent state action prevented utter disaster, but it could not ward off global recession, and world trade initially fell as fast as at the start of the 1930s Great Depression. National income went down, unemployment rose and living standards suffered almost everywhere.

Neoliberals need honestly to acknowledge the sheer scale and gravity of the costs imposed by the recession. This is important because after 2010 they and their media allies imposed a completely false mindset on public debate, in Britain at least. In the argument about where the roots of the crisis lay – either 'overspending' by government or in irresponsible lending by bankers – the neoliberals certainly trumpeted their case the loudest. Inevitably many people swallowed it, and backed calls for a purge on public spending, so delaying the day when the economy would recover from recession.

As was noted earlier, the direct costs to the state of bank bailouts to rescue failing financial systems formed only part of the burden born by taxpayers in fighting the recession that began in 2008. From their analysis of 66 countries over nearly eight centuries, Reinhart and Rogoff found that the deepest and most protracted recessions tend to be those associated with severe systemic banking crises. And indeed, German Chancellor Angela Merkel and IMF Chief Economist Olivier Blanchard both acknowledged that tackling the worst recession since the 1930s was always going to be a marathon, not a sprint.

The direct costs of bank bailouts constituted only the down payment in an instalment plan for promoting recovery which would last years. Again, the UK taxpayer was far from alone in bearing such costs. Over the period 2007–09 these direct fiscal outlays totalled 8.7 per cent of GDP in the UK (mainly by recapitalising RBS, Lloyds

Bank and Northern Rock plus loans to Northern Rock and Bradford & Bingley). The corresponding figures were 1.0 per cent of GDP in France, 1.4 in Germany, 3.1 in Denmark, 4.1 in Austria, 4.9 in the US, 5.0 in Belgium, 7.6 per cent in Ireland, 12.7 in the Netherlands and 13.0 in Iceland.[23]

But much greater than these initial direct costs have always been the broader fiscal cost of the recessions induced by financial crises. Typically the deep recessions that accompany severe financial crises have led to huge increases in public debt to which bank bailout costs have made only a minor contribution. Contrary to neoliberal accusations, it tends to be a sharp drop in tax revenue rather than a rise in public spending that drives the increase in government borrowing and rise in national debt.[24] Before the impact of the crisis, annual UK public sector borrowing under Labour had been projected in March 2008 to reach £38 billion in 2009–10. It actually leapt *four times* that projection to £156 billion. The annual budget deficit rose from 2.6 per cent of GDP in 2007–08 to again *four times* that amount or 11.0 per cent in 2009–10, a post-war peak.

Even higher still was the ongoing annual loss to all citizens – taxpayers and non-taxpayers alike – represented by the value of national output forgone. Recession and a plodding recovery led UK national income to fall well short of its long-term growth trend. In 2013 output was still over 3 per cent below its 2008 peak and about 16 per cent below where the pre-crisis growth trend would have taken it, an annual loss of national income in excess of £200 billion and a cumulative loss over five years of about half a year's total production: truly calamitous losses which meant each British household was penalised by an annual average of over £5,500.

Rising public borrowing and falling national income as the economy slid into recession pushed up the burden of UK national debt. Public sector net debt, forecast in March 2008 to reach 39 per cent of GDP in 2009–10, actually hit 56 per cent because of the banking crisis. In December 2013 the Office for Budget Responsibility forecast net debt to peak at 80 per cent of GDP in 2015–16 (£1,451 billion).[25] That compared with Labour's 2006–07 level of 36 per cent (£498 billion). Over nine years a private sector banking crisis will have cost UK taxpayers nearly an extra £1,000 billion of debt.

The Institute for Fiscal Studies estimated in April 2009 that Labour's 2008–09 fiscal stimulus accounted for a fraction – less than *one fifteenth* – of the total rise in debt expected between 2009 and 2012, a pointer to the importance of allowing the automatic stabilisers to come into play and to the need for care if contemplating imposing arbitrary caps on social security budgets. It is another nail in the coffin of the deceitful Tory version of the recession as being all down to 'Labour spending profligacy'.

By the first half of 2010 both the UK and the US economies were making tentative recoveries. But then their paths diverged as the UK abandoned Keynes for neoliberal dogma under the Conservative/Liberal Democrat government. While US GDP kept growing, the UK experienced its slowest recovery from recession since the 19th century. Having shrunk by 7 per cent from its 2008 peak to its 2009 trough, UK GDP began expanding again in early 2010. But growth was brought to an abrupt halt by Chancellor of the Exchequer George Osborne's 2010 emergency budget and spending review. A harsh fiscal squeeze, coupled with Osborne's nightmare scenarios about a Britain 'on the brink of bankruptcy', shattered consumer confidence and business optimism. Household spending and business investment promptly dropped through the floor and the UK economy stagnated for three years.

By the end of 2013, UK GDP was still well short of its 2008 peak, in contrast to the US and Germany, which both passed their pre-crisis peaks in 2011. It had taken them three years to recover. Over five years after the financial crisis the UK economy was still in a shrunken state. Something had stymied the pace of recovery and left the UK economy lagging behind our leading trading partners. That something was a programme of brutal cuts in public investment and expenditure which meant that the best Britain could hope for was to get back to square one by 2014, having taken *six* years to achieve what our friends abroad did in *three*. The National Institute of Economic and Social Research (NIESR) has pointed out how much worse Britain has done in *this* recession even than in the 1930s when Britain's GDP regained its previous peak by the *fourth* year after the 1929 Great Depression.[26]

Adair Turner summed up the situation in January 2014: 'We have spent the last few years talking about the need to rebalance the economy away from a focus on property and financial services and towards investment and exports. We are now back to growth without any rebalancing at all.' He added: 'If you chuck enough monetary stimulus at an economy something happens. It is as if we have had a cracking great hangover, had a stiff drink and off we go again.'[27]

Some anti-globalisation campaigners miss the point that it is the globalisation of finance and gambling rather than the globalisation of production and trade that has exposed entire economic systems to risk of meltdown. Huge financial flows across international borders have done nothing to boost international trade in goods and services. Instead they have undermined domestic economies by encouraging speculative bubbles that trigger collapse when they burst. Thus the proportion of world GDP held as reserves by the central banks of countries running balance of payments surpluses, most notably China, more than doubled from 5.6 per cent to 11.7 per cent. But instead of being recycled into the global economy as extra consumer spending at home on imported goods and services from abroad, they became 'hot capital' that was lent to advanced economies like the US and the UK where they fuelled the subprime housing bubble.[28]

This New Finance has done absolutely nothing for what we used to call 'the manufacturing base' of the UK economy, which has shrunk disastrously. This is partly because domestic consumers now spend a smaller share of their income on goods, switching instead to services, and because firms are replacing workers with plant and equipment and making more efficient use of the people they retain. But it is also because British manufacturing firms failed to compete on price and quality, leading them to lose orders at home and abroad. They could not match low-cost foreign competitors or rivals who invested more in their future and were backed by governments which provided a more supportive business and banking environment. The clearest contrast is with Germany which has retained its export market for manufactured products by a much more supportive financial system, enabling it to exploit its comparative advantage in high quality, reliable, precision-engineered products, built by highly skilled workers using the best kit. Britain's or Germany's? No prizes for guessing which economy became stronger.

The new capitalism

Capitalism has evolved into a system which now generates greater inequalities of income and wealth than ever, with negative social consequences: unequal societies tend also to become unhealthy and unsafe ones.[29] Privilege is still perpetuated from one generation to the next, reserving the best opportunities for the favoured few and limiting social mobility.

Today's capitalism also underinvests in human capital, preparing our young people poorly for a fast changing world while insisting that competitiveness requires adaptability and flexibility. It emphasises innovation while granting the highest rewards in sectors like finance with the least socially beneficial technological breakthroughs. It encourages patterns of production that pay little heed to their social and environmental consequences by the over-exploitation of natural assets. It combines a relentless focus on future opportunities for profit with a stunning disregard for the environmental damage and clean-up costs it has dumped on society in the past.

The leaders of today's capitalism demand less state regulation but more government guarantees. They want public spending for others to shrink but government contracts for them to expand. They can't stand social welfare but are all for corporate welfare whereby the state provides massive support for the private sector. They want a level playing field in product markets and free movement in capital markets, yet practise discrimination, blacklists and unfair treatment in labour markets. They call for transparency while rigging interest rates on interbank borrowing like LIBOR and mis-selling products like payment protection insurance. They preach open competition while shrouding predatory pricing in a cloak of commercial confidentiality.

The result is not simply to trap a substantial group at the bottom – almost an underclass – but to squeeze the majority of society: Britain's 'squeezed middle' has suffered real cuts in relative living standards for years, similar to the US where the median wage of its employees is now lower than in the 1980s despite substantial growth. On current policy trends this is likely to worsen for the next generation, placing huge stresses on social cohesion.

Without fundamental financial reform, once economies have recovered from recession and resumed steady growth, competition between the banks will push them back into their bad habit of taking ever higher risks. Because that is what bank bonus and incentive payment systems encourage, and because that is the way to meet shareholder demands for ever higher returns on equity capital. This is where neoliberalism leads: to catastrophe, not to any sort of platform for stability.

To the brink

Tony Crosland's confidence in the likelihood of capitalism delivering ongoing economic growth and financial stability proved sadly misplaced. It was overtaken by events. The relative financial calm of the 1950s gave way to a transformed financial system in which lightly regulated big banks and unregulated 'shadow banks' interacted with one another in a frenzy of financial deals quite unrelated to the needs of the real economy.

The traditional notion of banks as intermediaries between individuals, companies or governments who want to borrow and people with money to lend or invest has not completely disappeared. But it is now a minor part of what banking is about. The financial system has become a gambling emporium rather than a mainstay of domestic and international trade. It is now self-serving rather than servicing the needs of the economy. As such, it now poses a lethal threat to the stability of economies and to the viability of state finances.

The neoliberal experiment with deregulated financial markets that New Labour warmly embraced led the global economy to the very brink of complete economic collapse and to well-founded fears of civil disorder. Avoiding any repetition must be a policy imperative for the left, with reform and tough regulation of financial systems. For democratic socialists across the world to even partially concede the neoliberal case would render our cause, and our potential, worthless.

CHAPTER 4

Growth not cuts

Britain's budget deficit has been at the centre of public debate since the financial crisis broke out in 2008 and the economic downturn began. Every pre-budget report, every budget and every public spending review has been assessed for its implications for government borrowing and national debt. Yet the key consequence each time has been what it has meant for the growth rate of the UK economy, for it is on growth that both deficits and debt ultimately depend.

The recession that started in 2008 lasted longer in some countries than others, the difference owing as much to fiscal policy and the degree to which governments made *austerity* rather than *recovery* their aim. At the G20 summits in London and Pittsburgh in April and September 2009 global leaders agreed to cooperate to ensure that growth was sustained. But Labour had lost the election by the time of the Toronto summit in June 2010 which sadly abandoned that stance. It committed the advanced economies to at least halving their budget deficits by 2013 instead of prioritising growth.

Even so, few finance ministers pursued austerity with more vigour than Britain's George Osborne. He gripped the UK economy in a budget squeeze far tighter than that in the US and twice as tight as in the eurozone.[1]

The consequences of austerity

The result? In the growing American economy by 2013 the actual budget deficit had fallen by over 40 per cent since 2010. In the stagnant UK economy, it had dropped by only 31 per cent. Osborne was borrowing £217 billion more between 2011–12 and 2015–16 than he had said he would just three years before in his June 2010 emergency budget, £539 billion against the £322 billion forecast. Austerity had left Britain's budget deficit 68 per cent above target.[2]

In 2012–13 George Osborne's first *target deficit* (the cyclically adjusted current deficit as a share of GDP) turned out twice what he originally said it would be: 3.6 per cent in 2012–13 compared with 1.9 per cent forecast in June 2010. By 2013–14, according to the Office for Budget Responsibility (OBR), it was expected to be four times what Osborne planned in June 2010: 2.9 per cent against 0.7 per cent forecast in 2010.[3] Hardly what David Cameron presumably meant when he told Parliament his government was going 'further and faster on the deficit': falling short of his deficit target by ever wider margins. OBR Director Robert Chote recognised in April 2013 that progress in cutting the deficit had stalled. The Chancellor was both wildly off course and behind schedule on the deficit.

His second *target* from 2010 was to see public sector *debt* falling as a proportion of GDP by 2015–16. But he missed that too. His original plan saw debt falling to 67 per cent of GDP in 2015–16, but the March 2013 budget saw it falling to 85 per cent in 2017–18: a surreal definition of success – debt falling upwards: Salvador Dalí would have been proud. In December 2013 the OBR was forecasting debt still to be rising in 2015–16 to a peak of 80 per cent of GDP.

The Americans took the route of economic stimulus and stuck to it. They reaped the reward and kept growing. The British set out on the same path under Labour and the economy began to pick up. But the Tory/Lib Dem coalition veered off as soon as they took office, turning the road to recovery into the road to ruin for millions, especially young people desperate for work. Osborne turned a growing economy into a slowing economy. He took recovery from start to stop.

And, contrary to Osborne's claims at the time, it was not the eurozone that had been holding Britain back. By backing austerity instead of growth, both British and European governments dragged each other down. Problems in the eurozone spell trouble for the UK economy – of course they do, with half Britain's trade being with the EU. But the Chancellor conveniently said nothing about how Britain had been benefiting from the recovery of the US economy, which accounts for 20 per cent of our trade, and which was growing while the eurozone was slowing. American growth offset much eurozone sloth. By leaving the American recovery out of the picture in order to serve his political purposes, Osborne presented a false prospectus.

Debt, deficits and growth

What we witnessed in that period was part of an established historical pattern across the globe. It is private sector financial crises that have led to public sector fiscal strain, not the other way round. Increases in public debt have proved a poor predictor of subsequent financial crises. Growth of private credit has proved a better augury of such emergencies.[4]

But that was not the story conveyed by David Cameron and George Osborne. As was shown in Chapter 2, they deliberately peddled a myth that the worst global recession for 80 years stemmed from wildly excessive spending by the last Labour government. Their mantra, relentlessly repeated like an old gramophone record stuck in the same groove, gained powerful traction in shaping UK political and public debate, and Labour – preoccupied after its 2010 defeat with a leadership election which lasted far too long, twice as long as David Cameron's 2005 election as Tory Party leader – did much too little, much too late to stop it taking hold. In this vacuum, Labour allowed discussion to be dominated by the level of national debt and the size of budget deficits, rather than the growth rate of the economy on which they both depend.

It serves the right's ideological purposes to paint a picture of public spending as a 'bad', a negative for the wealth creation, for entrepreneurialism and for the risk taking upon which, most certainly, all economies depend in order to prosper. Their argument is that public spending 'crowds out' private investment in market economies.

But that is obvious nonsense in a recession when a drop in private sector spending, especially business investment, leads to spare industrial capacity and growing unemployment. Extra public spending is needed to fill the gap caused by shrinking private sector spending, to put people back to work and to get the economy growing again. But a growing economy needs public spending too, to provide the educated and healthy workforce, the system for enforcing property rights, the essential infrastructure, and the social safety net on which a dynamic private sector depends. In reality, in economies like the UK a proper balance between the market and the state is vital for both to work well. Starving the public services does not 'liberate' entrepreneurs, it undermines the foundations on which a civilised society is built. Cutting the number of NHS nurses does not promote a healthier community by 'freeing up' private health care that most people cannot afford and which only meets a limited range of medical needs. Cutting police numbers does not reduce crime, it raises insurance premiums. Few contributors have acknowledged that the UK has a startlingly good record of reducing its debt burden *while* improving public services in a growing economy.

For that reason Tony Crosland was relatively unworried about debt and deficit hangovers from the Second World War effort in the mid-1950s – and it is easy to see that he was right. The Radcliffe Committee reviewed the working of the UK monetary system in 1959. It noted that while public sector net debt had risen from £27 billion in 1952 to over £30 billion by 1958, as a proportion of national income the debt burden had fallen from 213 per cent to 168 per cent.[5] The growing UK economy, coupled with inflation, was bringing down the burden of debt despite budget deficits which were in the region of 2–3 per cent of GDP for most of the 1950s and 1960s.[6]

In relation to GDP, national debt fell from its postwar peak of 238 per cent in 1947 to 42 per cent under the Tories in 1997 and 36 per cent under Labour in 2007, rising to 52 per cent by 2010 as recession hit.

Debt is more sustainable *with* growth. The Tories' own record in government proves the point. Between 1979 and 1997 the Thatcher and Major governments ran a budget surplus only twice, and overall there was a net deficit adding up to 35 per cent of GDP. Yet the economy grew by 57 per cent and national debt fell from 47 per cent to 42 per cent of GDP.[7]

Moreover, predictions that debt levels of the order forecast for the UK would lead financial institutions to refuse to lend to the British government by stopping buying government bonds or by insisting on much higher interest rates from public sector borrowers have proved totally false. Such debt levels in a country like the UK simply do not mean a bond market veto on government borrowing that some headline-seekers suggest – even under New Labour at the height of the crisis, the markets were not 'selling shares in Britain' as Tory/Lib Dems pretended would have happened without their post-2010 cuts.

Borrowing and spending

Conservative ministers like Chancellor George Osborne claimed that Labour took the country to the 'brink of bankruptcy', or 'maxed out on the country's credit card'. Had there been any substance to this myth, the warning signs would have been flashing all over the City of London. In fact they had been signalling steady as she goes ever since the financial crisis erupted in 2008, for yields on British government bonds remained low. In March 2009 yields on ten-year government bonds fell to 2.95 per cent, the lowest since 1958. City investors were keen to lend to the Labour government at low rates because they had confidence in the UK's public finances – and with good reason. If Britain really had been a bankrupt borrower, no investor would have bought government bonds on such terms. In fact in 2009 City investors lent £30 billion to the British government. In the first quarter of 2010 the bond market financed 87 per cent of the UK budget deficit, at even lower yields than it had done during 2009. What kind of City investor lends £30 billion to a 'bankrupt' borrower?

On taking office in May 2010 Osborne pledged to slash government borrowing, warning that otherwise interest rates and yields on government bonds would soar as investors lost confidence. Yet while he borrowed over £200 billion *more* than he forecast in 2010, yields on government bonds continued to drop, the yield on ten-year government bonds reaching a record low in May 2012 of 1.87 per cent, the lowest since Bank of England records began in 1703.

The UK lost its 'triple A' credit rating but the government could still borrow at low rates. Bill Gross of bond investor Pimco had claimed in January 2010 that the UK finances were so precarious they were 'resting on a bed of nitro-glycerine'. But he was proved wrong:

borrowing rose but there was no big bang. His and Osborne's claim that interest rates would rocket unless government borrowing was slashed has been comprehensively contradicted by the facts. Nobel economist Paul Krugman has convincingly demonstrated that, with sensible economic management, neither the UK nor the US needed to fear the 'bond market vigilantes'.

Nevertheless, some Labour colleagues passively accepted the neoliberal orthodoxy presented in the OBR analysis of Britain's scope for economic growth and the prospects for the public finances. A New Labour chorus took up this orthodoxy early. In September 2010 the pro-Labour analyst Peter Kellner announced that 'social democracy, as we have come to understand it, has become unaffordable'. In November 2010 Tony Blair's former policy adviser Patrick Diamond wrote: 'Labour must be much clearer on the specifics of spending cuts it will support if it is to restore fiscal credibility with a public that understands fiscal retrenchment is needed.' In 2012 former Labour government advisers Gavin Kelly and Nick Pearce of the Resolution Foundation and the Institute for Public Policy Research dismissed the prospects for Croslandite social democracy up to 2020 as 'vanishingly thin' and the outlook for public spending as 'unremittingly bleak'. They did so because they took as given what they called 'the scale of the hole to be filled' without considering whether the OBR could have got its sums and indeed its whole analysis wrong. This was even before the OBR's July 2013 fiscal sustainability report calling for further permanent spending cuts or tax increases of £19 billion in 2018–19 if governments wanted to reduce national debt to 40 per cent of GDP by 2062–63.

In April 2013 Tony Blair's former Europe adviser Roger Liddle went further, advising European social democrats to impose 'ruthless financial discipline' by sticking within existing public finance envelopes 'verified independently by bodies independent of the nation state'. By February 2014 Patrick Diamond was back, as pessimistic as ever about Britain's growth prospects and with new euphemisms for cuts: 'Labour cannot rely on economic growth to render strategic prioritisation irrelevant. The short- and long-term pressures on the state will continue. In all likelihood, growth will remain anaemic, given uncertainty in the global economy. The modern social settlement will have to be renegotiated.' This was the same week that the Governor of the Bank of England Mark Carney forecast that UK economic growth would hit 3.4 per cent in 2014, though Carney did acknowledge that 'as yet the recovery is neither balanced nor sustainable. A few quarters of above-trend growth driven by household spending are a good start, but they aren't sufficient for sustained momentum.'[8]

Spare capacity for growth

The analysis on which the OBR forecasts were based has been hotly disputed by critics, who argued that the amount of spare capacity in the economy (capital equipment left idle plus unemployed or underemployed labour) far exceeds that assumed by the OBR. Since 2008 the economy has *actually* been producing less than it *could* be producing. The actual level of GDP has fallen short of where the past trend (or potential) level of GDP would have been but for the recession. By the beginning of 2014 this difference, the amount of 'slack' in the economy, was about 15 per cent of GDP, or over £200 billion worth of output forgone due to recession. If this spare capacity was put to work, total output in the economy could grow quite quickly, at least until the economy had used up the slack and begun to produce at close to full capacity again, when production could expand only as fast as capacity itself grew.

This 'output gap' – the difference between actual and potential output – far exceeded the modest 3 per cent of GDP assumed for 2011 by the OBR in March 2012 and continued to exceed it in 2014. The OBR assumption in December 2013 of an output gap of only 1.8 per cent of GDP for 2014 was disputed by authoritative critics, who saw much greater scope for growth, including the International Monetary Fund and the Institute for Fiscal Studies.[9]

In 2014 UK spare capacity was much more than twice that assumed conservatively by the OBR. That meant the size of the structural budget deficit – the bit that would persist even after a return to full-capacity working – was very much smaller than in OBR forecasts. The implications are critically important for economic policy, for the future of Britain and indeed for the future of democratic socialism.

First, the fiscal squeeze needed to end the deficit could be far less tight and public spending cuts far less deep than planned by George Osborne (or backed by those New Labour loyalists who see calls for public spending cuts as key to Labour's *political* credibility in a neoliberal-dominated climate even if the *economics* is deeply flawed). The squeeze could be relaxed, not intensified, without damaging confidence or sending the deficit and debt sky high.

Second, the scope for 'catch-up growth' could be far greater than the OBR assumed, making rapid recovery and ongoing expansion entirely feasible. That is what Alistair Darling expected in 2009: 'After a downturn like the ones we had in the 1980s and 1990s, growth tends to bounce back, sometimes hitting as much as 4 per cent, as people get back to work, produce more goods and sell more services,' he wrote.[10] It is what happened in the 1930s. The Great Depression hit bottom in 1932 and the period 1933–36 saw very strong recovery with annual UK growth of over 4 per cent (not the under 3 per cent forecast by the OBR for 2013–18), significantly fuelled by a house-building boom.[11] Catch-up growth is also what happened in the US: between 1933 and 1937 America's GDP grew at a startling average annual rate of 9.5 per cent.[12]

When growth of 2.4 per cent at an annual rate appeared to have returned at last to the UK economy in the middle of 2013, Simon Wren-Lewis noted: 'We should really be looking for rates of GDP growth of 4% or more if we are going to start utilising those resources which are currently being wasted.'[13]

In February 2014 Oxford Economics forecast that UK GDP growth would average 2.6 per cent per year from 2014 to 2018.[14] But its belief that UK spare capacity was so great gave it grounds for expecting the UK economy 'to be able to sustain several years of above trend growth beyond 2018–19 and that we could plan for much less fiscal consolidation [cuts] as more of the deficit would prove to be a temporary phenomenon.' They added: 'If the most optimistic forecasters prove correct then none of the spending cuts planned beyond 2014–15 would be needed to return the deficit to pre-crisis levels.'[15]

All the talk about sorting out the public finances by yet more cuts always misses the point about growth. Under the Tory/Lib Dem government there was plenty of spare capacity in the UK economy. Maybe unemployment rose less during their 2010–13 recession than forecast from past experience because businesses hoarded labour, masking the degree of spare capacity, and because far too many new jobs were part-time and insecure, with a high level of underemployment. The economy could easily have grown quite quickly for several years by taking up the slack. As Jonathan Portes of the National Institute of Economic and Social Research and former chief economist at the Cabinet Office commented in 2013: 'A few years of 3 per cent growth – and given the amount of spare capacity in the UK economy, there is no reason that should be infeasible … – and much of the problem will simply vanish.' Another respected economist William Keegan has summed up the situation perfectly: 'Experience shows that it is surprising how, during a period of rapid "cyclical" growth, a "structural" deficit can evaporate.'[16]

In short, the name of the game is growth. Throughout modern history getting the economy growing again after recessions has been the key to cutting the deficit and stabilising, and then bringing down, the debt burden. With the economy growing again it is always much easier to deliver any remaining tax rises or spending cuts that may still be necessary to rebalance public finances post-recession and make the growth sustainable. This is because, as Jonathan Portes argued, jobs will be plentiful, with real incomes rising and companies investing again. Just as exercise is the magic bullet for improving the nation's health, economic growth is the direct line towards overcoming deficit and debt problems.

Alternative to austerity

The relentless Tory charge remained that Labour would 'increase borrowing'. The answer should be clear: in the short term, yes, but in the medium to longer term, no. Boosting economic recovery may well require more public borrowing in the short term. It is the right thing to do to get the economy growing again, to maintain the momentum of growth and *reduce borrowing* over the medium term. Higher public spending and borrowing *today* can mean lower borrowing *tomorrow* if it gets the economy growing again, with tax revenues rising as total spending in the economy increases, and welfare bills falling as unemployment comes down. It has been tried before and it has worked. President Obama's 2009 stimulus package added to the US federal deficit, but US interest rates fell, spending and output rose, and dole queues shortened. And as a proportion of its expanding GDP, America's overall deficit shrank every year from 2009 to 2013.

Although there was never going to be a painless way out of the banking crisis, easing the squeeze and getting the economy growing again could have produced much, though not all, of the extra tax revenue and the spending cuts needed steadily to bring the budget back into balance. The urgency for cuts in order to reduce UK debt to 60 per cent of GDP by 2030, as outlined by the IMF, would also be less pressing if the size of the adjustment required were to be lower.

From a New Labour standpoint, Nick Pearce proposed in March 2013 that Labour commit to reducing the ratio of debt to GDP ratio by 15 per cent, from 80 to 65 per cent, between 2015 and 2025, independently enforced by the OBR, to demonstrate seriousness and credibility about debt reduction. But the last time the debt burden was cut by 15 per cent it took eight years longer – 18 years, from 1984 to 2002. And three quarters of the way through New Labour was complaining, justifiably, that the Tory public spending squeeze had left public services seriously underfunded and important parts of public infrastructure – from railways to hospitals – in abject decay.

Another reason to doubt Nick Pearce's assessment is because he was so casual about welfare spending. In May 2013 he and Graeme Cooke argued, correctly, that the benefits bill must rise during a recession. But they also claimed 'the problem is that it does not fall when there is growth'. This claim cannot be squared with the evidence. At the bottom of the previous recession in 1993 the UK benefits bill was 12.69 per cent of GDP. At the peak of the following boom in 2008 it had fallen to 11.37 per cent of GDP.[17] That is a difference worth some £20 billion per year.

The consequences of sticking with a right-wing economic agenda – extreme under another Tory-led government or moderate under a Labour-led one – could prove fearful. Despite this the Tories set upon compounding their failures in government to repeat the mistake that British governments made in the 1920s. George Osborne told the September 2013 Tory Party conference that he wanted to run a budget surplus in the Parliament to be elected in 2015, and to do so without raising taxes. It is not difficult to see where his thoughts were leading: he could call for ten years of structural budget *surpluses* to bring the 2030 debt burden down below 40 per cent of GDP – its pre-2008 level – presumably in order to give government the borrowing ability to bail out the banks again when they next crash. Even more extreme, City analyst Roger Bootle suggested cutting debt to only 20 per cent of GDP, lower than its 1914 level and on a par with Britain at the beginning of the 18th century when public infrastructure and public services were almost non-existent. This is serious small-state political dogma, not serious economics.

There is a practical and credible alternative to such stifling and reactionary neoliberal ideology. A future Labour government could back sustained recovery by reinstating many of the public investment plans which Osborne inherited from Labour and cancelled. One option is a substantial stimulus focused on public investment until recovery proves self-sustaining, especially house building and infrastructure, including acting on Ed Miliband's call for a commitment to decarbonise the UK power sector by 2030.

From the bottom of the previous recession in 1993 to the peak of the boom in 2008 the economy grew steadily, bringing down the UK debt burden despite public sector deficits in most years and despite significant increases in public spending by Labour after 2000. Economic growth remains a fundamental factor in shaping possibilities. Restoring growth and keeping it going must always be Labour's top priority – and only the state can do that.

Of course Labour always has to manage the public finances responsibly. That includes recognising the evidence that economies falling into financial crises with high levels of public debt appear to sink deeper into recession and take longer to recover. But the roots of Britain's contemporary debt and deficit problems do not lie in excessive state spending. They stem from a build-up of private sector borrowing and reckless bank and shadow bank lending that culminated in the world's worst ever financial crisis, one which required state rescue on an unprecedented scale to forestall an unparalleled threat.

The cure is not still more cuts and continued deregulation. It is to remind ourselves of one of Keynes' verities which inspired Crosland, as it still should all of us today: 'The boom, not the slump, is the time for austerity.' For the foreseeable future the imperative is targeted growth which only active government can lead. Government should be spending more not less – until the private sector is strong enough to take the economy forward.

CHAPTER 5

Growth by active government

Britain was still undergoing post-war reconstruction when Tony Crosland wrote *The Future of Socialism*. The West European economies had benefited from American assistance through the European Recovery Program (the 'Marshall Plan') in rebuilding their shattered economies. The balance between state-led and market-led initiatives differed from nation to nation: more nationalisation and state intervention in France, more reliance on private enterprise in West Germany, for instance.

In Britain the government took on new responsibilities, both in promoting prosperity and in supporting social change as our 'mixed economy' emerged. For instance, it built record numbers of council houses and regulated consumer credit through controls on hire purchase and mortgage lending. Fortunately for Britain the terms of trade (how much we had to export to pay for a given volume of imports) moved in our favour during the 1950s, helping the economy to grow and giving living standards a boost as a consumer boom began, with ordinary families getting cars, fridges, TV sets and washing machines for the first time.

The part played by government continued to evolve in the decades that followed. Crosland would have approved of how the pattern of government spending changed under New Labour between 1997 and 2010, and of how it illustrated government's key role in pursuing socialist objectives.

According to the Institute for Fiscal Studies, over the period 1998–99 to 2010–11, there was a doubling in real terms of spending on health from £63 billion to £121 billion – an average annual real growth of 5.6 per cent as New Labour raised UK health spending closer to international levels, dramatically improved service standards like waiting times, and dealt with demographic and relative inflation pressures: all completely consistent with the socialist values espoused by Crosland.

New Labour also managed to switch spending from the costs of failure to investing in success. The big increases in shares of total public spending were health and education. The main falls were debt interest, defence and social protection (ie social security benefits, including tax credits and state pensions, whose combined share fell by 1.3 per cent, due in part to record employment levels).

However, in common with all governments since the late 1970s, there were cuts in the shares of total public spending on social housing (aggravating housing shortages), trade, industry, energy, employment and the environment (all key to economic progress).[1]

A financial not a spending crisis

Yet, contrary to subsequent rewrites of history, the fiercest challenge the last Labour government faced was not in setting its public spending priorities. It was the 2008 financial crisis that threatened to undo a decade of good since 1997. Labour met the immediate challenge, stopped a recession becoming a depression, and got the economy growing again. But the economy remained as vulnerable as ever to turmoil from the financial system. That is capitalism's exposed flank and where government must play a particularly vigorous reforming role if we are to avoid being bushwhacked by the bankers again.

Frankly, nothing fundamental changed after the crisis, except that the stakes kept rising every year because the banks still acted irresponsibly. They continued speculating with other people's money, still practising casino banking. Britain's banking culture remained fundamentally the same, as the scandals over payment protection insurance, rigged Libor rates, mis-sold credit card and identity protection policies, foreign exchange rate fixing and fee-paying 'packaged' current accounts all showed.

The banks continued clinging to their security blanket, simply relying upon being bailed out the next time they screwed up capitalism big time: this year, next year, sometime, whenever. They continued to subscribe resolutely to the neoliberal fiction that a so-called free market economy produces the best results for all concerned, while quietly pocketing the profits that come from the implicit backstop of a state 'get out of jail free' card.

They did not accept that the way the financial system had developed since the 1970s had led to a massive loss of trust both *in* banks and *between* banks, one which caused enormous damage across wider society. They refused to recognise the fundamental role that government plays in underpinning markets by setting a responsible framework of rules which markets need to rely on if they are to function at all. Or if they did acknowledge it, they became the men with means behind the scenes who lobbied discreetly and curried favour in private to get a regulatory regime that they found easy to live with.

The coming decades require governments that understand how a market economy fits into wider society and the vital role the state must play in preserving and promoting trust among all the members of that society. That means appreciating some fundamentals about human development and social trust, and their implications for the role of government.

Social cohesion depends upon active government

There is an African proverb which says: 'If you want to travel *fast*, travel alone. If you want to travel *far*, travel together.'

Humans are a social species. We live in groups that range from families and neighbourhoods, through cities and regions to sovereign nation states and fully integrated federal states like the US, Canada and Australia, or looser political structures in which nation states share sovereignty and abide by common policies like the European Union. In democratic states like the UK individuals enjoy certain rights and responsibilities according to a set of rules agreed between us which enshrine key values we hold in common that we agree to uphold. What brings us together are what Gordon Brown once called 'the shared needs, mutual interests and linked destinies that unite working people'. Membership of such a society confers citizenship, with entitlements and obligations which give us all a share in the benefit from belonging to a common community and a stake in that society's survival and in its success.

A share and a stake, but not necessarily equal shares, the same stake or equivalent status as each other. Fortunately, the upstairs/downstairs days have gone and Britain is no longer the kind of deferential, divided and class-conscious society it once was, even in Crosland's 1950s. But some of the old inequalities have returned in recent years, reviving social tensions that we thought we had seen the back of, and straining the bonds between us. The old social stigma that used to be attached to council estates or manual jobs still surfaces from time to time, such as when applications for admission to Tony Crosland's old university, Oxford, are being considered. A study for the Tory/Lib Dem government, chaired by the former New Labour Cabinet minister Alan Milburn, showed in 2013 that social mobility had reduced over recent years to a startling degree.

For socialists, the core responsibility of government should be to maintain the cohesion of society and to guard against social breakdown, although that has not always been possible. In 1922 the Irish Free State and the rest of the UK went their separate ways, by negotiation and agreement but only after a long and often violent struggle whose echoes we are still living with today. The 2006 St Andrews Agreement – and the subsequent 2007 agreement – on the devolution of power to the Northern Ireland Assembly showed how politics can find a peaceful path to settling differences that might otherwise cause internal conflict and shatter society. Sometimes, as I experienced directly over the case of Gibraltar in 2001–02, the gap between opposing parties appears momentarily bridgeable, only for a feasible way forward to dissolve at the last minute as one side or another retreats to the comfort zone of an entrenched position.[2] Politics can only work where there is at least a minimum of mutual trust between the parties concerned.

The possibility of a breakdown of civil order and of rioting in the streets was part of the apocalyptic vision that US Treasury Secretary Hank Paulson and Federal Reserve Chairman Ben Bernanke put before the leaders of the US Congress in September 2008 in their (initially unsuccessful) bid for Congressional backing for what became the $700 billion Troubled Assets Relief Program (TARP).[3] But it did not take a riot on Main Street, it took a 10 per cent fall in the Dow Jones index of share prices on Wall Street to convince Congress to back the programme.

Labour's Chancellor Alistair Darling described in more measured terms how he came close to considering panicking on Tuesday, 7 October 2008, the day when Royal Bank of Scotland came within hours of collapse: 'If we didn't act immediately, the bank's doors would close, cash machines would be switched off, cheques would not be honoured, people would not be paid ... If RBS closed its doors, the banking system would freeze, not just in the UK but around the globe,' he wrote.[4]

The grounds for possible panic were the quite conceivable breakdown of law and order if people were unable to access cash, food, fuel or medicines. The state could hardly expect everyone to join patient orderly queues like those that had formed outside Northern Rock branches in September 2007 when word spread that this modest building society was short of cash and depositors feared that their savings might not be safe. RBS was one of the world's biggest banks and the knock-on effects of failure could have been enormous, making RBS Mr Hyde to Lehman Brothers' Dr Jekyll.

The events of October 2008 showed how fragile are the bonds that hold society together and how close we came to social breakdown.

Neoliberalism tries to explain how we interact with one another in terms of independent individuals all maximising their own self-interest in markets free from government regulation and linked by a price mechanism that covers all conceivable contracts into the infinite future. In reality markets function within a framework of rules set by society – such as government guarantees that customers' bank deposits are safe up to £85,000 – and societies are about interdependence and mutual trust. As Ed Miliband memorably put it: 'markets don't just drop down from outer space, perfectly formed.'[5]

Societies and markets depend on cooperation and reciprocity as well as on competition and self-interest, and cooperation and reciprocity require a foundation of trust.[6] Markets only work when customers have an ability to pay and trust the supplier offering the product or service that is for sale. If the object on offer becomes suspect for any reason it may become impossible to find a buyer or to do a deal. Markets depend on the maintenance of mutual trust too. Britain's modern market economy has proved fertile but, like society, it also remains fragile and must be managed with care. Too much regulation could stifle initiative and frustrate growth. That was the complaint commonly made before the 2008 crisis and still heard from business today. Too little regulation can expose both markets and society to disaster, as the 2008 banking crisis demonstrated when trust between banks evaporated. The biggest single recent threat to social cohesion in the UK came from the financial system – and it still does.

In common with almost every other government, Labour got regulation of the financial system wrong last time and paid a heavy price. The party can't afford to make the same mistake again. But the lessons go wider than just the banking system. The 2008 credit crunch and subsequent recession alerted people to the limitations of the market mechanism and led many to look to the state for help in troubled times. Sudden insecurity for *some* brought home the vulnerability of *all* to unpredictable developments. It highlighted how dependent we all are upon each other in the face of common threats, and revived both concerns for fairness in society and the importance of government protecting us.

In 2008–09 state action was the only game in town to stop the situation going from very bad to even worse, despite the government's failure to see the trouble coming. Sadly, much of the state's capacity to help those hardest hit was subsequently scrapped in the Tory/Lib Dem scramble to cut public spending, reduce the budget deficit and shrink Britain's debt burden. Premature Tory talk about running a budget surplus is simply another instalment in their campaign to make public spending cuts permanent and to reduce the role of the state, confirmed by David Cameron in his 2013 Lord Mayor's Banquet speech. It is the same 'starve the beast' argument that the Republican right have been pushing for years in the US: set an arbitrary debt ceiling, slash taxes at the top and demand public spending cuts, especially on welfare benefits, to bring borrowing down – nominal financial prudence which cloaks the real neoliberal agenda for small government, a stand-on-your-own-two-feet society, and a second-rate economy.

Why growth depends on government

What drives economic growth, what it means for the typical citizen's standard of living and quality of life, and what governments can do to encourage faster sustainable growth is a complex matter.

Until the 19th century the world was caught in the Malthusian trap whereby any gains in income through gradual technological advance were matched by population growth, which drove average living standards back down towards subsistence levels. A real rise in average incomes could not be sustained while technology improved slowly, and the typical rate of technological advance before 1800 was less than 0.05 per cent per year, a 30th of the modern rate.[7]

However, the establishment of market economies after about 1800 and the industrial revolution changed things. From the mid-19th century the British economy normally grew at a positive pace, save for depression years in the 1870s, the 1920s and the 1930s. UK growth was markedly faster post-1945 than in the interwar years, one reason why Tony Crosland was so confident about the prospects for the British economy and about the future of socialism in the 1950s and 1960s.

He was right to argue that growth holds the key to delivering the kind of society that the Labour Party stands for, one in which the gains are fairly shared. Where he proved to be wrong was in adopting the view, standard for that time, of what drives growth, and in his optimistic assumptions about both the durability of the political and economic consensus that prevailed between the parties in the 1950s and the kind of capitalism that succeeding generations would face.

Crosland saw a high rate of capital investment as the dominant factor driving growth. He therefore called for government fiscal and monetary policies based on a Keynesian analysis to induce such investment. Although his understanding of what drives economic growth was widely shared in the mid-1950s, it proved to be flawed. While Crosland was writing *The Future of Socialism* in London, in Cambridge, Massachusetts, Robert Solow, in two pioneering articles, was transforming our understanding of the drivers of growth and their relative importance. He provided a more convincing explanation of what determines an economy's long-run rate of growth: one in which the contributions made by capital investment and an expanding labour force are far outweighed by that made by innovation.[8]

That explanation, refined in the 1990s and more recently, has become an important rationale for 'active' government, undermining the neoliberal case that governments should get out of the way and simply let the outcome be determined by market forces. Government support for innovation, for investment in both physical and human capital, and for improvements in the social infrastructure holds the key to technological and organisational change which underpins growth and prosperity in modern economies. It was a rationale that New Labour proved reluctant to act upon until late in its time in office, but which provides the intellectual basis for a much more active and interventionist role for the state in promoting growth by backing innovation.

Technological innovation

Solow showed first that, without technological advance, extra capital investment runs into diminishing returns, output eventually only grows at the rate of population growth, and income per head stops growing altogether. It was only when he introduced technological progress to his theory of growth that it predicted the sustained growth in per capita income of the kind displayed by the North American, British and other European economies since the mid-19th century.

Solow's next key contribution was to estimate the relative importance of each factor contributing to growth. He found that half of the growth of American output and two thirds of the rise in output per capita was due to this third factor, innovation, rather than to increases in physical capital or labour inputs. Innovation was the driving force behind sustained per capita growth.

Tony Crosland devoted five chapters of his book to the question of economic growth. None of them mentioned technical innovation. He only discussed innovation elsewhere, in a chapter examining the pattern of consumption where he noted the fleeting ability of the rich to display their special status through the purchase of the latest prestige products before the masses started doing so too.

For Robert Solow innovation really represented the combined influence of several changes contributing to higher productivity: new technology, new forms of business organisation, and new markets – all of which had combined to grow worldwide productivity 18-fold since 1800. If the emergence of market economies since 1800 has *doubled* worldwide productivity gains since then, there remains a *nine-fold* worldwide productivity gain from breakthroughs in business organisation and technological innovation.[9] Innovation, both technological and organisational, is enormously significant to long-run growth in market economies, and points to where the focus of long-run public policy should lie.

The government factor

However, what determines the pace of technical progress – and therefore whether government can influence that pace – remained unexplained until the 1990s. Then Paul Romer suggested a neoclassical growth model (in broad terms, a free market model) which linked technical progress to the number of researchers trying to come up with new ideas and new inventions from which they might profit.[10] A further explanation – albeit one which made a rather undignified and confused entry into UK political debate in 1994 – came when Gordon Brown was mocked for making a speech referring to 'post neoclassical endogenous growth theory'. His critics missed the point of the *post* neoclassical reference. For he was acknowledging a different set of ideas suggesting – contrary to the Solow and Romer models – that governments can influence economic growth rates by the decisions they take on taxes, public spending, regulation of markets and investment incentives. This is the new, radically different idea that government, by investing in the social infrastructure of physical and human capital, can encourage innovation and investment and thereby promote economic growth.

A good social infrastructure means more than just a dependable power grid and water supply, extensive road and rail networks, reliable telecommunication systems, an efficient banking system, and health and education services that meet high standards. It encompasses the rules and regulations, institutions and policies that primarily determine how willing people are to make the long-term investments in new technology, capital and skills that drive long-run growth.

It means policies and laws that encourage domestic investment in new production facilities, inward investment by foreign firms that effectively transfers new technology, and personal and corporate investment in skills training by individuals. It means a business environment which inspires entrepreneurs to risk launching new products and processes, which encourages organisations to introduce new ways of working and fresh methods of managing their people, and which prompts talented individuals and groups to try out new ideas and come up with inventions.

It means an openness to international trade and competition backed by stable institutions and the rule of law. It means a legal system that protects intellectual property rights, enforces contracts, ensures compliance with statutory obligations like health and safety rules and duties of care, and sees that individual rights are respected, including employment rights and consumer rights. It means a ban on blacklisting of potential recruits and on unfair discrimination.

A good social infrastructure provides incentives to encourage investment and production over consumption and activities which merely syphon off output rather than increase it. Such activities include what economists term 'rent-seeking activities' like crime, tax evasion, corruption, political lobbying for tax concessions, and boosting profits and bonuses by rigging interest rates and misleading customers.

Yet against these important factors, the UK banking system appears to be an important syphon that has *held back* UK economic growth. The former chairman of the Financial Services Authority, Adair Turner, has shown that Britain's banking boom in the last 30 to 50 years has involved transactions among financial institutions rather than between them and the real economy, transactions which extract rent from the real economy rather than add value. The UK banking system has played only a minor role in channelling household savings into corporate investment. For instance, manufacturing is only a marginal net borrower from the banking system. Sadly, most UK bank and building society lending goes either into smoothing consumption over individual lifecycles or into investment in *existing* assets, especially residential and commercial property, rather than into financing new production. Since only some goes into financing new construction, there has been only a limited link between mortgage finance and building *new* homes.[11]

Hall and Jones have shown that higher rates of investment in physical and human capital and higher 'total factor productivity' levels – Solow's third source of growth, innovation in all its forms – tend to be associated with better social infrastructures.[12]

Examples of countries that appear to have experienced so-called 'growth miracles' – but only because their governments intervened to identify and support new business opportunities and improve social infrastructure – include South Korea and Singapore in the early 1960s. They both raised their rate of investment in capital and in education and underwent unprecedented growth rates. Another glaring example is China, which introduced reforms that coupled market freedoms with massive state investment in new transport networks, education and health, and urban development at the end of the 1970s and experienced double digit average annual growth between 1979 and 2010.

Social infrastructure and public investment

To promote economic growth, even the Tory/Lib Dem government appeared unequivocally to agree in December 2013 that high-quality social infrastructure is absolutely essential – both to underpin innovation and to ensure the physical and human capital without which modern economies cannot prosper. Temporarily parking its neoliberalism, it made an important admission:

> The quality of a nation's infrastructure is one of the foundations of its rate of growth and the living standards of its people. That is why the government has put long term investment in roads, railways, energy, telecommunications and flood defences at the heart of its growth plan. Successive governments have failed to invest sufficiently in the UK's infrastructure. In making a long-term commitment to infrastructure investment,

the government's ambition is to reverse the effect of this historic underinvestment and equip the UK with world class infrastructure.[13]

Yet the very same day as this admission the Chancellor George Osborne announced plans to cut the share of GDP devoted to public investment to 2003 levels by 2018. Osborne's double-edged declaration came straight after Richard Threlfall, consultancy firm KPMG's head of infrastructure, had acknowledged more than 30 years of underinvestment in the UK's infrastructure, the UK having invested less than any of its major competitors and typically less than 1 per cent of its GDP.[14] Threlfall subsequently noted that George Osborne counted £20 million to be spent on repairs to historic cathedrals as infrastructure investment.[15] Osborne's 2018 target was for net public investment to equal 1.3 per cent of GDP.

Yet he set his target only weeks after the annual report of the World Economic Forum (WEF) on global competitiveness had ranked the UK just 28th in 'quality of overall infrastructure' in 2013, down from 24th in 2008;[16] after the energy regulator Ofgem had warned of a possible drop in spare electricity capacity from a 14 per cent margin to one of only 4 per cent by 2015;[17] backed up by the Royal Academy of Engineering warning that by winter 2015 'the capacity margin could reduce to a level that puts security of supply at risk'.[18]

The WEF report also provided pointers to how the UK had got its priorities wrong in the allocation of scarce educational resources in particular. The UK ranked only 26th for the quality of its educational system, 31st for the quality of its primary education, 36th for its tertiary education enrolments and 50th for the quality of its maths and science education – but third for the quality of its management schools where a favoured few able to pay sky-high fees reap rich rewards.

Unsurprisingly the UK ranked 105th for the soundness of its banks, and 56th for government procurement of advanced technological products. Its only 'achievement' was a dizzy 12th for its much vaunted wage flexibility. Yet, although that may have delivered relatively high employment levels, it has only done so on a basis of poor wages, endemic job insecurity, widespread 'zero hours' contracts (totalling

1.4 million in 2014) and high levels of 'underemployment' (in 2013, 3 million workers stated they were being forced to work fewer hours than they wished or needed). Over recent years there has been an increasing reliance upon a casualised, hire-and-fire workforce which lacks the most basic rights like paid holidays, with in-work benefits cut too and a jump in self-employment which in practice means barely subsistent self-underemployment. All these are characteristics of a low-quality economy.

The UK is unique in that, following the privatisations of the 1980s and 1990s, some 60 per cent of this country's key economic infrastructure is privately owned.[19] So the condition of Britain's infrastructure depends on both private and public investment. Michael Heseltine's 2012 review, *No stone unturned in pursuit of growth*, reckoned that the UK required over £250 billion of infrastructure investment over the next five years, most of which in his view would need to be provided by the private sector.[20] Yet in June 2013 the Tory/Lib Dem coalition which had commissioned Heseltine's report responded timidly. It extended by two years the guarantees that government provides to encourage private sector investment in infrastructure, and committed itself to publicly fund projects worth just £100 billion by 2020.[21]

If the size of these figures was meant to wow the public, government spending proposals on this scale are actually less substantial than they look. They meant devoting the same share of GDP to net public investment in 2018 as the UK averaged over the 25, mainly Tory, years ending in 2005, when the foundations of our poor place in international infrastructure quality rankings were laid. Our infrastructure compares poorly because, instead of investing, successive governments since the 1970s gave priority to selling off state-owned assets and cutting back on public sector capital spending.

This long-lasting squeeze showed up in the falling share of GDP devoted to net public investment as each succeeding decade began: from 6.2 per cent in 1970 to 1.9 per cent in 1980, 1.3 per cent in 1990, and 0.5 per cent in 2000.[22] In some years, notably at the height of the 'boom' in 1988 under Nigel Lawson as Chancellor of the Exchequer, public investment was so low that the stock of public capital assets, including key parts of the UK infrastructure, came close to wearing out faster than it could be replaced – demonstrating the fundamentally flawed nature of Thatcherite 'success'.

The inevitable consequences were contra-flows and cones on our roads, dilapidated schools and hospitals with long backlogs of needed repairs. They also included 1,200 safety-inspired speed restrictions across the rail network and a nationwide track replacement programme after the fatal Hatfield train crash in October 2000. This followed what a judge called 'sustained negligence' by the privatised Railtrack (later the partially renationalised Network Rail) and its maintenance contractor Balfour Beatty – negligence itself also a product of chronic underinvestment by the Thatcher and Major Tory governments, because privatised or not, our railways required huge public subsidy just like every successful railway in the world.

In office from 1997 New Labour made a slow start to reviving Britain's straining infrastructure. UK infrastructure investment was lower in 2000 than in 1997 and lower still by the beginning of 2007.[23] However, Labour's response to the financial crisis was to boost public investment by over £30 billion over the three years 2008/09 to 2010/11, taking the share of GDP devoted to public investment to its highest for over 30 years. Net public investment in real terms suddenly shot up to a 40-year high, taking Britain's construction industry infrastructure work from famine to feast as it increased by 74 per cent between 2007 and 2011.[24]

But the bonanza was short-lived because Labour planned to pay for the extra public investment by making offsetting cuts in the following two years, to help reduce the budget deficit. Bringing forward future infrastructure spending did little more than change the time profile of public investment over a five-year period. This was a practical response to an economic emergency, an entirely appropriate short-term spending surge to stop the economy sliding into slump. It was not an attempt to redefine the role of the state and put Britain's infrastructure on a firmer footing by establishing a new, higher plateau of public investment, which is what Britain clearly needed then – and still needs now.

The cuts which Labour planned for 2012 would have taken public investment back to its pre-crisis 2006 level. In 2013 the Tory/Lib Dems went further: Osborne's 2018 target meant cutting the share of GDP devoted to net public investment to 2003 levels.[25] Some lyrics from Melanie Safka's 'Nickel song' come to mind: 'They're only putting in a nickel but they want a dollar song. They're only putting in a little to put right a lot that's wrong.'

Challenging old ideas

The economist J.K. Galbraith used the phrase 'the conventional wisdom' in the 1950s to draw attention to the widely shared ideas and assumptions which constitute orthodox opinion and set the limits of acceptable policy. For its first ten years in office the Labour government that was elected in 1997 challenged relatively few of the prevailing 'conventional wisdoms' inherited from the Thatcher/ Major era about how to run the economy. Despite being seen as a quintessential New Labourite, David Sainsbury, Minister of Science and Innovation at the Department of Trade and Industry (DTI) from 1998 to 2006, has acknowledged how New Labour's ministerial thinking 'largely reflected the dominant neoliberal political economy of the time'.[26] He now accepts that the financial crisis following the Lehman Brothers bankruptcy demolished the argument that the market system is self-regulating, with the state consigned to only a minimal role in the economy.

But the rot had set into Labour under its Prime Minister Jim Callaghan back in 1976. He anticipated the neoliberal outlook that came to dominate orthodox opinion after 1979 once Margaret Thatcher became Prime Minister when he dismissed Keynesian fiscal policy as a recipe for full employment. Thirty years later New Labour's leaders proved no less averse than Callaghan to accepting the logic of neoliberalism with its emphasis on supposedly efficient and self-regulating markets and a role for government only in rare situations of market failure.

Experience has taught us that government cannot simply stand aside. In the face of the most severe downturn in the world economy since the Great Depression radical steps were the only way to save the economic system. Along with our G20 partners Labour adopted unorthodox measures to tackle a threat that was unprecedented in the post-war period. Contrary to the then conventional wisdom that fiscal policy took too long to work to warrant more than a minor role in countering any threat of recession, twelve of the advanced economies including the UK announced a substantial fiscal stimulus within two months of the Lehman Brothers collapse.[27]

Financial reform

The 2008 economic crisis showed that a credit crunch can pull the plug on a business, put jobs in jeopardy and cause families to fear for their future as abruptly as a power cut, a fire or a flood. The modern economy depends on financial and credit networks as much as it does on utilities like water, gas and electricity supplies. Failure anywhere within such interconnected systems risks catastrophic consequences, and the financial system proved in 2008 that it is prone to seizure.

The destabilising role played by the banks which culminated in the 2008 crisis has confirmed the need for vigorous state action to reform the financial system. The idea that the financial system has inherently self-stabilising properties proved to be neoliberal fiction. In reality it is a powder keg that could explode again with even more destructive force next time unless government gets a tight regulatory grip on the whole financial system, including the shadow banking sector and hedge funds.

In these circumstances the government has an overriding obligation to intervene, to protect the public interest. A much firmer framework of active government involvement and tighter regulation is required, with stricter rules for all financial institutions, to promote the common good.

In 2011 the Independent Banking Commission chaired by Sir John Vickers proposed new rules for UK banks. It called for banks like Barclays, HSBC and Royal Bank of Scotland to ring-fence their retail banking operations from their investment banking activities by building an internal firewall between them. In February 2013 George Osborne agreed to 'electrify' the ring fence by allowing the banking regulator to break up any bank that it believes to be undermining the purpose of the fence. Unsurprisingly the British Bankers Association opposed any idea of 'electrifying' the ring fence. If only the Tory

Party were to devote as much effort to questioning the BBA as it has done to criticising the BBC.

One person's internal firewall is another's Chinese wall and the story goes in the City of London that you can tell a Chinese wall by the grapevine growing over it. Far better than uncertain financial firewalls would be to separate retail banking from investment banking altogether by breaking up the big banks, with taxpayers only guaranteeing the socially essential parts like payment systems and customers' deposits, and not the risky casino side, most of which is reported to have been described by the former Chairman of the UK Financial Services Authority, Lord Turner, as 'socially useless'.[28]

The Vickers Commission also proposed requiring UK banks to expand their top quality equity capital safety cushion to at least 10 per cent of capital, provided they also have genuinely loss-absorbing debt on their balance sheets. This is better than the 7 per cent in the 2010 international agreement by the Basel Committee on Banking Supervision, but it falls well short of what is required to protect against banks that are 'too big to fail' and that have to be rescued by taxpayers.

For instance, it is much lower than the 19 per cent required by Swiss regulators of Credit Suisse and UBS and the 20 per cent suggested by Professor David Miles of the Bank of England Monetary Policy Committee.[29] Much higher capital requirements, twice as high as those proposed by the Vickers Commission, are needed. They could be varied according to financial conditions in the economy, and raised if signs emerged of a bubble in asset values like property prices, to choke off speculation. They could also be targeted so that the biggest, most complex and most interconnected banks have to hold higher amounts of loss-absorbing capital,[30] to limit contagion when one bank fails.

A start could be made on building up such buffers by temporarily restricting bank dividends and requiring that profits be ploughed back into the business instead of distributed to shareholders or paid out in bonuses to directors, senior executives and top traders. Some signs of movement in this direction began to appear in 2013 on both sides of the Atlantic. In the UK the Bank of England regulator called on five banks (Barclays, the Cooperative Bank, Lloyds, Nationwide and RBS) to increase their capital by a combined £27 billion to fill holes in their balance sheets. The Swiss National Bank urged UBS and Credit Suisse to focus on capital building to comply with the 3 per cent simple leverage ratio (the most basic standard for safe banking set by the Basel Committee of international banking supervisors in 2010). US regulators were also reported to be considering doubling the minimum capital requirement for the biggest American banks to 6 per cent, obliging banks like Goldman Sachs, J.P. Morgan and Morgan Stanley to hold back on dividend payments.

The Vice Chairman of the Federal Deposit Insurance Corporation in the US called for the replacement of complicated risk-based rules that attach different weights to different categories of capital by a 10 per cent leverage ratio which defines capital more tightly and includes more off-balance sheet assets than allowed under Basel rules. Such a step might mean the three largest US banks having to stop paying out dividends for about five years.[31] The cloud of confusion that envelops these issues is made worse by the fact that banks do not report what their capital or leverage ratios would be according to new Basel definitions for calculating assets or off-balance-sheet items.

Even much tighter capital requirements could still leave bank bosses and their senior staff liable to take excessive risks, pocket obscene bonuses from the resulting artificial profits, and leave with golden goodbyes if their institution fails and has to be rescued by the taxpayer. As a safeguard there should be a rule that no board member or senior executive of a failing bank would be allowed to hold a similar post at a bank unless they can prove to the regulator that they warned against the risk taking that led to failure and tried to reduce it.[32] Such a lifetime ban would weaken the addiction to risk so rife in the financial sector.

The change in the way top bankers in Britain and the US have been paid since the 1980s has spread beyond the boundaries of the financial system. Over the past 20 years it has begun to infect non-financial companies too, the big ones at least, also with damaging effects. Companies in the UK and the US started behaving differently from the way they used to, and from the way their counterparts in other major economies do.[33] Like the banks they chose to restructure their balance sheets, increasing leverage by borrowing more rather than issue equity capital. They have been doing so partly under the influence of tax rules that treated interest paid on debt as a tax deductible expense, unlike dividends paid to shareholders.

The bonus culture has led them to adopt increasingly short-term horizons, preferring higher profit margins over capital investment and steering cash flow into share buybacks, instead of into new capital equipment, in order to reduce their equity capital, boost earnings per share and raise their share price. They are tending to opt for the longer-term risk that lower investment and loss of market share involves, rather than take the short-term risk that cutting profit margins would represent. So they invest less and have higher profit margins than would have been the case before the bonus culture took hold. Under this model, business investment as a share of GDP has fluctuated with the cyclical state of the economy but shown a distinct downward trend in both the UK and the US.

Traditionally big businesses in Britain and the US tended to finance their investment from ploughed-back profits rather than by borrowing medium to long term from banks. Over the past decade they have run a substantial cash surplus, conserving their cash instead of investing while they wait for signs of a sustained recovery and barely bothering the banks.

Ensuring banking backs growth

On the other hand, small and medium-sized firms in the UK have long been more dependent on banks for financial support and were quickly hit by the 2008 credit crunch and subsequent squeeze, as banks were reluctant to lend during recession. What Britain's small, often family-based businesses lack is the kind of supportive network of long-term lending and modest amounts of equity capital from regional and industrial banks that is enjoyed, for instance, by small and medium-sized enterprises (SMEs) from the state-owned development bank Kreditanstalt für Wiederaufbau (KfW) in Germany.

Germany has more than five times as many banks as the UK, so there is more competition to lend. This shows in the fact that loan rejection rates in the UK are twice those in Germany, where the banks have a much tighter focus on small and medium-sized firms and a less arm's length relationship. Often they take long-term equity stakes in the businesses to which they lend, so ensuring they have an obligation to help those businesses succeed, rather than as in Britain simply getting their money back in the short term.[34] Their pattern of regional banking also encourages a more supportive albeit commercial relationship tailored to the needs of local economies.

Nicholas Tott's 2013 report for the Labour Party's leadership proposed the creation of a British investment bank. It pointed out that the UK is the only member of the G8 not to have a dedicated institution dealing with SME financing issues. Nothing to compare with Germany's KfW or the Small Business Administration in the US or the Business Development Bank of Canada, 90 per cent of whose customers are SMEs with fewer than 50 employees.[35] Significantly, KfW's lending *increased* following the credit crunch, a valuable countercyclical approach to lending which helped to keep small firms alive during a tough time, when in Britain they were being strangled by a banking system for which SMEs were almost the last concern.

Such a British investment bank could also help to finance investment in infrastructure, including accelerating investment in housing and in low-carbon innovation by attracting funding from pension funds and insurance companies. The latter need to acquire long-term assets to match their long-term liabilities. Australian and Canadian pension funds already seem to be ahead in this game. We should study their experience.

George Osborne took some hesitant steps in this direction in his 2012 Mansion House speech when he offered government guarantees on private sector investments in house-building and infrastructure projects. But Jonathan Portes of the NIESR and Martin Wolf of the *Financial Times* pointed out how marginal are the differences between this and the government borrowing from the private sector to finance public sector investment in infrastructure improvements, especially as real interest rates on government borrowing at the time were close to zero.[36]

Marginal but not insignificant. First, because Osborne's approach leaves the government supporting projects that the private sector is prepared to undertake only with government backing, *not* the investments that are highest priority for the government. Second, because even private funding guaranteed by government may end up more expensive than government borrowing, especially at a time like mid-2012 when the government's real cost of borrowing was close to zero. Third, because what was driving Osborne's policy was his fixation with shifting funding off the government's published balance sheet, which is why he favoured a form of funding investment that makes debt 'disappear' from the public accounts, though the potential public sector liability represented by the government guarantee still exists. There is a certain Treasury smoke and mirrors here.

Professor Alasdair Smith of the University of Sussex also pointed out how daft using private finance for public infrastructure can become, both because the former's apparent advantage is only illusory, being based on bad practice in public accounting, and because of how much more costly private finance can be than public finance. He estimated in mid-2012 that the regulated UK water companies could borrow money for 25 years at an interest rate of 5 per cent, that is, about 2 per cent above the rate at which the government could borrow by selling bonds. Or, if the companies raised the funds by a mix of borrowing and selling new shares, at an overall rate of about 7 per cent, the higher rate being required because of the extra risk involved to shareholders. 'A £20 million school rebuild funded by private finance will therefore cost £400,000 to £800,000 more per year in loan interest than one financed by direct government borrowing. The publicly funded school could afford to employ perhaps 10 or 20 more teachers.'[37]

The upshot was that Britain faced the opportunity of a lifetime to repair and upgrade its capital stock on incredibly favourable terms. Portes called for an immediate £30 billion public investment programme; Wolf suggested far more. But Osborne postponed any increase in public investment until 2015–16 and limited it to £3 billion. What a missed opportunity to transform our creaking infrastructure.

The 'greed is good' culture of the top bankers has damaged the lives of millions. Staff at the Federal Reserve Bank of Dallas estimated the costs of the 2007–09 financial crisis to the US by comparing the value of lost output, reduced wealth and increased federal debt. They found that the crisis cost between 40 and 90 per cent of 2007 GDP or between $6 trillion and $14 trillion. Their assessment of who bore what share of the pain attracted the following verdict:

> In sum almost everyone lost during the financial crisis, with households losing most, but Wall Street lost least. The reason is that its losses were covered by capital injection by the corporate and household sector, and there was huge government support. No wonder there was an Occupy Wall Street movement.[38]

The fall in the UK stock market in 2008 alone resulted in a £228 billion drop in the value of all investments held by pension funds and unit trusts.[39] The 'official' cost of UK austerity, the cumulative loss of GDP due to fiscal tightening from 2010 to 2013, exceeded 5 per cent or about £75 billion, according to the Office for Budget Responsibility.[40] Yet the bankers have been able to hang onto the huge bonuses they pocketed in the years of illusory profits. Few lost their top jobs and those who did suffered little by way of personal sanction, receiving generous golden goodbyes and compensation packages.

Unless the rules are changed, Britain's bankers will face the same temptation to take irresponsible risks with other people's money, confident that if the worst happens the state will step in to save them. Except that next time the potential bailout bill may exceed even what the state can afford. Without radical reform the banks may become too big to save, leaving everyone to wonder when, not if, the financial Sword of Damocles will fall.

Geoff Hodgson has assessed how far reform has progressed since 'the Great Crash' of 2008: 'Subsequent reform of international financial arrangements, to help create greater stability, has been minimal, and the institutional and political bases for such measures are frayed. Another major global financial crash in the next fifty years is more likely than not.'[41] The situation has been summed up by former IMF chief economist Simon Johnson: 'We are nearing the end of our fiscal and monetary ability to bail out the system. We are steadily becoming vulnerable to disaster on an epic scale.'[42]

National Economic Development Council

Our readiness to respond to reality by challenging old ideas and adopting a fresh approach eventually showed also in the Labour government's approach to industrial policy, but only after years of reluctance to embrace the evidence that government has a key role to play in promoting economic growth, especially by promoting innovation. That reluctance stemmed in part from a perceived need to distance New Labour from the record of previous Labour administrations, in part from doubting the efficacy of an interventionist approach to industrial policy.

The hub of Labour's 1997 election campaign was its media centre in Millbank Tower. A few floors above was the conference room where the National Economic Development Council (NEDC) used to meet. For three decades government, employers and unions would gather together regularly, normally under the chairmanship of the Chancellor of the Exchequer, sometimes that of the Prime Minister, for a candid exchange of views on issues of economic and industrial policy.

The NEDC was a 'one nation' initiative launched by Harold Macmillan in 1962 that survived the Alec Douglas-Home, Harold Wilson, Ted Heath, Jim Callaghan and Margaret Thatcher years, only to be abolished when John Major took over at No. 10. It drew on French experience with 'indicative planning', exemplified the kind of consensus approach to economic management that Tony Crosland expected, and was consistent with his only vaguely expressed ideas about how planning might promote faster economic growth. Since the NEDC's demise in 1992 there has been no neutral forum where government can meet both sides of industry to assess Britain's economic problems and the prospects for tackling them together. Yet few participants have ever mourned the NEDC's passing, and New Labour avoided reviving it. Gordon Brown, as Chancellor, launched a series of Treasury initiatives involving task groups with specific remits, notably on productivity, but New Labour never pursued broader consultation with both sides of industry on a systematic basis.

In its time the NEDC steered clear of troubled water. Productivity was discussed but not pay and prices. Skill shortages yes, strikes no.

The NEDC was never a place where deals were done. Members met as colleagues around a conference table, not as negotiators across a bargaining table. Maybe that was why it survived for so long.

Its record was a mixture of modest success, missed opportunity and unrealised potential. NEDC members were consulted in the preparation of Labour's elaborate 1965 National Plan for growth. But the plan proved short-lived and government policy became dominated by prices and incomes considerations from which the NEDC was kept at arm's length. In 1973 the Confederation of British Industry (CBI) tried to use the NEDC to engineer an end to the three-day week. The attempt failed in the face of an adamant Ted Heath. In 1984 Margaret Thatcher was intent on defeating the miners, not in using the NEDC as a forum for finding a compromise and settling the coal dispute. Jim Callaghan used the NEDC in 1978 to alert British industry to the importance of microchip technology. The UK might have been better prepared for the single European market in 1992 if Michael Heseltine had stayed in government after 1986, able to challenge employers and unions at the NEDC about their plans. Instead 1992 was dominated by devaluation day when the UK crashed out of the European Exchange Rate Mechanism. Had the NEDC survived in the 1990s the annual white paper on UK competitiveness that Heseltine introduced might have become the focus of national debate, much as Gordon Brown's pre-budget reports did.

By failing to address the fundamentals of economic policy, the NEDC seemed always to be standing on the sidelines whenever matters came to a crunch. It led a kind of twilight life existing in parallel with, but rarely being part of, key government decision-making. This was highlighted during 1975–79 when the NEDC's profile was at its peak. The appearance was of both sides of industry tied into an interventionist government Industrial Strategy. The reality was the Social Contract, a prices and incomes policy negotiated outside the auspices of the NEDC, and from 1976 ongoing monetary and fiscal restraint.

The Industrial Strategy involved a network of 39 tripartite working parties and economic development committees covering particular sectors of industry, backing up the overall NEDC. However, government intervention was limited to its shareholding in British Leyland, nationalisation of shipbuilding and aerospace, some modest schemes of industrial assistance, and minor measures aimed at specific industries, sometimes adopted by the DTI and Treasury behind the backs of the relevant NEDC working party.

But when inflation threatened to lead to economic collapse the public spending boom of 1974 gave way in 1975 to a budgetary squeeze and adoption of the 'Social Contract' – a bargain promising wage restraint on the one hand in return for improvements to the 'social wage' (like better welfare benefits and stronger employment protection laws) on the other – following talks with the Trades Union Congress. From 1976 it was fiscal and monetary policy and prices and incomes policy that mattered most to the Cabinet, not industrial policy. Although the TUC continued to be consulted closely about economic policy, ultimately it was the IMF, not the NEDC, CBI or TUC that mattered most in the corridors of power in Whitehall.

New Labour non-interventionism

Small wonder perhaps that, despite New Labour's fondness for commissions and quangos, Tony Blair showed no interest in resurrecting the NEDC. Or that in New Labour's early years in office ministers responsible for industry saw little scope for industrial policy to encourage investment and innovation. Desperate to proclaim Labour's free market credentials, Stephen Byers in 2000 described the role of government as 'active but not interventionist', whatever that means. Patricia Hewitt's 2002 manufacturing strategy statement dismissed aid to industry as 'handouts to domestic companies', without acknowledging that the average EU member state's aid to industry was three times the UK level at the time.

This was a time when the *Financial Times* was reporting that Edmund Stoiber, Minister President in Bavaria and leader of Germany's conservative Christian Social Union Party, had used over £3 billion from selling off state assets to fund investment in 'growth-oriented industries' like the media and science-related sectors.[43] In other words, state intervention in the economy.

Patricia Hewitt's 2002 statement cited NIESR research attributing the manufacturing productivity gaps between the UK and the US and Germany to three factors: less physical capital per worker in the UK, explaining 20–30 per cent of the gaps; poorer skills in the UK, explaining about 25 per cent of the UK/Germany gap; and poor ways of organising work in the UK, explaining 50–75 per cent of the gaps. Unfortunately the June 2002 response from the House of Commons Trade and Industry Committee claimed that the 'main obstacle' to improving UK manufacturing productivity was the shortfall in UK capital investment, when the research evidence clearly shows that this is only part of a bigger problem and is outweighed by obsolete ways of organising work and managing people.

Contemporary research findings from Toby Wall of Sheffield University and an International Labour Organization study by David Ashton and Johnny Sung showed the effectiveness of high performance ways of working and people management practices, and thus the importance of encouraging a partnership approach at work, perhaps along the lines of German practice where cooperation is routine.

The DTI's 2002 formal endorsement of partnership between both sides of industry was lukewarm and belied by New Labour's actual record in office: reluctant to require companies to train their workforce, restrained in its backing for partnership at work, and resistant to an EU information and consultation rights directive.[44]

Patricia Hewitt's 2003 DTI statement 'Prosperity for all' simply pooh-poohed industrial policy as 'protecting companies from competition and propping them up with subsidies' – the Treasury-speak of the time, before and after. That was when New Labour made most plain its acceptance of neoliberalism as the basis for industrial policy.

Market failure

The framework for intervention spelled out in the 2003 DTI policy statement was simply stated. The job of public policy was 'to correct for market failures' where outcomes generated by unregulated markets were 'not the "right" result from the perspective of society as a whole'.[45] The statement acknowledged four sets of circumstances in which market failures might occur that justified state intervention. First, where externalities or spillover effects cause the social rate of return from research and development spending to exceed the private rate due to some of the benefits from the investment being shared by other firms. Second, where barriers to entry prevent potential rivals from breaking into a market. Third, where imperfect information or uncertainty causes resources to be allocated inefficiently. Fourth, in the case of 'public goods' – products or services like street lighting where one person's consumption of it does not mean there is less to go round and it is impossible to prevent anyone else from using it once it has been produced.

But invoking market failure as the sole basis for state intervention implies accepting the notion from neoclassical economic theory that a society of self-centred optimising individuals competing with one another in markets which cater for all eventualities will deliver some kind of socially optimal allocation and distribution of resources. A result that is efficient in the sense that production costs are minimised and no one can be made better off without someone else simultaneously being made worse off (turning a blind eye to the fairness or otherwise of the current distribution of income and wealth).

In reality we have seen what happens when markets are left (largely) to their own devices. They can work well for long periods and deliver the dynamism on which higher material living standards depend, albeit with the downside of a grossly unequal distribution of rewards, perpetuation of privilege and discrimination, and harsh neglect of those who are simply unlucky. But sooner or later the market system always stalls. The most significant market failure has been seen again and again throughout economic history. It has been the failure of the market system to shield society from the threat of catastrophic collapse without state intervention to save the day. We saw it in its most acute form in the 1930s Great Depression and we saw it on a similar scale again in 2008.

The American venture capitalist William Janeway has pointed out how inconsequential the market failure argument for state action has been in reality:

> Writ large, the strategic interventions that have shaped
> the market economy over generations have depended
> on grander themes – national development, national
> security, social justice, liberation from disease – that
> transcend the calculus of welfare economics and the
> logic of market failure … interventions at systematic
> scale, such as Britain's National Health Service, could
> only be established and maintained by collective action
> in response to motives (such as compassion and solidarity)
> not reducible to individual, material incentives.[46]

In practice the state has played a major role in promoting economic growth ever since the industrial revolution. First and fundamentally, by encouraging the culture of cooperation and reciprocity that makes us one society with a shared identity, fostering both specialisation and mutual interdependence whereby we all achieve more together than we could as competing individuals unconcerned for the community of which we are each a part. That has involved fulfilling basic functions like promoting public health, housing the homeless, educating the young, supporting the old, caring for social casualties of all kinds, enforcing the law and defending the nation against threats from abroad. Secondly, the state has kept the show on the road. Often, as during the banking crises of the 19th century and when they began to occur again after 1974, especially in 2008, the state has had to restore stability and maintain continuity by saving the banking system from itself and protecting the real economy from financial collapse.

Government's key role

Increasingly since the Second World War, and especially in capitalist economies like the US, South Korea, Israel, Taiwan, Germany and more recently Brazil, the state has done more than just fix market failure, by funding the basic research that leads to discovery and invention, educating young people and providing the infrastructure on which the market economy depends.

David Mowery, a specialist on the impact of technological change on economic growth, argues that a better explanation of the part played by government in promoting innovation is provided by a 'systems of innovation' approach. This is one in which R&D is geared more to the particular missions of government agencies, such as via programmes decided by policy makers at the Defence Advanced Research Projects Agency or the Small Business Innovation Research programme, rather than to the general advancement of knowledge to fill gaps caused by market failure, such as curious academic researchers might make. Mowery points out that most public R&D spending in the leading economies is now mission oriented rather than linked to the general advancement of knowledge, and decided by policy makers based on their assessments of the research needs of specific agencies, not by detached 'scientists', whether of the pure or applied kind. Albert Einstein came up with the equation $e = mc^2$ and Robert Oppenheimer was Scientific Director for the Manhattan Project that developed the atomic bomb, advising General Leslie Groves, who was in overall charge, but their budget was set by a five-man policy group responsible only to President Roosevelt. The scientists were on tap but the policy makers were on top.

The 'systems failure' argument for government intervention to encourage innovation and economic growth was noted in Labour's September 2003 statement on industrial policy. But that was just two paragraphs in the middle of 24 pages explaining DTI strategic priorities within the traditional market failure approach to intervention. The DTI acknowledged that firms exist within a network of interconnected institutions that generate, store and diffuse new knowledge and skills, a network which constitutes a national innovation system. And that such institutions may have inconsistent objectives. For instance, the incentives facing research centres may lead them to strike a poor balance between publishing results and cooperating with business, leading society to lose out unless the state takes corrective action.

In both these approaches to intervention – market failure or systems failure – the state's role remains one of plugging the gaps, creating the conditions for private sector innovation, putting right what the market economy gets wrong. Mariana Mazzucato recognises the validity of both bases for state intervention but insists that this is only part of the story because market failure accounts for less than one quarter of the R&D investments made in the US. David Mowery has summarised the situation as follows: 'Although the market failure rationale retains great rhetorical influence in justifying public investments in R&D programs, casual empiricism suggest that its influence over such public investments is modest at best.'[47]

Economist John Llewellyn showed how government can encourage innovation more broadly, and that the private sector often has to be pointed in the right direction to meet a change, either by regulation or active intervention:

> This typically requires government to be involved: to identify the problem; specify it; corral key people; offer the prize; provide funding. Witness the Second World War, which on that basis produced radar, radio navigation, the jet engine, rocketry and nuclear energy. Or space exploration: while increasingly now a private sector venture, would it have started without government involvement? Would nuclear energy?[48]

Entrepreneurial government

Mazzucato argues most persuasively that in modern advanced economies the state can also play a far more active and entrepreneurial role, both as lead risk taker and as creator and shaper of new product markets. She cites evidence from the recent record of the US where the state has been the source of dynamism and innovation, taking investment risks in areas shunned by a risk-averse private sector, and triggering technological advance in areas as diverse as aviation, computers, the internet, biotechnology, nuclear energy and green technology. The recent US shale gas success stemmed from geological knowledge based on government-funded research going back to the 1980s.[49] In Israel the Office of the Chief Scientist within the Ministry of Economy also invests in ventures which the private sector deems too risky. It played a supporting role in Waze, the navigation software company that Google bought in 2013 for $1 billion. In the 1990s it helped to establish Israel's venture capital industry through its Yozma ('initiative') programme.[50]

Mazzucato points out that all the technologies making the iPhone so smart originated from research funded by the US government: not just the internet, but GPS, touch-screen display and even the Siri voice-activated personal assistant. 'All of these came out of government agencies that were driven by missions, mainly around security – and funding not only the upstream "public good" research but also applied research and early-stage funding for companies.' Tellingly, she added:

> But while it's great that Steve Jobs had the genius to put those technologies into a well-designed gadget, and great more generally, for entrepreneurs to surf this publicly funded wave, who will fund the next wave with starved public budgets and a financialised and tax-avoiding private sector? New missions today should be expanded around problems posed by climate change, ageing, inequality and youth unemployment.

This is the key role for a dynamic state as the initiator of change, not just a fallback role responding to the inadequacies of the market system.[51]

With other leading economists, Mazzucato views innovation systems as networks of interacting institutions, both public and private, through which new knowledge is widely diffused and whose collective outcome is technological and structural change. Systems in which the state can drive technological advance, playing a developmental role in priority areas by pushing early-stage, risky research, encouraging the spread of resultant new knowledge, and providing vital funding at the commercial viability stage, especially via its procurement policies. This means more than the state creating the conditions in which innovation might occur. It means active state involvement all the way through from funding the first stages of risky, radical research, to facilitating commercial development, spurring innovation on.

In addition to the Defence Advanced Research Projects Agency, helping firms develop new products and processes in areas including computers, jet aircraft, civilian nuclear energy, lasers and biotechnology, and the Small Business Innovation Research programme, which has been making early-stage and seed funding awards to high tech firms and new enterprises since the early 1980s, key American examples include the 1983 Orphan Drug Act, providing both small and giant pharmaceutical firms with tax incentives, subsidies, fast track approval and stronger intellectual property rights for drugs aimed at treating rare conditions, and the National Nanotechnology Initiative from the 1990s, making investments in both research and commercialisation and in reviewing rules and regulations.

Mazzucato emphasises that much radical new technology stems from funding by a risk-taking state, estimating that 75 per cent of new drugs in the US trace their research to publicly funded National Institutes of Health laboratories, whereas the private pharmaceutical firms prefer to invest in safer variations of existing drugs. She notes that venture capital only invested in biotechnology, nanotechnology and the internet 15–20 years after the most important investments were made by public sector agencies.

She also cited two powerful and recent examples in Britain which demonstrated the leadership that public agencies can deliver compared with the private sector. 'When the BBC invested in iPlayer – the world's most innovative platform for online broadcasting – instead of outsourcing it, it went against the grain. It brought brains and knowledge into a public sector institution.' The same was true of the Government Digital Services when it wanted to create its own advanced website. Dissatisfied with the fashion for outsourcing because the recipient for many such contracts, Serco, had produced only a mediocre site, 'GDS brought in coders and engineers with iPlayer experience, who went on to produce an award-winning website that is costing the government a fraction of what Serco was charging. And in so doing also made government smarter – attracting, not haemorrhaging, the knowledge and capabilities required for dreaming up the missions of the future.'

But ominously, Mazzucato points out:

> By privatising public goods, outsourcing government functions, and constant state-bashing (government as 'meddler', at best 'de-risker') we are inevitably killing

the ability of government to think big and make things happen that otherwise would not have happened. The state starts to lose its capabilities, capacity, knowledge and expertise.

Which is exactly the consequence of neoliberalism and the contemporary fad for austerity.

Janeway has pointed out that 80 per cent of all American venture capitalist investments have consistently been ploughed into just two sectors, information and communications technology and biomedical, both beneficiaries of huge state funding ranging from scientific discovery to technological innovation: 'Through the Defense Department and the [National Institutes of Health] the federal government funded construction of a platform on which entrepreneurs and venture capitalists could dance.'[52] When the pharmaceutical company Pfizer moved its largest research laboratory from England to the US, Conservatives saw this as a search for lower taxes and less regulation. Actually it was nothing of the kind: it was to benefit from more than £30 billion of public funding for biomedical knowledge. More generally for biotech, private companies and venture capital, Mazzucato points out, 'entered the game 15 years after the state did the hard stuff'.

Active industrial policy

What David Sainsbury has called an 'enabling state', Mariana Mazzucato an 'entrepreneurial state' and Fred Block a 'development state' share a key common feature. They all envisage the state playing a vital role in encouraging economic growth, in part by actively promoting innovation. Unless this lesson is understood and implemented by Britain we will inevitably trail behind other countries, putting all our eggs in the basket of a self-serving private sector.

Industry Secretary Peter Mandelson's 2009 'New industry, new jobs' statement marked a significant shift in Labour government thinking towards a more active industrial strategy, one closer to that belatedly backed by David Sainsbury than the still bolder role for the state highlighted by Mariana Mazzucato. Mandelson acknowledged that his new statement of policy had removed a negative check on the subject that had prevailed for more than 20 years. But only under the pressure of the banking crisis had New Labour broken free from one of the deepest neoliberal conventional wisdoms.

'New industry, new jobs' accepted that suitably tailored state action could complement markets, notably in respect of infrastructure, training or investment in innovation. It could shape the business environment without seeking to substitute for markets, such as through public procurement of goods and services where large private sector investments depend on government commitments.

Business leaders often make the case for action learning, for learning on the job. That is what the Labour government experienced – albeit only through a crisis. We belatedly felt able to proclaim that government does indeed have a vital role to play in promoting investment in the new high technology jobs of the future: in the digital economy, in low carbon, in renewables and in bioscience.

Labour identified seven key areas where government action could help to restore strong, sustainable, long-term growth.

First, by *backing enterprise*, especially by improving access to finance required by starting and growing firms. Our UK Innovation Investment Fund provided a new source of equity capital for high tech firms.

Second, by *backing university spin-outs* through our Higher Education Innovation Fund, to help foster knowledge, transfer it from university to business, and so help to transform it into innovation and economic growth. We expanded centres of excellence developing British capabilities in plastic electronics, composites and industrial biotechnology, as well as investing in carbon-capture technology.

Third, by *building the skills* on which future jobs and living standards depend by adopting a fresh focus on vocational training, one aimed at ensuring that three quarters of people should take part in higher education or complete an advanced apprenticeship or equivalent technician level course by the age of 30.

Fourth, by *modernising Britain's infrastructure* and adapting it to the requirements of a low-carbon economy by bringing forward £3 billion of capital spending. To encourage private investment we pushed ahead with plans for high speed rail links and for next-generation broadband.

Fifth, by helping to ensure *open and competitive markets* that drive innovation and boost productivity by pressing for full implementation of an open EU market for business services.

Sixth, by building on Britain's *industrial strengths* by committing nearly £1 billion to the Strategic Investment Fund to bring government action to bear on areas where it could help unlock potential, like electric vehicles, offshore wind and other renewable energies.

Finally, by adopting a more strategic and coordinated approach to *clear away unnecessary blockages* to major inward and domestic investment projects.

Such an active industrial policy reflects the experience of countries which have rejected the low-wage strategy championed by so many of Britain's business elite. It recognises that there is no future for Britain trying to compete at the shoddy end of the quality spectrum, charging rock-bottom prices for copycat products made using clapped out kit by unskilled labour on poor pay. David Stout, Economics Director at the National Economic Development Office, drew attention in the 1970s to the vital importance of non-price factors to UK competitiveness. John Edmonds, GMB General Secretary and one of the TUC members of the NEDC in 1990, pressed for Stout's evidence to be updated. The results confirmed that the UK was still losing competitiveness in non-price terms, still drifting downmarket.[53] Today China is competing in global markets not just in low-cost, low-value markets but at the high quality end of the spectrum too.

Yet the so-called low-wage, low-price competitive strategy is commonly endorsed among leaders of British business, heavyweights who have enjoyed too many CBI lunches and Institute of Directors dinners listening to each other blame the workers, the government and the EU for their sinking market shares. Ha-Joon Chang has spelled out the implications of such a low-wage strategy: to compete with China, British wages would have to fall by 85 per cent; to contend with Vietnam they would have to be cut again by a further 75 per cent; then they would have to drop by another 66 per cent to match the Ethiopias and Burundis of this world. His conclusion: 'Britain can never win that game.'[54]

Britain needs an active industrial policy to rebuild our position in high quality high value markets and to encourage UK expansion in key sectors like the life sciences, health care, civil engineering, the automotive sector, renewable energy technology and educational services. Michael Heseltine introduced his October 2012 report *No stone unturned in pursuit of growth* with the comment: 'But what strikes me – and encourages me – is the unanimity of, among others, the CBI, TUC and *The Times* that Britain needs an industrial strategy … In their own way all our competitor economies manage their systems along these lines. We are the ones out of step.'

The single most successful European economy, Germany, has powered ahead of the pack by setting standards of customer service that its rivals have been unable to match. It has developed its people, its product range and its production methods. Germany's competitive edge has come from persistent investment in design, precision, quality and reliability on a scale unmatched by any of its EU partners. Of course, keeping costs down has also played an important part in building a world-class competitive economy, especially since German reunification. But by choosing as a society to invest in vocational education and training, to prepare for change and embrace it rather than resist it, and to make workplace cooperation commonplace, Germany has developed a source of real competitive advantage that has helped it to enjoy the fruits of growth. Labour's colleagues in the German Social Democratic Party (SPD) have suffered fewer of the frustrations that we in Britain have experienced as a result. Like ours, theirs is also a far from perfect society but Germany is only one of Britain's EU partners from whom we could learn some useful lessons – including from the German banking system, which is geared to long-term business investment, even common equity stakes in businesses to which they lend.

Only active government which makes a virtue not a vice of state intervention can enable Britain to succeed in a way that our more interventionist and successful competitors have done. A 'downsized', 'lean' or 'small' state is not the answer in the modern age – if it ever was. A smarter, interventionist, risk-taking state is.

CHAPTER 6

Fraternity, cooperation, trade unionism

Tony Crosland was candid about citizen cooperation as an imperative for societal success: he wasn't at all sure where it fitted into his vision of socialism. He did not doubt that fraternity and cooperation formed one of the five basic socialist aspirations, but was uncertain how to translate that ideal into practical proposals. He acknowledged that working together for a common goal could provide powerful incentives of fulfilment, a sense of satisfaction and fewer grievances. But he accepted, too, that differential rewards boosted economic growth and living standards, because people generally worked for personal material gain, not for some social good. Each motive, individual self-advantage or a shared purpose, worked well in appropriate circumstances.

The one area where Crosland certainly saw individuals joining forces in a practical way was in the workplace, where differences of reward, of status, of opportunity and of treatment by management were generating discontent and resentment rather than teamworking and high morale, holding growth back instead of pushing it forward.

Britain in the 1950s was a class-conscious society in which the working classes were still expected to know their place, show due deference and keep clear of first-class carriages. These were the days of the tradesmen's entrance, of petty status distinctions, and of Received Pronunciation. Of bowler hats, trilbies and cloth caps – when who you knew counted more than what you knew. When golf-playing board members could enjoy long lunches in the directors' dining room while their employees took short breaks in the company canteen listening to '*Workers' playtime*'.[1] When much of British industry was led by a privileged elite of amateurs in an increasingly professional post-war world. In 1957, when sociologist Michael Young first coined the term 'meritocracy', the establishment twisted it into an endorsement of their deserved place on the bridge of the ship of state and in the driving seat of British business, summed up in Prime Minister Harold Macmillan's 1957 claim 'You've never had it so good.'

You did not have to be Fred Kite (the caricature trade union shop steward of the era) to want to say no to nepotism, to understand why an underlying atmosphere of conflict seemed ever present in British workplaces, or to see how collective bargaining by trade unions might be an effective way of winning a better deal for blue- and white-collar workers alike, and of bringing the UK economy up to date.

Crosland thought that unions could promote cooperation rather than conflict at work by bringing management and labour together. He never denied that there were two sides in industry with divergent interests. But he saw no reason why industrial relations should be endless pitched battles between belligerent bosses and uncompromising unions. He reckoned that, by abandoning outdated attitudes on both sides of the bargaining table, deadlocks could be replaced by breakthroughs, and disputes by deals. He accepted that management and labour's common interest in keeping production going demanded a high degree of cooperation, though not one which could wholly override other potential points of conflict. He insisted that unions must stay independent of management, responsible to their members and keen to represent them robustly while ready to give members frank and even unwelcome advice, if necessary.

He envisaged unions delivering better terms and conditions of employment for their members by expanding their collective bargaining agenda, from its traditional tight focus on pay to wider issues like pensions, holidays and sickness benefits. They could press for single status agreements (agreements with employers on pay and conditions treating all grades of employee equally, so that no one felt like a second-class employee). And they could increase the involvement of workers in decisions that affected them by negotiating better information and consultation rights. But he regretted that British unions, unlike their Swedish counterparts, had rarely sought to extend the scope of collective bargaining to cover subjects such as investment and labour force plans, managerial efficiency, profit margins and productivity, and business prospects.

Tony Crosland was optimistic about the prospects for change at work. He believed that full employment had transformed the balance of power between employers and unions, with the unions' new bargaining strength ruling out wage cuts imposed by bosses. He dismissed any likelihood of anti-union legislation by a Tory government in view of their rejection in 1955 of proposals to outlaw even unofficial strikes. And, apart from Ted Heath's short-lived attempt in the early 1970s to rig industrial relations law against unions, Crosland's expectation of a relatively benign legal climate for unions proved true – until the arrival of Thatcherism changed everything.

Cooperation spurned

But until the 1980s most unions saw no need for the kind of cooperation at work that Crosland favoured, the kind that is standard today in some other parts of Europe, notably Germany and Scandinavia. Union membership had reached a record high of 13 million in 1979, helped by a favourable economic environment with full employment most of the time, and buttressed by Labour's pro-worker legal regime of the 1960s and 1970s which included allowing closed shops covering more than five million workers who were obliged to join a trade union to keep their job.[2] A 1977 proposal from the Labour government's Bullock Committee for employee representation on company boards was torpedoed in a pincer attack by unions and employers. The former feared losing their independence and letting non-union members have a say, the latter feared losing management prerogatives and ultimate shareholder control. The cautious outlook shared by union activists and full-time officials kept them in their comfort zone, tied to a traditional bargaining agenda and at ease with antagonistic relationships between management and labour.

The unions were slow to see things Tony Crosland's way. It was not until the 1970s that the GMB union became the first to appoint a full-time specialist national pensions officer, and 1990 before it adopted a mission statement which included the goal of working in partnership with responsible employers. It was also 1990 before the unions affiliated to the TUC backed a joint initiative by the Union of Communication Workers and GMB and formally committed themselves to pursue a new, broader bargaining agenda. (Both I and Phil Wyatt, then Heads of Research for these two unions, worked on this agenda.) It emphasised prospects as well as pay, with the focus falling particularly on training since low skills meant low pay and no skills increasingly meant no jobs. The 1980s had ended with unions only tackling management about training and skills in two out of every ten workplaces where they were recognised, according to the Advisory Conciliation and Arbitration Service.

Britain's unions had been influenced in part by the example set by the German engineering union IG Metall which was pursuing five days training per year for all its members, and under the German 'co-determination' model was involved in all stages of setting training standards. They also hoped to build upon the lifetime training rights provided for in article 15 of the European Social Charter agreed at the December 1989 EU summit, Margaret Thatcher dissenting. That ambition was frustrated when John Major opted out of the social 'chapter' of the 1991 EU Maastricht treaty. Although Tony Blair opted back in, he went cold on the European 'social dimension' which included such measures.

As the respected economics commentator Larry Elliott noted, at the start of the 1980s Britain faced a choice between 'the consensual German way, with trade unions seen by management as partners rather than adversaries, or there was the American model, which saw labour as an enemy'.[3] Britain with Mrs Thatcher at the helm chose the latter.

The whole idea of closer cooperation between unions and employers had been under strain throughout the 1980s, as union membership sank under the onslaught of a five-pronged Tory attack that Crosland would have regarded with both incomprehension and anger. First, a deliberate fiscal squeeze in Geoffrey Howe's 1981 budget that pushed the economy into recession, forced unemployment up above 3 million and kept it there for four years. Second, anti-union laws that banned the closed shop, restricted industrial action and limited workers' legal protection against unfair dismissal. Third, privatisation of state-owned industries and compulsory competitive tendering for local government services, which led to massive job losses, slashed union memberships and disrupted union relationships with employers. Fourth, a huge decline in manufacturing jobs and a consequential collapse of union membership as big industrial centres shrank right across the spectrum from clothing and textiles to chemicals and heavy engineering and mining. Fifth, a campaign of anti-union abuse that included Margaret Thatcher labelling unions 'the enemy within', culminating in the year-long 1984–85 miners' strike which saw unprecedented and ruthless state power deployed to decimate both mining and the iconic National Union of Mineworkers.[4] Cooperation between both sides of industry was further undermined in 1992 when John Major scrapped the National Economic Development Council, a 1962 Tory 'one nation' initiative that had survived every Prime Minister from Harold Macmillan to Margaret Thatcher.

The years leading up to the 2008 financial crisis should have been the decade when the flexible firm met the ubiquitous union. It was a period which witnessed steady economic growth, new union recognition rights and fairer rights at work delivered by New Labour. But the unions failed to bounce back and union membership barely changed. Had the share of the workforce in unions kept pace with the rise in employment since the mid-1990s, the TUC would have represented over a million more members than it did by 2008. If unions represented today the same share of the workforce that they did in 1991, when I gave up my union post to become MP for Neath, TUC membership would now be some 9 million strong, not under 7 million. The gap between where unions are today and where they could be is getting wider. This is not a new problem but it is becoming steadily more serious.

British trade unionism at the crossroads

The union conference season opens every Easter and runs until the TUC Congress in September. A chorus of complaint about various aspects of Labour policy and leadership performance is par for the course, whether it is in or out of office. The toughest strictures usually come, more in sorrow than in anger, from speakers who see themselves as Labour's critical friends. That's fine. Ministers and shadow ministers need candid feedback to keep them on their toes and to help them raise their game – though sometimes it feels less like a half-time team talk from José Mourinho and more like a verbal assault from Sir Alex Ferguson.

As is sadly too often the case within the left, those nearest to you can become bigger targets than your opponents – moaning about Labour seems easier than attacking the Tories. Typical was the occasion a month before polling day in 2010, when the able left-wing civil service trade union leader Mark Serwotka hit the front page with this astonishing gem attacking Labour's record: 'I have to say to you this – that if you judge a government by how it behaves as an employer, this is the worst government in the history of this country.' His members – their ranks swelled among the 800,000 additional public sector workers recruited under New Labour, and their pay having risen sharply – were about to find out just how much 'worse' it could get under the Tory/Lib Dems. Serwotka accepted not the slightest responsibility for Labour's crushing defeat at the polls: as usual it was all 'the party leadership's fault'. I commend to his ilk some words written in 1653 by Anne Collins: 'They that faint with complaint therefore are to blame. They add to their afflictions and amplify the same.'[5]

No one ever succeeded in a union by settling for second best and there are few prizes for patience in union politics. Ernest Bevin warned against poverty of ambition in the labour movement. So unions rightly set exacting standards and make strong demands. I spent 14 years as a research officer proudly helping the Union of Communication Workers to do exactly that. It's what unions are for.

But negotiators know that what goes around comes around. The halving of union membership since 1980 to only 23 per cent of those in employment in 2013, and 14 per cent in the private sector where 70 per cent of the jobs are, is not a picture of trade unions closely attuned to the needs of working people. It is compounded by an even bigger drop (by two thirds) in the number of union activists. Relatively few members now take part in electing union national executive bodies, and many successful candidates fill uncontested seats. Union committees setting policy and bargaining priorities in particular sectors often include retired members who are poorly placed to assess current shop-floor opinion. Turnouts in recent elections for union general secretaries have been woeful: USDAW 13 per cent in 2008, Unison 15 per cent in 2010 and Unite 15 per cent in 2013.

Although hardly a ringing democratic endorsement of the Thatcherite insistence on individual membership ballots for union leaders, and on a par with the average 15 per cent turnout in elections for Tory-imposed Police Crime Commissioners, all this threatens the foundations of trade unions' claim to represent working people, and their legitimacy in helping decide Labour Party policy and in electing Labour's leaders. It reflects something that Tony Crosland highlighted in the 1950s, namely that, for all their progressive rhetoric, unions have been captured by their own conservative culture. Instead of embracing change by backing cooperation at work, they too often talk the language of reform while seeking to stick with rigid procedures, outdated pay structures and obsolete ways of working. Union officials sometimes seem in no need of a sat nav because they never intend to change their position, treating their negotiating mandate as a season ticket back to square one. Like England cricketer Chris Tavare, whose run rate was once so slow that he was said to have dropped anchor at the crease, some union representatives habitually adopt a fixed negotiating stance and play a dead bat at everything employers send their way, resisting change without always even knowing why.

Fighting developments that may even be in their members' best interests, or failing to come forward with alternative proposals of their own, is a form of union leadership that is both lazy and lousy. Union officials serve their members poorly when all they can do is provide a predictable quote condemning bad news instead of working together with employers on ways to pre-empt problems and overcome obstacles.

Sometimes trade unions do have to take a stand and defend their members' interests through confrontation rather than cooperation, and every new generation of union leaders gets labelled by the media as the awkward squad, as if their predecessors were merely the mild bunch. But unless they can switch off the autopilot and chart a fresh course Britain's unions could slide into the long-run steady state into which David Metcalf of the London School of Economics has forecast their past performance will take them, representing only 20 per cent of the workforce and only 12 per cent in the private sector.[6]

Nevertheless, some notable union successes have been overlooked by commentators. For instance, a 2006 article by Anne Perkins found the union movement to be 'in remorseless decline', in part because 'there are no more mass employers, except the state'.[7] But this missed the fact that Britain's second biggest employer, Tesco, then had 250,000 employees in the UK. Tesco now has over 280,000 UK employees, 164,000 of whom are USDAW members covered by the partnership agreement between USDAW and Tesco Retail, the biggest private sector collective bargaining agreement in the UK. But the inability of unions in general to recover past strength despite record levels of employment tells a different story. Regrettably TUC talk about a union revival stems from wishful thinking and union leaders have been slow to accept that they speak on behalf of a shrinking share of the workforce and quick to blame globalisation or government or greedy hostile bosses.

I have been a trade union member all my working life. And I make no apology for actively supporting strikes like those in 1976–77 by Grunwick workers and in 1984–85 by miners.[8] As a union official for 14 years I was involved in difficult negotiations, brinkmanship and the occasional strike. Without effective trade unions our democracy would be impoverished, working people damaged and our economy would suffer serious loss. Despite huge membership losses, trade unions are still by far the largest democratic movement in Britain, representing *over nine times* the combined membership of the main political parties – something Conservatives may care to acknowledge when they repeatedly attack unions as lacking legitimacy.

The blunt truth is that declining trade union influence has been paralleled by the richest 1 per cent getting steadily richer and the rest of us getting steadily poorer. And this was worsened in Britain by the impact of the Tory/Lib Dem government's public sector pay freeze and pension cap on low to middle income workers who experienced a loss of earnings of up to 20 per cent in real terms according to an analysis by the Public and Commercial Services union in July 2014. Public sector workers with annual earnings of £20,000 in 2011 should have been earning upwards of £22,750 by 2015 just by keeping up with the retail price index; instead they were frozen at £20,000.

Indeed, because union decline has encouraged a small elite to take a larger share of our national incomes, the rest of the population has been borrowing more to maintain living standards, in turn encouraging the explosion of debt and reckless finance which produced the meltdown of 2007–08. As a 2010 IMF working paper concluded:

> Without a recovery in the incomes of poor and middle income households, the inevitable result is that loans keep growing and therefore so does ... the probability of a major crisis ... Restoration of poor and middle income households' bargaining power can be very effective, leading to the prospect of a sustained reduction in leverage that should reduce the probability of a further crisis.[9]

Rebuilding trade union strength could be one helpful crisis-avoidance step.

We need stronger, more effective unions with a much wider and bigger membership, because workplace injustice and job insecurity remain rife today; many rights and benefits, hard-won over generations of struggle – from pay to pensions to facilities for union representatives like office space, computer equipment and somewhere to meet members – have been rolled back as an elite at the very top of the earnings tree has advanced while everyone else has experienced falls in real income. But righting these wrongs won't occur unless unions tackle some uncomfortable truths about their own performance and the results they are delivering to their members.

Union priorities

In this light, the policy priorities that union leaders pressed upon the last Labour government seemed questionable if not bizarre. They had three in the key area of rights at work: to bring back the closed shop, provided employers agreed; to encourage strikes to last longer by dropping the eight-week rule limiting the time during which it was automatically unfair to sack someone taking industrial action; and to force very small firms to recognise unions, by scrapping the 20-employee threshold.

Were these really the rights-at-work issues that union members were most concerned about? I had expected union leaders to champion other issues that mattered more to their members. Three came to mind. First, equal pay: top of the equal rights agenda for both men and women workers. Second, effective enforcement of current health and safety laws by increased funding for Health and Safety Executive workplace checks, and corporate manslaughter, both of which were big issues among union members. Third, although the unions rightly welcomed moves by the government to tackle work–life balance issues through rights to apply to work flexible hours and childcare support, I had also expected to see stronger union pressure on Labour to tackle harassment and bullying at work, which union members saw as an acute problem.

The unions failed to grasp the opportunities for recruitment and recognition that New Labour delivered: record levels of employment, a statutory right to union recognition, a new right to accompany workers at grievance and disciplinary hearings, union involvement in sector skills councils and statutory recognition for union learning representatives, fresh rights at work (often implementing EU directives on issues like information and consultation, age discrimination, working time and part-time work), better protection against unfair dismissal, and even state financial support for partnership at work and union modernisation.

Decades of dependence on closed shops had made unions complacent about recruiting new members in the growing, small-firm dominated service sector to replace those lost in the shrinking, large-firm dominated manufacturing sector; about winning recognition from employers in both existing and new workplaces; about the standard of service they supplied to members; and about the support they provided at grassroots level to their largely voluntary workplace representatives and local branch officers.

Their loss of membership strength has weakened unions' ability to deliver. The proportion of workers whose pay is affected by collective agreements has dropped significantly, the union 'wage premium' (higher pay in unionised workplaces) has fallen from about 10 per cent in the private sector in the early 1990s to under 3 per cent now (allowing for differences in skill and qualifications), and the scope for negotiations between unions and employers has narrowed, despite formal union pledges to pursue a broader bargaining agenda.

The frustration is that I see in my constituency advice surgeries regular casualties of these shortcomings: workers who are not in unions being victimised or treated shoddily. And also that real wages for the average worker have fallen by 8–10 per cent since the financial crunch of 2008, while boardroom pay has soared.[10]

A shrinking rank and file base

Although trade unions have professionalised their back-up staff and their full-time officials, with impressive and modern membership support services providing help on key areas from law to pensions via experienced union officers, their frontline strength has shrunk as the number of lay representatives – volunteer workplace-based activists like union stewards and staff representatives – has dwindled. By 1998 some 25 per cent of workplaces where unions were recognised had no union steward – meaning no one to represent existing union members and no one to enrol new recruits as existing members retire, switch employers or lose their jobs. By 2004 fewer than half the members of unions recognised by employers had access to a lay representative at their own workplace.

With stewards stretched so thinly, unions have struggled to maintain standards of service to members. Unions can lose a fifth of their members each year. Many leavers go partly because they are unhappy with some aspect of the service they receive: too little contact from workplace representatives, not enough help given to members with problems at work, and rare letters or magazines to their homes reminding them that their union is only a phone call away if needed.

Between the bottom of recession in 1993 and the peak of the boom in 2008 the number of private sector service jobs rose far faster than public service jobs. But union recruitment priorities lay elsewhere. They tried to stay on familiar territory of public services and manufacturing. They also kidded themselves that by admirably recruiting women working part-time they had taken a bold step forwards, when recruitment of the traditional male full-time worker was falling. In fact they were not even standing still.

Only a minority of union stewards rank recruitment among their most important duties. Workplace employment relations surveys show that even where unions have access to induction sessions and lists of new starters this has made little difference to union recruitment.

In 2002 the prize for best publication at the annual TUC Press and PR Awards had to be awarded posthumously. The winning magazine had already been scrapped. That same year the TUC highlighted insurance for pets as a major new union service, turning an obviously blind eye to the evidence that few people join unions for financial services.

It was also a time when only 6 per cent of union members were aged 16–24 and unions needed to boost their appeal to young people. Unfortunately, many unions prioritised recruitment among full-time students who worked part-time, a group that was outnumbered eight to one by non-students in the same age range who were already in regular work.

Despite extensive evidence of unfair management treatment of employees, many people remain reluctant to turn to a union for fear it may make an awkward situation worse. In fact union stewards usually intervene to take the heat out of difficult situations and to calm matters down. They are peacemakers, not troublemakers. Their key role in practice is to help solve problems at work, not to cause them. This is especially true of union safety representatives. Independent evidence shows that workplaces where unions are recognised have *half* the accidents of those where unions are absent. So unions often work to the benefit of management and employees alike, but that is rarely if ever trumpeted.

Strangely union support provided to key activists has also become patchy. In some cases barely half the stewards regularly receive union materials like handbooks, employment law guides, bargaining briefs or health and safety advice. Many stewards now feel isolated, being the only union representative at their workplace. In a TUC survey 9 per cent of union representatives said they received no paid time off at all to carry out their duties. Many others cannot take the paid time off to which they are entitled, due to lack of cover if they do so, and pressure to meet work targets.

Their lack of workplace representatives handicaps many unions in protecting members at work. Only two thirds of the members of major unions have a steward at their workplace. Yet the focus of union lobbying in Labour's 2005 review of employment rights was not on time off or facilities for workplace representatives. It was on extending the 1999 Employment Relations Act to very small firms where few unions have any members at all.

Recognition by employers

David Metcalf's team at the London School of Economics has shown one area where union performance has been particularly poor. That is in winning recognition from employers in new workplaces. The reluctance of many union leaders openly to acknowledge how much responsible employers can gain from a union presence is short-sighted. Workplace employment relations surveys confirm that most managers remain indifferent rather than hostile to unions. They are open to persuasion but will only recognise an organisation that they can see bringing something to the party. Convincing them that it is a myth that 'TUC spells trouble' is usually the first step.

A 2003 TUC report emphasised that effective union representation depends crucially on employer support in the workplace.[11] But rants betraying a taste for conflict, with union leaders talking a good fight to *Morning Star* readers, denouncing Britain's overpaid bosses as 'a bunch of greedy bastards', and blood-curdling threats of campaigns of civil disobedience have handicapped union recognition without boosting recruitment.

The latest development is for employers setting up new workplaces to treat potential union partners as they would a preferred suppliers list, only recognising unions that can contribute by boosting customer service. That means unions which want to encourage teamworking, minimise labour turnover, support continuous improvement programmes, promote quality and reliability, and encourage safety.

Workers want their unions to cooperate with employers in such ways, not wage class warfare in the workplace – even if strikes remain an important and legitimate tactic when all else fails. That is made more difficult when the CBI and the Institute of Directors call for the scrapping of almost all rights at work, while some of their members practise illegal blacklisting of union members, discriminate illegally against employees on age, gender and sexual orientation grounds, sack loyal workers unfairly, or exploit zero-hours contracts unmercifully. Or when victims of unfair dismissal and discrimination fighting for their rights must pay fees to take their case to an employment tribunal. And when recession has caused the number of people feeling insecure at work to double in three years, as it did between 2010 and 2013, rising from 6.5 million to 13 million.

What a contrast with Germany where *Mitbestimmung* or co-determination builds in cooperation between both sides of industry and where union candidates have to win contested elections to leadership positions on works councils, helping to keep them in touch with workplace priorities and making working together with employers a routine imperative, not a cause for questioning loyalties. The German approach has been far more successful than the British, both macro-economically and in securing good, well-paid jobs and conditions.

Equally, however, that has not saved the German unions from a similar struggle to retain support as that being fought by unions in the UK. Germany had over 8 million union members in 2010 representing some 19 per cent of employees – a fall from 24 per cent in 2000. Parallel de-unionisation trends illustrate a societal problem for trade unionism, not a problem peculiar to British union leadership and organisation.

Job losses and therefore union membership losses have been most acute in manufacturing both in the UK and in Germany, as elsewhere in the advanced world, symbolised by the closures of the Ravenscraig steelworks here and the Rheinhausen plant there. Although Germany still has one of the biggest and most successful manufacturing sectors in the world, like the UK the German economy is now predominantly a service-based one without the tradition of union membership typical of heavy industry and concentrated workplaces. Both economies have seen sites change. The iconic Hoover domestic appliance plant at Perivale in West London and the Bowater paper mill in Gillingham, Kent are now both Tesco supermarkets. The workforces have also changed, from mainly men in boiler suits working full-time to mainly women in workwear working part-time. Germany's much stronger small-firm sector, often family based, poses unique challenges to unions. Neither country has seen unions do well at winning recognition in new green-field sites, though de-recognition has been a rarity. No one can say that change has passed either workforce by, or the unions that aim to give them a voice at work. But the question is not which union movement has got most members. It's which country's system yields best results for working people. And there is no doubt that Germany comes up trumps.

Working together for results

The way work is organised and how people are managed are key factors determining workplace performance results. Yet too many traditional UK methods of doing so are out of date, hindering rather than helping firms' efforts to match their product or service to customers' requirements. They undermine rather than underpin employers' efforts to keep up with their competitors. And they often alienate rather than motivate employees by treating them unfairly or locking them into unrewarding routine tasks.[12]

By working together, unions and employers have the potential to deliver dramatic improvements in performance, boosting productivity and profitability and enhancing living standards and future prospects. A mutual commitment to accident prevention and risk avoidance can streamline production, boost reliability and make workplaces safer. A shared resolve to boost training and personal development can make continuous improvement a reality, ease the take-up of new technology, promote quality and precision, and enhance employability and pay. An agreed undertaking to find more flexible ways of working that suit both employer and employee can cut customer order lead times, boost motivation and morale, and enhance job satisfaction and earnings. A joint commitment to customers, colleagues and the company can reduce labour turnover, cut absenteeism and produce a better work–family life balance. A mutual pledge to cooperation and a problem-solving approach to employment relations can free up management time, promote effective team working and improve dignity at work.[13]

None of this need undermine unions' ability to deliver positive results for their members. Nor need it mean unions meekly accepting the employers' agenda. Unions can still press pay, pensions, skills, fair treatment, equal pay and work–life balance issues onto the bargaining agenda. Why are German workers better paid, why do they have more job security and why are their companies more competitive? The agenda suggested above is often greeted by union leaders and activists as being too 'soft'. Actually it would be more successful, as German unions have proved. It can also be more hard-headed. German trade unions were not reticent, especially during the height of the financial crisis, in negotiating earnings freezes or even cuts in return for maintaining jobs. They showed that a bit of flexibility can be a fillip to a company facing a serious drop in orders and cash flow problems because of the onset of recession. In similar circumstances British union officials who stick too rigidly to standing orders may get their members their marching orders, because rigid negotiating positions just cause everyone a pain in the neck.

How well unions perform their fundamental role of recruiting and representing working people also determines how much political weight they carry in society, whatever the institutional link between some unions and the Labour Party. In their political role unions expand the contribution to popular debate made by working people and promote a more representative democracy. In particular, many workers take part in Labour Party activities via their union. Unions bring colleagues together, provide platforms for protagonists, and create a focus for argument, for example by submitting motions to party conferences, proposing amendments to draft policy documents, arranging fringe meetings at party and union events, and issuing statements and articles through the media. By leading debate in this way the unions affiliated to the Labour Party encourage accountability, inspire alternative perspectives, stimulate exchanges of views, and enhance democratic debate. But unless unions rebuild their strengths in workplaces their hopes of playing a more prominent and influential role in the political arena will remain unfulfilled.

A Labour government can and should help by enforcing the law on blacklisting and all forms of discrimination, by providing stronger protection against unfair dismissal from the day that someone starts working for an employer, and by taking tough action to enforce the national minimum wage and bring it up to a living wage level. It can and should crack down on zero-hours contracts by banning employers from insisting that zero-hours workers be available even when there is no guarantee of any work, stopping zero-hours contracts that require workers to work exclusively for one business, and ending the misuse of such contracts where employees are in practice working regular hours over a sustained period. It can and should oblige employers to conduct equal pay audits (as recommended by the Equal Opportunities Commission over a decade ago).

But ultimately the unions' future lies in their own hands, not with government. They have to recognise that they operate at the interface between employees and employers, and cannot succeed for either unless they bring benefits for both. That means learning from their colleagues' experience elsewhere in Europe, and showing what genuine cooperation can mean in the workplace, just as Tony Crosland proposed.

Although unions have rarely, and usually reluctantly, embraced Crosland's concept of cooperation between management and labour, they have reached some pioneering partnership deals in the past that show how different the future could look.

A union agreement with United Distillers linked improvements in employment security with new ways of working and opportunities for training and personal development. It helped the United Distillers plant at Leven in Scotland to win the 1997 Management Today/Cranfield School of Management 'Best Factory of the Year' award. A union-backed annualised hours agreement helped MD Foods to win the 1998 Chartered Institute of Personnel and Development 'People Management' award. These were way ahead of the CBI Headstart service, aimed at helping firms to develop world-class standards of people management.

More recently, too, unions have sometimes escaped the oppositional culture which has held them back for decades by pursuing a robust relationship with employers that brings benefits to both sides. A June 2012 two-year agreement between GMB and the Asda supermarket chain covering 10,000 union members working in 20 distribution centres was hailed by management and union alike as one that brought working practices up to date, secured jobs and supported growth.

In the summer of 2012 the security company G4S fell out of favour with the public and the government for failing to provide over 10,000 guards for the London Olympics. The GMB General Secretary Paul Kenny came to the company's defence, describing this employer of 23,000 GMB members as significantly better than others in the security business. G4S had paid for 5,900 security guards to get Security Industry Authority (SIA) qualifications – making them more employable after the Games – and recruited 2,000 more with SIA licences (ensuring people working in the security industry are properly trained and qualified to do their job), about 7,000 of whom had joined the union.[14]

In June 2014 Nestlé UK won accreditation as a 'living wage' employer following work with its trade unions GMB, Unite and USDAW. The company's direct employees already earn the living wage but Nestlé committed to work with its contractors to ensure that agency and contract staff are paid it too by December 2017. Paul Kenny of GMB said: 'It just shows what can be achieved when a decent employer works together with progressive unions.' Unite's Len McCluskey added that the agreement was won 'in the spirit of cooperation and a willingness to start to tackle poverty pay in a traditionally low paying sector'.[15]

These agreements and others, like the relationship between Unite and Jaguar Land Rover which helped to turn the company around, show that trade unions can deliver high-performance ways of working which employees support, at a price that employers are willing to pay. They demonstrate how a union can help to build trust and overcome initial anxieties about change among employees and management alike, in the process enhancing job security. But unfortunately they are exceptions, not the rule. Britain's unions have never queued up to sign partnership agreements with employers. Routine robust cooperation with employers of the kind practised by the German unions has never become the norm in the UK. That is what has to change. Otherwise, in an era where individualism has been allowed to flourish at the expense of the security and opportunity that only collectivism can bring, unions will continue to weaken   tragically for workers and tragically for British competitiveness and economic success.

New framework for cooperation

The way to bring about such change is for Parliament to create a new framework for cooperation at work, one that conservatism on both sides of British industry has been blocking for decades, exemplified by the inability of management and unions to forge fresh relationships since new EU information and consultation rights took effect in the UK in 2005 under Labour. A framework which acknowledges that one of the biggest broken markets of all is Britain's labour market, where a long-lasting mutual failure to find better ways of working together by unions and employers has cost them both, and the country, dear. A framework for relationships between employees and employers like the co-determination system that has been one of the sources of Germany's postwar economic success. The German model, sniffily derided in the British media, British management and in New Labour circles for its 'high social costs', has in fact delivered higher wages, better pensions, enhanced job security, and helped power German manufacturing industry to be the envy of the world.

British society has paid a heavy price for clinging so closely to its outdated adversarial system of industrial relations that has done so little to deliver employee involvement. It is the conflict at the core, the real factory flaw. Mutual suspicion has led both sides of the bargaining table to conduct negotiations haunted by nightmares about the other side's supposed hidden agenda. The damage has taken many forms: low employee motivation, lagging productivity, lost competitiveness and lousy job security; shocking skills gaps, grossly unequal rewards, and grotesque discrimination. Instead of world-class standards of product quality and customer service British business has too often settled for second best, and – with a few notable exceptions – we have seen our market share drop and jobs disappear.

Instead of work that they find fulfilling and rewarding, with opportunities for advancement, too many employees feel locked into undemanding humdrum jobs, prisoners of rigid rules, hierarchical structures and narrow horizons. When it comes to information about mergers, reorganisations or new technology they are first in the firing line but the last to know. Too many managers cling to a command and control approach, fearful of sharing information with employees and union representatives, while talking a good game about teamworking and joint endeavour. Too many union representatives deliver a backdated brand of alphabet soup at meetings with management: A for antagonism instead of arbitration, B for belligerence instead of breakthrough, C for confrontation instead of conciliation and D for deadlock instead of deal.

A works council approach along German lines would mean applying internationally proven best practice to Britain's way of doing business. Although it wouldn't turn shop stewards into industrial pacifists – the bed of nails wouldn't become a bed of roses – and although the need for independent trade unions would remain, such an approach could help to match UK performance closer to that of our leading international rival in markets at home and abroad. When Angela Merkel, leader of Germany's Christian Democratic Union Party, spoke to the 2005 national conference of the German chemical workers union IG Chemie, she assured them that *Mitbestimmung* or cooperation had been one of the secrets of Germany's post-war economic success, and she was refusing pressure from her allies in the right-wing Christian Social Union Party to abandon it. And she subsequently maintained this position. The results speak for themselves, including high living standards, unparalleled export success, a strong manufacturing base, world-class training and skills and greater social cohesion.

Such cooperation at work was the kind Tony Crosland had been searching for. The co-determination system was in its infancy in West Germany when he was writing *The Future of Socialism*, though its roots can be traced back to Germany's 1920 Works Council Act requiring firms with over 20 employees to set up consultative bodies. After being banned by the Nazis, works councils were revived in 1947 by the Allied occupying powers (Britain, ironically, most prominent among them: what helped the Germans apparently hindered the Brits). Today, although every German workplace with at least five employees *could* elect a works council, in practice large firms are much more likely than small ones to have one. In private sector workplaces in Germany with more than 500 employees in 2011, about 90 per cent had works councils.[16] Three quarters of the people elected in 2010 to represent workers on German works councils were members of unions linked to the DGB (the German TUC) – so this approach is entirely compatible with vibrant trade unionism.

When Crosland admitted to uncertainty about the relevance of cooperation to the Britain of the 1950s, but saw some practical prospects in the world of work, it was harmonious industrial relations in the emerging, enviable success of Sweden rather than one of the sources of the nascent German economic miracle that caught his attention. But that is no reason to blind Labour to 60 years of unparalleled German success. Any more than it should allow us to overlook home-grown models of practical success with stronger worker participation and a stake in the future of the business shown by organisations like the employee-owned John Lewis Partnership (encompassing workers in John Lewis and Peter Jones department stores and the Waitrose supermarket chain), and the string of case studies of high-performance workplaces practising employee involvement that the Involvement and Participation Association has collected.

Cooperation at work can deliver results that benefit employees and employers alike, especially when it is backed by trade unions that want relationships with employers that are both robust *and* productive. This is not an argument for trade unions and managers being passive or weak, but rather for both being *different*, in the interests of better economic performance and prosperity – for them, and for the country.

CHAPTER 7

But what *sort* of socialist state?

If there is a strong case for greater not less state intervention, does that, as the right charges, inevitably mean a 'Big State' with its overtures of remote, inflexible bureaucracy and even authoritarianism?

The answer is emphatically no. The right cannot be allowed to get away with such a caricature. But equally the left must be very clear what our vision for the state is – what *sort* of socialist state do we envisage?

Democratic socialism should mean an active, democratically accountable state to underpin individual freedom and deliver the conditions for everyone to be empowered regardless of who they are or what their income is. It should be complemented by decentralisation and empowerment to achieve increased democracy and social justice.

And whereas the right advocates a small state for public services, it runs a big state for those who challenge its policies.

Neoliberalism, democratic legitimacy and society

The right's neoliberalism means the smallest small state possible, out of the way to leave space for a free-for-all. In schools for example, the left aims to empower parents, teachers and school governors within a framework of strong support for, and enforcement of minimum standards by the local and national state to ensure equal opportunities for all, rich or poor. Whereas for the right, schools should be 'set free' to compete in a marketplace – hence 'free schools', grammar schools and private schools.

Yet, despite being promoted in the name of 'individual freedom', the more ascendant the right's agenda has become, the more disempowered all but a few feel and the more democratic legitimacy has been endangered. Political cynicism and disaffection is probably greater than ever before in industrially advanced, democratic societies. In Britain, democratic accountability has been undermined both by a powerful global economy and by the centrifugal impact of the right's agenda of privatisation, contracting out and marketisation, including in the NHS and schools. In turn, popular support for parliamentary democracy has been undermined because, for the ordinary citizen, it no longer seems in charge of the vital public services that matter in daily life.

The response to this from the right has been to exploit its compliant media crescendo for austerity by promoting still further marketisation and government downsizing, on the one hand, and centralised bureaucracy to police the consequences, on the other.

Thus, under free market capitalism, the state gets out of the way of the market and public expenditure is cut, with well-known consequences: tax dodging, insider trading, City fraud, pension rip-offs and bloated bonuses for the elite. Finance is structured in such a way that asset-holders rather than wealth creators are rewarded. Lord Adair Turner, former chairman of the Financial Services Authority and former director of the CBI, has made the point forcibly that Britain's banks tend to finance investment in existing houses and commercial property, rather than fund expanding production.

At the same time this neoliberal state punishes welfare claimants and encourages job insecurity, with those at the bottom typically consigned to a world of zero-hours contracts and minimal employee protection. Values of justice, morality, mutual care and mutual cooperation are subordinated to individual self-interest. Income inequalities widen, the poor get poorer and the ultra-rich richer. Communities disintegrate, as does family life generally, but certainly among the poor: a trend supposedly antithetical to the 'conservative values' claimed by the right and which has been for this reason the subject of a critique by Blue Labour apostles, notably Maurice Glassman.[1]

Although the neoliberal state may be *small*, it is emphatically *strong*. It may *preach* localism but it *practises* centralism. As the commentator John Harris explains:

> the modern Conservative party evidently wants to accelerate Britain's progress towards being a country of spot checks and roving billboards instructing illicit migrants to hand themselves in, and the rest of us to grass them up. Large parts of the welfare state increasingly look not like a safety net, but a mess of traps, intended to enforce complete obedience under pain of destitution. Doctors, nurses and teachers work to central diktat as never before. And from the role of private firms in our penal and borders system to the ties that bind the internet's corporate providers to government (something at the heart of the storm over data collection ...), it is increasingly hard to tell where government ends and the private realm begins: what blurs the two is effectively a shadow state, which gets bigger and bigger.[2]

For neoliberals there is no respect for the state as enabler, and where necessary as enforcer of equality before the law, and consequently there is 'no such thing as society' in Margaret Thatcher's immortal and very revealing words. David Cameron – in his 'compassionate Conservatism' phase – sought to distance himself from Mrs Thatcher's brutally crude give-away with his concept of 'The Big Society'. But in practice that became little more than a ruse to dump responsibility for providing community services onto a voluntary sector itself experiencing a huge capacity collapse driven by government cuts. In 2010 the Conservative MP Jesse Norman set out a valiant and much discussed neoliberal prospectus for the concept of individual citizens taking responsibility for local services.[3] But his case was rapidly swept aside under the torrent of cuts as 'The Big Society' was forgotten by the government. Unsurprisingly the prospectus became viewed as spin rather than substance.

Meanwhile dominant economic trends have pushed back against statist forms of economic organisation – in Britain, for instance, nationalised monopolies like British Gas and British Telecom have been privatised. Throughout the world, but especially in Western Europe and the US, the market and privatisation triumphed over public planning and public ownership during a period of significant change in the system of production – until the financial crisis struck in 2008 when it became clear that sometimes there is no substitute for state intervention. Before then, corporate ownership had become even more globalised, making it difficult to apply the nationalisation model.

Difficult maybe, but hardly impossible. In 2008 the British state found it easy either to nationalise or to take big and expensive ownership stakes in banks as part of rescuing them. It also took over and ran some failing railway services from private train operating companies, like East Coast through Directly Operated Railways Ltd, with public ownership becoming more attractive as franchises expired and private companies walked away. Moreover, Arriva Trains Wales which runs most rail services in Wales belongs to the Arriva Group, part of Deutsche Bahn which is majority-owned by the German federal government. Deutsche Bahn/Arriva also own CrossCountry Trains and Chiltern Railways in the UK.

Although huge nationwide distribution networks (like Amazon for example) and new giants like Microsoft and Google have risen, so too have new forms of production which are more flexible and specialised, moving industry away from mass production on one site, away from the pattern of heavy industry with a large-scale concentrated workforce which was dominant during past industrialisation. The trend to smaller and more diversified industry is likely to be maintained as digital technology not only permits but encourages economic decentralisation and specialisation. The internet and broadband allow an information superhighway into every home and workplace to empower consumers and permit more individualised services, localised manufacturing, neighbourhood employment and decentralised economic activity.

But, uncomfortably for neoliberalism, this form of production can only succeed by more cooperative relationships between employer and employee, between government and enterprise – and also with government structures sufficiently close to local economies to understand and respond to their characteristics, and therefore decentralised. Modern production depends upon the active participation of employees who become the principal agents for innovation, high quality and therefore market performance. It also requires government to promote key sectors, to sponsor investment and to ensure the provision of high-quality infrastructure and skills. In short the new industrial age brings an imperative for a *libertarian socialist* alternative to neoliberalism.

British socialist roots

For although, as we have seen, neoliberalism cannot deliver fairness for all – or even a sustainable, stable economy – its deliberate conflation of socialism with statism does still resonate and engender unease. That makes it even more critical to establish a future for socialism founded upon a tradition which, though rich and deeply rooted, has tended to be in the shadows of socialist thought and practice. The left has been cursed by its long association with the socialism of the centralised state. Yet there always was a different socialism with deep roots, a socialism which was libertarian, empowering and decentralised.

Socialism, a term which first came into general use in France and Britain around 1830, sprang essentially from a critique of capitalism and an indictment of its political alibi, liberalism. As Noam Chomsky, a modern libertarian socialist, pointed out, classical liberalism's most appealing features – its stress on individual freedom, its insistence upon tolerance and its respect for human rights – were perverted by its failure to address the demand for equality, especially at the critical juncture following the French Revolution of 1789 and the long process of industrial revolution which so ferociously transformed the lives of the ordinary people of Europe. Chomsky argued: 'With the development of industrial capitalism, a new and unanticipated system of injustice, it is libertarian socialism that has preserved and extended the radical humanist message of the Enlightenment and the classical liberal ideas that were perverted into an ideology to sustain the emerging social order ...'[4]

However a millstone around the left for far too long was that, for many of its founders in Western Europe, socialism was defined as

137

'the abolition of private property'. Another curse was revolutionary communism, which was sown on fertile ground amidst the deep inequalities and injustices in industrialising nations of the 19th and early 20th centuries. Whereas *socialists* were prepared to accept the industrial revolution and to tame it by eradicating the consequent poverty inflicted upon the masses; *communists*, by contrast, were more radically egalitarian and proletarian and wanted violently to overthrow it. *Socialists* also wanted democratically to build upon the elements of civilisation which had been established in Europe, especially Britain; *communists* wanted none of this, favouring instead a transitional revolutionary dictatorship. Yet both were part of the left, enabling democratic socialism to be tarnished by association.

In Britain a libertarian socialist tradition was more strongly rooted, with direct and continuing relevance for the future of the left. Its antecedents are very mixed and they are not cited in the pretence that there was something coherent called 'British libertarian socialism': very far from it. Many who can be identified in its supporting cast did not use the term as such; the contributions of some were partial and contradictory. But the point is that the crucial elements of libertarian socialism – decentralisation, democracy, popular sovereignty and a refusal to accept that collective provision of social standards and public services meant subjugating individual liberty – were present in their writings and activist advocacy. Together they stand in a line which provides a robust alternative to statism.

Fenner Brockway, a longstanding member of the Labour left, linked himself in *Britain's First Socialists* to a tradition dating back to the mid-17th century and the English Civil War. He pinpointed the radical activists of that age: the Levellers, Agitators and Diggers. For Brockway, socialism was about democracy and liberty or it was about nothing. He showed that the ideas motivating the three groups were precursors to socialism:'The Levellers were pioneers of political democracy and the sovereignty of the people; the Agitators were the pioneers of participatory control by the ranks at their workplace; and the Diggers were pioneers of communal ownership, cooperation and egalitarianism. All three equate with democratic socialism.'[5]

As historians have noted, the Levellers were the first democratic political movement in modern history, presaging at least a century earlier the demands for democracy which erupted in America, France and Britain. They demanded a democratic Parliament, the abolition of the House of Lords and democratic reform of the whole state, including even the judiciary and the army. Their insistence upon decentralisation of government and the army, coupled with their proposals for public health, education services and the right to work, showed they were indeed premature libertarian socialists. So were the Agitators with their stress upon workplace democracy. The Diggers' advocate Gerrard Winstanley was a socialist pioneer, with his proposals both for common ownership of land in an era of landed aristocracies and for egalitarian communities.

During the late 18th and early 19th centuries, the foundations of the British labour movement in the emerging proletariat shared similar libertarian socialist affinities. Trade unions and political organisations evolved from a series of self-governing societies, groups and institutions established in Britain. Local craft-based trade clubs, 'friendly societies' (providing rudimentary social welfare for members), early trade unions and (later) cooperatives were all examples of the way in which working people organised and combined collectively from the bottom upwards. These were models of local self-organisation not dependent upon some central apparatus and they led some towards local socialism as a model for society.

There were also libertarian socialist elements to other initiatives at the turn of the century. Tom Paine's *Rights of Man* in 1791 was for that period a radical democratic manifesto and also expressed an ambition for equality which Tony Crosland would have admired: 'The contrast of affluence and wretchedness continually meeting and offending the eye, is like dead and living bodies chained together,' Paine wrote. Geoff Hodgson notes: 'Over two hundred years ago he [Paine] proposed a one-off, state-funded, distribution "to every person, when arrived at the age of twenty-one years, the sum of fifteen pounds sterling, as a compensation in part, for the loss of his or her natural inheritance, by the introduction of the system of landed property".' Hodgson also points out:

> The effect of this benefit would be to provide every adult
> with an amount of wealth that could be used to invest

in property or personal development, irrespective of the income or status of his or her parents. The £15 converts to roughly £1,300 or $2,000 in terms of purchasing power in 2011. But as a fraction of 1797 UK GDP, £15 converts to about £79,000 or $120,000 as an equivalent share of 2011 UK GDP.[6]

Another notable contribution from Paine's time was Mary Wollstonecraft's 1792 *A Vindication of the Rights of Woman* – significant not least because of the serious neglect of women's rights. Abolitionists protesting against the racism and oppression of slavery added an important and again neglected dimension. These precursors were part of a radical democratic tradition later joined by the Chartists and still later by the suffragettes.

The term 'socialist' was first used in the British *Cooperative Magazine* in November 1827, its chief exponent being Robert Owen, a founder of the cooperative movement in 1844. Owen's ideas on common ownership and industrial democracy through cooperatives coincide with those of modern libertarian socialism. Meanwhile groups of workers such as the Rochdale Pioneers in 1844 were putting into practical effect local socialist ideas for workers' shops, insurance societies, credit unions and companies. Through such initiatives, these early trade unionists and socialists invented and practised what the historian A.H. Halsey described as 'the social forms of modern participatory democracy'.

Significantly, some Owenite socialists also developed early feminist ideas.[7] One Owenite convert, Anna Wheeler, co-authored *Appeal to one-half of the human race*, a pamphlet which first put a socialist feminist case: 'All women and particularly women living with men in marriage … are more in need of political rights than any other portion of human beings.' She also argued that women could only achieve happiness through general cooperation, not selfish competition. Another Owenite feminist, Frances Morrison, insisted that the only way to end the treatment of women as property was to abolish private property itself. Two more Owenites, Margaret Chappellsmith and Eliza Macauley, argued for reform of financial institutions. And by the early 1830s, Owen's Charlotte Street Institution was sponsoring large meetings of working women who formed cooperatives and trade unions, not just in London but in towns like Manchester and Leicester too.

Later, William Morris made another important contribution with his ethical socialism, concerned about the way people reacted to each other, the moral values underpinning these relationships, and unusually for the time emphasising sexual equality. His was also a cultural socialism, a sharp counter to the seductions of materialistic consumption: 'Have nothing in your home which you do not either believe to be beautiful or know to be useful,' he said. He also stressed the importance of the quality of life and of protecting the environment – his was a green socialism. He was critical of state socialism – what he called 'semi-demi-socialism', believing that it would result in upholding the status quo of a centralised, unequal society. Over 50 years later, Morris's contribution was acknowledged by the guild socialist advocate G.D.H. Cole: 'It was Morris who made me a socialist,' he said.

Trade unionism provided a continuing conduit for non-state socialism, especially through the syndicalists. From 1910 the British trade union leader Tom Mann started introducing ideas about workers' control, gleaned from French and American syndicalists, in his journal *The Industrial Syndicalist*. Especially in the period before the First World War, syndicalist ideas were widespread in the British trade union movement. For example, the South Wales Miners in 1917 put forward a programme for industrial democratisation of the privately owned coal industry under public ownership.

On the eve of the First World War, anti-statism was rife. Within the left there was a revolt against leaders of the Fabian Society (an influential Labour Party pressure group) who advocated 'administrative socialism' because it designated a pre-eminent role for the state. As the historian Ernest Barker noted, this was because it was believed that 'the governing class under State-Socialism becomes a bureaucracy, regimenting and controlling the life of the citizen'.

Instead, many on the left were attracted by the ideas of syndicalism and guild socialism. However, the need for collective action and the use of state machinery to mobilise for war quickly prevailed. And from the Labour Party a leading Fabian Sidney Webb wrote in 1917:

'we have had ... a great deal of control of capital ... *can we afford to relinquish that control when peace comes?*' (Webb's emphasis). This was reflected in Labour policy statements after the war and in the famous Clause IV, part 4 of the Labour Party's 1918 constitution.[8]

Retreat from libertarian socialism

Understandably after the First World War – and especially in the depression of the 1930s – Labour and the wider left saw nationalisation as a model, with the emphasis upon planning and state ownership of still hierarchically run enterprises, rather than turning them over to employees. This stance was magnified by the shift away from the turn-of-the-century 'municipal socialism' of the Fabians such as George Bernard Shaw and Sidney Webb in his more radical, younger phase. They had seen local government as an important source of socialist change. As the younger Webb had written in 1910, it was a form of 'democratic organisation on the basis of the association of consumers for the supply of their own needs'. Municipal socialism can be seen as standing alongside the libertarian or decentralist school; its supporters at the time remained concerned however that it would be extinguished by the growing power of central government.

These worries proved valid. Labour's increasing strength at a parliamentary level led to a retreat from municipal socialism: instead, Labour local authorities became 'handmaidens of parliamentary socialism'.[9] With the growth of working-class representation in local government, there was a parallel anxiety from the dominant class that Labour local government was a troublesome threat to the state, and that it must be made subordinate to central government. This was perhaps best symbolised by the clashes between Whitehall and the Labour-controlled Poplar Council in the 1920s. Under George Lansbury, Poplar refused to implement cuts in unemployment and poor relief, and 30 of its councillors were imprisoned in the fiercest rebellion against central government of the century. In the early 1930s, over 20 councils, mostly Labour, refused to implement means testing for unemployment assistance, until the Conservative-led government was forced to 'nationalise' assistance by transferring the administration to a central board. But 'Poplarism' was as much a threat to the Labour Party establishment as to the Conservatives.

It became common ground between the leaderships of both parties that, instead of autonomous agencies for 'bottom up' democracy, local authorities should be conduits for the state to dispense services efficiently. Partly in response to this concern for administrative efficiency, Sidney and Beatrice Webb had meanwhile developed a theory of 'administrative socialism', in which experts, professionals and bureaucrats played a key role. Such administrative collectivism may have addressed the need for socialists to run the machinery of government in a different way, but it offered little hope to notions of empowerment, as G.D.H. Cole, the principal advocate of 'guild socialism', was quick to point out. In 1921 he wrote of the importance of building mechanisms for popular participation into local government. In 1947 he sought to reconcile the importance of local democracy with the centralising pull of efficiency in a modern state by proposing both larger and smaller authorities, at 'regional' and 'neighbourhood' levels. The latter would be powerful agencies for local socialism, he asserted.

Guild socialism

From 1912, the guild socialist movement had taken up the themes of industrial democracy and decentralised socialism. In 1917 G.D.H. Cole distinguished the guild socialists' belief in *decentralisation* from the syndicalist belief in *federation* (ie power delegated upward from below) and the state socialist belief in *centralisation*.[10] Decentralisation, he argued, sees society in the national terms which characterise the modern state, and devolves power from the centre. Nevertheless, he insisted, 'it is the essence of the Guild idea that it means government from below'. He believed that 'capitalist supremacy can only be overthrown by a system of industrial democracy in which the worker will control industry in conjunction with a democratised State'. Cole argued 'that there can be no guarantee, except democracy, that the resources of production will, in fact, be used for the benefit of all'. Hence, socialists should seek 'to bring about the widest possible diffusion both of political and economic and social power and of the knowledge needed for putting such power to effective use'.

Three main forms of guilds were proposed: industrial, distributive and civic (the latter being, for example, the professions, educationalists, lawyers). These would be federated up to a national level and come together in a Guild Congress. Workers would participate at all levels in the direction of the guilds, which would cooperate with other guilds but be sovereign within their own sphere (except insofar as their policies affected consumers, for example, prices). Ownership would be vested in the guilds, with nationalisation being advocated only where it seemed to be the most rational approach.

As Anthony Wright argues, Cole was a 'leading theorist of a school of participatory democracy and socialist pluralism'.[11] It is not necessary to accept uncritically the tenets of guild socialism for Cole's importance in the libertarian socialist tradition to be recognised. In 1960 he used words later to be echoed (albeit seldom, if ever, acknowledged) by modern libertarian socialists:

> I am neither a Communist nor a Social Democrat, because I regard both as creeds of centralisation and bureaucracy, whereas I feel sure that a Socialist society that is to be true to its equalitarian principles of human brotherhood must rest on the widest possible diffusion of power and responsibility, so as to enlist the active participation of as many as possible of its citizens in the tasks of democratic self-government.

This means democracy in every area of social activity – the workplace, neighbourhood, educational institutions, and interest groups. Otherwise individuality and citizenship would be suffocated by capitalism and state socialism alike. Cole helps us to retrieve the tradition in socialist thought which does not accept the prevailing orthodoxy that the real choice for the left is a statist one.

Socialism is about *empowering* the citizen or it is about nothing. Although this verity has often been downgraded, it is another reason for Cole's significance. In 1917, when asked what the greatest evil in society was, he responded that most people would answer wrongly: 'They would answer POVERTY, when they ought to answer SLAVERY.' In other words, powerlessness is the overriding problem. Equality, freedom – neither of these cherished goals can be achieved without empowerment. Paternal government or state socialism, however well intentioned, is no answer because it breeds dependence. Liberty cannot be handed down, it must be confidently claimed, as of right. Cole believed in 'a participatory definition of freedom'. As Anthony Wright shows:

> Cole's commitment to activism ... provided the foundation for his democratic theory ... To Cole, men [sic] were born active; it was capitalism which rendered them passive. This attachment to participation as a fundamental human good in its own right, as a school of political education and personal development, places Cole in the mainstream of ... a theory of participatory democracy designed to provide ample scope for that active exercise of will which was seen as intrinsic to the definition of a human being, and which was negated by capitalism and state socialism alike.

Centralised collectivism

However the experience of the Second World War finally eclipsed the residual libertarian socialism within the British labour movement. It shaped a consensus for centralised collectivism which went far beyond socialists. With the success of wartime centralised planning of production and resources, and the imperatives of post-war reconstruction, statism became dominant, with few exceptions. For example, the 1947 Town and Country Planning Act effectively vested development rights in the community (without compensation) to be dealt with by local planning authorities, the planning committee of the relevant local elected council.

Statism was also encouraged by the failure of critically important private utilities and companies like railways which had to be saved by nationalisation. From 1945 onward nationalised coal, gas, electricity, transport (and later steel and shipbuilding) became the paradigm for public ownership. That model, promoted by Herbert Morrison, led to a total break from libertarian socialism: when poverty, inequality, unemployment and capitalist inefficiency were so widespread, it seemed irrelevant to the need for free health services, for full employment and modern public utilities. Decisive action and planning by central government was necessary, and indeed was successful, as now public health, education and social services were delivered for the first time.

Nevertheless, as society was reconstructed after the War, R.H. Tawney, for example, stressed that socialism was also about the distribution of power. In 1952, Aneurin Bevan recognised the shortcomings of nationalisation and the need for democratic participation. Although this did not figure prominently in his socialism, he argued: 'industrial democracy is the counterpart of political freedom. Liberty and responsibility must march together. They must be joined together in the workshop as in the legislative assembly.'[12]

Interestingly, in *The Future of Socialism* in 1956 Tony Crosland was already noting public dissatisfaction with the public corporation model and expressing some interest in a plurality of approaches to ownership and control, including 'competitive public enterprise'. Prominent left-wing writers of the time, such as Raymond Williams and E.P. Thompson, also stressed that democracy and socialism should be indistinguishable.

The growth of feminism in the 1970s nurtured such ideas because women's groups stressed their local autonomy from male-dominated, centralised institutions, including those within the left. They emphasised personal politics and argued that socialism's historic concern with class as a source of inequality and oppression ignored other forms of oppression, especially patriarchy (the economic, social and political forces which produce male supremacy). In 1979 a seminal text for socialist feminism presented a devastating attack on the Leninist left, Sheila Rowbotham specifically urging a recovery of the libertarian socialist tradition.[13] Her co-author Hilary Wainwright argued: 'Much of the oppression of women takes place in "private", in areas of life considered "personal" … this has radically extended the scope of politics.' In 1987, the third co-author, Lynne Segal, called for 'a renewal of that more democratic and participatory vision of socialism which reaches out to include all social relationships and to give people a sense of greater control over their own lives.'[14]

Impact upon Labour

These changes on the left affected the Labour Party too, albeit hesitantly and spasmodically. After Labour's defeat in 1970, a prominent former Cabinet minister, Tony Benn, published a Fabian pamphlet in September 1970, *The New Politics: A Socialist Reconnaissance*. In it he took account of the growing 'grass roots socialism' and put forward ideas for decentralisation, workers' control and popular participation.

Decentralised socialist ideas started to gain more credence in the wider labour movement. There was a growing critique of nationalisation and increased support for industrial democracy. In 1978 the Labour government issued a White Paper endorsing the Bullock Report's recommendations for worker participation at company board level – though proposing initially only one third of the seats for employee representatives, not the parity with management recommended by Bullock. Although its proposals were demolished under a twin attack from trade unionists (who saw it as a threat to traditional collective bargaining) and employers (who saw it as a threat to their managerial prerogatives), the fact that it was sponsored by government was testimony to the growing interest in workers' participation.

But with the unions divided, the Labour government lacking a majority in Parliament, and grassroots union members seething over pay restraint under the 'Social Contract', the issue of industrial democracy was eclipsed by more pressing priorities – except in the nationalised industries, where two experiments were tried. The Post Office launched a two-year scheme that raised to seven the number of employee representatives on the 20-person main board. At British Steel six full-time employees joined the main board of 21. However, neither scheme proved long-lasting, as Margaret Thatcher became Prime Minister and these Labour initiatives were peremptorily abandoned.

Meanwhile there had been a growth of community action and demands for popular participation by council tenants' associations and radical groups, who saw local socialism as an alternative to parliamentary politics. Partly as a response to this, there was a revival of interest in 'municipal socialism', especially by the Labour left which, during the 1970s, was a growing force in the party, absorbing many of the 'extra-parliamentary' activists who were children of the1960s New Left. This revival – symbolised by the 1981–86 Greater London Council under Ken Livingstone – was both a challenge to the capitalist state and a rejection of bureaucratic labourism. As David Blunkett (then leader of Sheffield City Council) wrote in 1982, Labour local authorities had an admirable commitment to spending on public services, 'but they tended to be authoritarian: doing the right thing *for* people rather than with them'.

However, it is notable that as the Labour Party came increasingly under the control of its 'modernisers' during the latter stages of Neil Kinnock's leadership and then under that of John Smith and Tony Blair, this critique of labourism was sidelined. Except importantly for the devolution of power to Wales, Scotland and London, 'New Labour' did not stress the importance of popular participation and decentralisation. On the contrary, it gave pre-eminence to market forces.

A participatory democracy

Today democratic socialism's task is to recover the high ground on democracy and freedom through maximum decentralisation of control, ownership and decision making. For socialism can only be achieved if it springs from below by popular demand. The task of socialist government should be an enabling one, not an enforcing one. Its mission is to disperse rather than to concentrate power, with a pluralist notion of democracy at its heart.

The balance between having *active* government and *enabling* government is however the key one. Without active government the conditions for greater social equality cannot be secured. No ground should be surrendered in the quest for a broadly egalitarian society and a sustainable economy. On the other hand, without enabling government which decentralises power, neither individual liberty nor greater equality can be achieved because both depend upon each citizen having the power – at work, in the home, in the neighbourhood, over public services, as a consumer – to shape their own lives.

In place of the limited form of democracy inherent in the British system, the objective should be to create a 'participatory democracy' in which there is the greatest possible involvement of citizens. This will require two principal changes: making representatives much more accountable; and decentralising decision making as far as is compatible with wider interests. It will also involve not just the democratisation of government but of the whole of society.

If decentralisation were to be confined to government structures alone, it would simply reproduce the existing patterns of elitism and inequality at lower levels. The result would be a dispersal of administration, in which popular participation would still be blocked by the obstacles resulting from class, sex, race, age and disability inequalities: the face of government would be more local, but it would not be more representative and would still be constrained by extra-parliamentary forces favouring the interests of dominant groups in society.

However, power can only be spread downwards in an equitable manner if there is a national framework where opportunities (regardless of gender, sexual orientation, race or disability), resources, wealth and income are distributed equally, where democratic rights are constitutionally entrenched. Effective decentralisation will require the benefits of private ownership and wealth to be spread more evenly throughout the population. It will mean national redistribution of resources from prosperous to poor regions of the country, from the suburbs to the inner cities, from the dominant to the subordinate classes, from rich to poor, from men to women, from whites to blacks and from able to disabled. There will need to be nationally established minimum levels of public provision. High minimum levels and the relevant funding should be set centrally for affordable housing, public transport, social services, nursery schools, care services for the elderly, childcare and so on. The extent to which these would be 'topped up' and different priorities set between them would then be a matter for local decision. The statutory minimum wage is another example, above which pay levels could be negotiated by independent agreement to achieve a 'living wage'.

Nevertheless, trying to achieve all this through a 'statist' approach, despite worthy intentions, has led in practice to centralised, inefficient bureaucracies suffocating local initiative and reproducing hierarchical structures. Policies and programmes implemented through the state are necessary to clear away obstacles to democratic participation and freedom, but unless pressure is actively maintained through new democratic avenues from below, a participatory democracy will not take root. For example, universal childcare would be a national democratic socialist government policy. But the delivery would occur through local units and their exact forms of operating should be influenced by parents and local people in order best to reflect local needs and conditions.[15]

Ed Miliband was the first Labour leader to take up this cause in a lecture in February 2014 with this commitment: 'people-powered public services will be at the heart of the next Labour government. And it is rooted in the principle of equality that drives my politics.'[16] He denounced 'inequalities of power', arguing:

> Everyone – not just a few at the top – should have the chance to shape their own lives. I meet as many people coming to me frustrated by the unresponsive state as the untamed market. And the causes of the frustrations are often the same in the private and public sector: unaccountable power with the individual left powerless to act.

He made a series of important arguments to underline that principle:

> The challenges facing public services – from mental health, to autism, to care for the elderly, to giving kids the best start in the early years – are just too complex to impose solutions from the top without the active engagement of the people who use and rely upon them … decision-making structures in public services should

be thrown open to people so that we tackle inequalities of power at source – from personal budgets that help disabled people design their own care to councils that involve users in key decisions, to the empowerment of parents so that they don't have to wait for Ofsted [the schools inspectorate in England] if they believe things need to change in their school ... we should devolve power down not just to the user but also to the local level, because the national government's task is to set clear national standards for what people can expect, not to diagnose and solve every local problem from Whitehall. And if we are to succeed in devolving power to users, it is much easier to do it from a local level. In every service, from health to policing to education, and by devolving budgets more widely, we are determined to drive power closer to people.

There are severe limits to what can be achieved by a 'top down' focus. National, devolved and local government can facilitate wider democracy by spreading power from themselves. And on devolution we need to go further than New Labour's significant achievements, by answering 'The English question' left by an asymmetric devolution of power to Wales, Scotland and Northern Ireland, but – the special case of London aside – not England's regions or city regions. That is the unfinished business of devolution.

Despite devolution to Scotland, Wales and Northern Ireland the UK remains one of the most centralised states in Europe. This is especially true for England, where devolution has been addressed only half-heartedly. The Labour government's 2002 White Paper *Your Region, Your Choice: Revitalising The English Regions* envisaged eight regional bodies based on the eight economic planning regions, but it was not prescriptive, other than to insist, rightly, that any move to regional government in England must also mean a single layer of all-purpose local authorities, not an expensive three-tier region/county/district structure. The White Paper's very caution may have been the source of its undoing. The only referendum held to test whether there was popular support for an elected regional assembly was held in the North East of England in November 2004 and delivered a firmly negative verdict. Campaigning for a 'Yes' vote, I could sense that voters were suspicious of adding another tier of government which (unlike London) had minimal powers, especially when two tiers of local councils remained unreformed. Nevertheless, in 2007 regional development agencies were given executive responsibility for developing English regional strategy, subject to scrutiny by local authority leaders' boards, and each English region was allotted its own minister (policies abandoned by the Tory/Lib Dems).

This was a minimal response to the problem identified by Harold Wilson in 1973 when he pointed out the glaring gap between central government and local authorities, a gap bridged by a series of undemocratic expedients in which decisions are made at regional level by ad hoc agencies subject to no detailed control either by Parliament or by local authorities or by local people. Wilson saw that elected regional authorities in England could form a means of closing this gap and of giving the English as direct a say in decisions made in their name as 25 years later the Scots would have through a Scottish Parliament and the Welsh through a National Assembly for Wales. Harold Wilson encouraged discussion about English regional government within the Labour Party because he saw it as a way of giving everyone an equal voice in how they were governed.[17] He had no single solution to offer. Between them the 1969 Redcliffe-Maud report on local government in England and the 1973 Kilbrandon report on the constitution had put forward seven different schemes for regional authorities in England varying from five to 15 regions. It is time to revive that Labour Party debate.

Devolution or separatism?

But answering 'The English Question' has to be set within a different agenda following the unsuccessful Scottish push for independence which culminated in the referendum on 18 September 2014. Similar pressure from Catalans and Basques in Spain, Flemish in Belgium and Corsicans in France seems strangely contrary to historic trends which from at least the 19th century saw consolidation from regional and city statelets into nation states. It also seems to be running against increasing global economic integration and interdependence of countries (set out in the next chapter).

Nevertheless globalisation and the sheltering of nations under supranational trading umbrellas – the most advanced form being the European Union – has also provoked countervailing pressures as people turn away and towards their own communities, or, for those who feel excluded, to brashly populist politics: the UK Independence Party (UKIP) in Britain and similar right-wing parties across continental Europe from the Front National in France to Golden Dawn in Greece. Thus, as politics has gone more global it has also gone more local – or in the case of a constituent nation like Scotland, more nationalist.

The democratic socialist answer is or should be devolution, for which the former Labour Prime Minister Gordon Brown set out a compelling vision in rejecting Scottish independence, both in a speech on 10 March 2014 and in his book *My Scotland, Our Britain*.[18] He rightly insisted that the issue was not about patriotism: both pro- and anti-independence Scots could claim to be equally patriotic. Instead, Brown argues, the incontrovertible advantage of modern Britain is its 20th-century innovation: the pooling and sharing of risks and resources across the whole of the UK to ensure common welfare and decent standards of life for all citizens, regardless of nationality or where you live.

At the heart of that pooling and sharing of resources have been a set of path-breaking decisions throughout the 20th century – common welfare standards first introduced by Liberal governments and subsequently consolidated by Labour governments up until 2010 – ensuring common economic and social standards: common UK-wide old age pensions, common UK social insurance (sick pay, health insurance, unemployment insurance and labour exchanges), common UK child and family benefits, a common UK minimum wage, and a UK system of equalising resources, so that everyone irrespective of where they live has the same political, social and economic rights, and not simply equal civil and political rights.

Pooling and sharing the UK's resources also enables redistribution from richer to poorer parts of the UK – whether constituent parts of a nation like the coalfield communities of the South Wales Valleys or regions of England such as the North East. But although the Holtham Commission[19] in its case for devolving limited tax-varying and borrowing powers to Wales set out complex compensating arrangements which attempted to ensure that it did not fall behind richer parts of the UK, it could not guarantee the Treasury would always deliver this. With around 40 per cent of UK GDP concentrated in London and the South East of England, separatists have no answer to what is essentially the democratic socialist case for maintaining the integrity of the UK: redistributing resources from its better to less well-off parts, and guaranteeing equal opportunity and security for all UK citizens regardless of race, gender, sexual orientation, age, disability or faith.

That has meant, Brown showed, that while inside the European Union the average income of the typical citizen of the poorest country is just 20 per cent of that of the richest country, and in the US the income of the poorest state is 55 per cent of that of the richest, the average income of the typical Scot is 96 per cent the average income of an English citizen; for Wales the figure is 87 per cent.

Labour, he pointed out, created a universal right to free health care across the UK in the 1940s, and in the 1990s a UK-wide minimum wage and tax credits that guaranteed a minimum family income and stopped regions and nations undercutting each other by offering incoming businesses a lower-paid workforce, thus preventing a race to the bottom between the nations and regions within the UK. This sharing of resources through UK-wide pensions, UK-wide provision for social security and UK-wide National Insurance 'is now a defining feature of the Union and thus one of the core tasks of the Union is to secure cross-country fairness through the redistribution of resources and spreading of risks.'

Significantly, when Gordon Brown proposed a new purpose for the UK enshrined in a new constitution, he did not define it in terms of national identity: 'The Union exists to provide security and opportunity for all by pooling and sharing our resources for our defence, security and social and economic welfare, including to alleviate poverty and unemployment and to deliver healthcare free at the point of need for all.'

A positive alternative to separatism, he argued, requires a 'covenant' between the nations of the UK based upon its distinctive core as a social and economic union. And the clearest way to forward is to ensure that the legislatures for Scotland, Wales and Northern Ireland are enshrined as a permanent feature of the UK's 'constitution' in a section of a future Act of Parliament.

A more 'federal' UK?

This in turn means recognising the reality of a more 'federal' UK. But not one based upon an English Parliament to parallel Welsh, Scottish and (subject to the 1998 'Good Friday' settlement which permits unity with the Irish Republic should a referendum endorse that) Northern Ireland Parliaments. For the 1973 Kilbrandon Royal Commission made a convincing case against a separate English Parliament which has never been rebutted. Such a federation of four units would be 'so unbalanced as to be unworkable. It would be dominated by the overwhelming political importance and wealth of England ... [with] Scotland, Wales and Northern Ireland, together representing less than one fifth of the population.'[20] Instead, in a modern federal UK, English interests could be protected through regional devolution and by reforms within a continuing UK Westminster Parliament which both preserved the equality of MPs across the UK and introduced special procedures to ensure the voices of English MPs could have weight over English-specific legislation.[21] Such a Modern Britain, as Gordon Brown argues, would no longer be viewed as an 'all-powerful centralised unitary state ... but as a constitutional partnership of equals in what is in essence a voluntary multinational association'.[22]

The Westminster Parliament would have continuing responsibility for overall economic policy, taxation and spending totals, foreign and defence policy, security (including energy security) and social security. The devolved legislatures could then take responsibility for most other policy areas, by mutual agreement.

To underpin this, Gordon Brown proposed a new system of 'tax sharing', with partial tax devolution to ensure in devolved legislatures better accountability to the people for spending decisions.

But there is an important distinction between the Conservative-led government's endorsement of that objective and Brown's socialist perspective on it. For the right it is an ideological objective to shrink the Whitehall state, offloading as much responsibility as possible onto individual citizens to fend for themselves, outsourcing to private providers and 'subcontracting' tax and spending to devolved legislatures. Having strenuously opposed political devolution in the past, the Tories now see the virtues of economic devolution in neoliberal terms. And in that respect, at least, the outcomes if not the ideologies of nationalism and neoliberalism can be convergent, because under both the redistributive power of the UK state is either severed or stunted.

By contrast, Brown advanced an entirely different agenda, as he distinguished between maintaining high common social and economic standards which can only be achieved at a UK nation-state level, and providing the core resources for devolved levels. He points out that a cornerstone of our social rights is the common UK welfare system, which transfers resources between individuals, dependent on their circumstances, right across the whole Union. Therefore contributory benefits, especially old age pensions, should not be devolved. Moreover, pooling and sharing of resources at nation-state level must be sufficiently strong so as to guarantee free health care, pensions, a decent family income and universal education, as well as defence and security.

In turn the UK government should guarantee that no one in the Union – whether in Scotland or elsewhere in the UK – can be prevented from accessing these common social and economic rights, and the services that flow from them, by reason of shortage of resources. That is why it is right that all UK taxpayers – English, Welsh, Scottish and Northern Irish citizens together – contribute their taxes at a UK level to fund these common rights and services, thereby guaranteeing that the UK government and where relevant the Scottish Parliament, the Welsh Assembly and the Northern Ireland Assembly have the capacity to deliver them. So provision should be made for the Scottish Parliament, the Welsh Assembly and the Northern Ireland Assembly (*and* English regions or city-regions) to have the resources, whatever their own individual decisions on tax, to uphold these rights and deliver these services respectively to the people of Scotland, Wales, Northern Ireland and the English regions, cities and city regions, however these may be defined.

Pooling and sharing sufficient resources across the key services of the UK welfare state is essential to deliver the right to universal free health care, education, and the rights to a pension when elderly, help when unemployed, sick or disabled, under what Brown called 'covenanted expenditure'. That is to say, by providing the means for the UK to honour a 'covenant' through pooling our tax revenues from Scotland, England, Wales and Northern Ireland and sharing them based on need under the Barnett formula which distributes population-related block grants from the Treasury derived from changes in spending levels allocated to public services in England.

Under this model, revenue raised by the UK Parliament should cover non-devolved services and services vital to the maintenance of our welfare state for the young, the sick and the elderly, and the revenue that the devolved legislatures raised should cover other services, such as housing and agriculture. Such a demarcation, Brown estimates for Scotland, would enable devolved taxation to raise something like 40 per cent of the Scottish Parliament's expenditure. But it would still retain pooling and sharing of both resources and risks as a principal purpose of the UK, to build a society in which those with the broadest shoulders and greatest resources contribute most to the support of those in need.

He also proposes new power-sharing partnerships between the devolved legislatures and the UK Parliament to address common challenges, such as poverty, affordable housing, employment skills, science and innovation and aspects of transport and economic policy.

Thus we can glimpse a significantly different concept of socialism from Crosland's time. In the 1950s it was taken for granted that *British* socialism was a unitary idea applying across the nations, and there was no serious pressure to devolve power, with no Scottish or Welsh Nationalists elected to the Westminster Parliament in the 1955 general election. Today, as policies diverge under devolution and with nationalism's fresh impetus, that cannot be assumed. For example, there is free care for the elderly in Scotland but not in England or Wales. In Wales student tuition fees are a third of those in England, and relations between the trade unions and the Labour Party are closer. In Scotland and Wales collectivism is culturally more deeply rooted than in England, where Tory support is proportionately much greater.

Although socialists and Labour Party members right across Britain share common values of equality, social justice, democracy and liberty, these are increasingly expressed through different priorities and policies. Since New Labour – though to a lesser extent under Ed Miliband's leadership – the party in England has tacked more to the centre-right than in Wales or Scotland. There is – at least as yet – no recognisably Welsh or Scottish as opposed to English socialism, but there is a direction of travel which will only be accommodated under a British socialism that is much more participatory, pluralist and devolutionary than when Crosland wrote.

Devolving power can assist people to take greater control over their own lives, but government cannot force a participatory democracy onto people. Unless citizens have themselves participated in the process of gaining influence and pressing for greater control, they will not be prepared to take the new opportunities or exercise the extra responsibilities that go with increased decentralisation.

The crucial role of the socialist state is to assert the public or national interest, and to reconcile competing interests of different groups and associations in society – then to become an instrument for decentralisation rather than statism. Active devolution of power is intended to deliver a pluralist democracy in which the state, though pivotal, is not suffocatingly dominant over other associations in society. This stress on pluralism should be a key tenet in the future of socialism.

A Labour government, for example, should not be afraid to promote countervailing sources of power – for example, through an elected second chamber to replace the House of Lords and through devolution in England. Some Labour traditionalists of both left and right have balked at such democratic pluralism because, as has been the case in Scotland and London, these bodies are not necessarily Labour controlled. But that contradicts what ought to be a fundamental and defining characteristic of socialism, namely its essentially empowering ethos fit for the modern age. Today a truly democratic socialist state is an enabling one, though of course it needs to retain an enforcing role through upholding individual rights, asserting the common good on behalf of the community, and curbing excessive influence by the rich and powerful.

The failure of 'popular capitalism'

Although neoliberals might make parallel protestations for curbing the state's role – and indeed some term themselves 'libertarian'[23] – their vision is of individual empowerment through markets and extensive ownership of private property. This was the 'popular capitalism' of Thatcherism which for a time in the 1980s seemed to capture the high ground and was electorally successful, especially through selling council properties: a policy Labour, trapped in a statist mindset, wrongly opposed where we should have supported it – provided of course that the revenues were reinvested in replacement social housing. That did not occur under Thatcherism and the result has been a chronic shortage of affordable housing for both rent and purchase. But if Labour had pioneered it, we could have used the capital to invest in new council houses.

Through heavily discounted council home sales and cut-price share offers in privatised utilities, Conservative rhetoric promised each individual a stake in capitalism. But despite the fact that home ownership was more widespread for a time, it has since declined to a modern low. Government statistics showed that the proportion of homes lived in by owner occupiers in the year 2012–13 had dropped to 65.1 per cent – down from 71 per cent under Labour in 2003, and its lowest level for 25 years. The same year the number of households living in the private rented sector overtook those in social housing for the first time since 1980, and private rents have soared and, with them, homelessness. New social house building plummeted, leaving calamitous shortages of affordable housing for rent or sale, with young people finding it increasingly difficult to set up home, certainly in their own property. The neoliberal mantra has not worked: as a mechanism for delivering adequate housing, the market failed abysmally.

Neither did the much vaunted 'popular capitalism' materialise. According to the Office for National Statistics, by the end of 2012 individuals held 10.7 per cent of shares listed on the Stock Exchange, compared with 20 per cent in 1994 and 54 per cent in 1963. In 2012 there were actually more members of cooperatives in the UK – about 14 million – than individual shareholders – around 9 million. Most individuals who bought the heavily discounted privatisation shares cashed them in almost immediately: the motive was profit rather than any illusions about having real power under popular capitalism.

Individual share ownership has declined in proportion to institutional share ownership – power over, and ownership of, shares, capital and industry is now more centralised than ever before, whether at a national, European or global level. It may benefit the few but for the many empowerment cannot be realised by standing alone in such a marketplace. It is an open question as to how effective further tax incentives could be in transforming this situation by encouraging companies to adopt employee share-ownership schemes. Two schemes, Save As You Earn and Share Incentive Plan, already provide such help. Two new tax breaks were introduced in April 2014, raising taxpayer support by a further £75 million, despite claims by HM Treasury that most companies consulted on the issue did not see the tax system as a major barrier. Nevertheless, the idea of incentivising employee stakeholding should be explored.

Another case is local government. The Tory/Lib Dems preached what they termed 'localism' but practised centralism. Eighty-five per cent of local council spending in England continued to be financed from Whitehall, which constantly interfered and controlled. That had largely happened under Labour too, but the Tory/Lib Dems extended central control. Instead – and provided they meet the high minimum standards set nationally to avoid being trumped by New Right councils slashing services to reduce local taxes – councils should be much freer to choose how to spend their budgets, bearing in mind of course that schools and social services account for around three quarters of the total whichever party is in charge.

In July 2014 Labour leader Ed Miliband promised that a Labour government would devolve £30 billion of public spending to existing councils to pool their resources in 'combined authorities' to create 'economic powerhouses' to tackle housing, transport and employment problems. He charted what he called:

> a new course away from the old top-down command
> model and towards an era of people-powered public
> services. This will mean better accountability to the
> communities they serve, encouragement to cooperate
> and integrate with others, and a new emphasis on saving
> money by preventing problems rather than reacting
> to them ... This will begin to reverse a century of
> centralisation. [21]

Instead of Whitehall setting local authorities' annual budgets, Labour
would 'provide long-term funding settlements so councils can plan
ahead, improve their services, and reinvest the savings', Ed Miliband
argued. For instance, he would give local councils 'new powers and
access to central funding so they can keep elderly and vulnerable
people out of hospital with locally managed integration of health
and social care programmes, focused on the whole person, not just
their individual conditions' and 'equip young people with the skills
they need to succeed, by giving councils control over £1.5 bn of
funding for further education of 19–24-year-olds, and responsibility
for a new service for those under 21 years old looking for work'.

By contrast, however, it would be prudent to be wary of Tories
bearing gifts on devolution. Having been consistently hostile to
devolving power to Scotland and Wales, the Cameron government
embraced devolution of a proportion of income tax. The reason they
gave was 'greater tax accountability' – for which of course there is
merit. But then examine carefully the real motive. At least since the
banking crisis, David Cameron has been consistently explicit about
downsizing government and cutting spending. What better way to
do that in the case of Scotland, Wales and Northern Ireland than
cutting their central block grants distributed according to the 'Barnett
formula', and devolving responsibility for raising the shortfall? Then
add in an important consequence. Despite warm reassurances about
'indexation', divorced from a direct link to the tax revenues raised
nationally from by far the wealthiest part of the population – London
and South East England – Wales especially, as a low-income nation,
could be very badly short changed.

Here again is the stark ideological contrast between a socialist state and a neoliberal state. For democratic socialists the attraction of maximum *political* devolution while raising *income taxes* nationally within a unified British state is the ability to distribute wealth and income between richer English regions like the South East and poorer English regions like the South West and nations like Wales – so that the risks are pooled and the rewards shared. Equality and fairness should be just as important a goal for democratic socialists today as they were to Crosland decades ago.

The great majority of individuals need the state on their side, but not on their backs. They need active government which intervenes to curb market excess and market power. They need a social context to ownership. They need the assistance of strong communities. They need the solidarity which comes from acting collectively to exercise influence over the decisions which shape their lives, and to experience the fulfilment of active citizenship. They need power to be decentralised. This 'popular socialism' is the *real* alternative to the New Right 'popular capitalism', which has ideologically exhausted itself.

'Free' schools

'Free schools' – the ability of parents and others to establish their own schools with government funding (markedly more generous than to conventional state schools) – are a good example of the neoliberal approach to education. Presented as empowering local people by elevating 'choice' as an absolute priority, they brought into sharp focus the very different values which underpin a socialist approach.

In practice, free schools have eroded and fragmented universal state schooling provision, and risk promoting inequality and favouring articulate, well-informed, better-off and pushy parents over disadvantaged families. Charities, foundations, social enterprises and faith and community groups compete in place of common government schools provision open to all regardless of background, while businesses look to seek part of the action. The real risk is in the fragmentation of the school system which makes any coherent approach to planning places and raising standards very difficult indeed.

Furthermore, encouraging many faith providers to enter the market risks more ethnic and religious segregation.

Professor Stephen Ball has described the consequences:

> The English education system is being dismembered. Gradually but purposefully first New Labour and now the coalition government have been unpicking and disarticulating the national system of state schooling. With free schools and academies of various kinds, faith schools, studio schools and university technical colleges, the school system is beginning to resemble the patchwork of uneven and unequal provision that existed prior to the 1870 Education Act.[25]

Bypassing democratic accountability through elected local councils, free schools are commissioned and funded directly from the central state, again highlighting the dividing line between neoliberalism and socialism. In reality this is a huge power grab by the centre, leaving local communities (except for the few actually running these free schools) with little say over the shape of local provision. Instead the Department for Education in Whitehall is the boss, with free schools rhetorically decentralised but actually accountable to central diktat, ultimately the Secretary of State. An analogous example was Park View Academy in Birmingham which in June 2014 exploded into the headlines over allegations of jihadi Islamic extremism being preached to pupils. The episode revealed no proper system of accountability or meaningful oversight of the kind which traditionally operated through elected local councils.

For neoliberals, schools operate in a marketplace with parents made equivalent to customers, supposedly able to change if they are discontented. But such 'choice' is highly restricted to where you live: in most areas (especially rural ones) there is no choice at all. As Professor Ball concluded:

> There is no room in this for parents who just want to send their child to a good local state school – the one they attended, and friends, neighbours and relatives attend, that

is a real part of their community and history. Rather, this new education system is a market in which competitive individuals can seek to avoid others who are 'not like us'. The result, as in other choice-based systems (Chile, New Orleans, Sweden etc), is increased inequality and social segregation. In all the current political rhetoric around education, choice has almost totally displaced democracy as a positive social value. Parents can choose the school they want, or not, but communities cannot – unless they open their 'own' free school.

The socialist alternative for Labour should be to reclaim and capture the principle of autonomy for local school leaders and a degree of parental choice but to contain it in a fair, locally based regulatory structure so that, for example, every child has access to a school place, a basic curriculum entitlement and to be taught by a qualified teacher. Moreover some locally accountable body – ideally an elected local authority, but conceivably some other tier between central government and communities – must be empowered to consult with local people, plan places, intervene to prevent failure and ensure high standards in all local schools for all children. To achieve that Labour in 2014 called for new local Standards Commissioners, a modest though important reform to avoid the upheaval of unravelling the whole panoply of free schools, academies and state schools

There should also be tough regulation on admissions, exclusions and special needs provision so that schools cannot engineer themselves more favourable intakes using the freedoms that these market reforms have provided in the past. We know from international comparisons that it is real comprehensive schools with balanced intakes and minimal social segregation which provide the best educational environment for all children to succeed. Far better than the grammar/secondary modern 11-plus system to which Tony Crosland rightly took such strong objection.

Participatory socialism

In 1994 Ralph Miliband, a long-time supporter of a participatory socialism whose essence is democracy,[26] egalitarianism and socialisation, wrote that the socialist enterprise is sustained by

> a belief, inherited from the Enlightenment, in the infinite perfectibility of human beings; or, to put it in more contemporary terms, the belief that human beings are perfectly capable or organising themselves into cooperative, democratic, egalitarian and self-governing communities, in which all conflict would certainly not have been eliminated, but where it would become less and less frequent and acute.

This popular or libertarian socialism is underpinned by a different and distinct notion of politics. In the words of the 1962 Port Huron Statement from the American New Left: 'politics has the function of bringing the individual out of isolation and into community'. Its mission is to find a meaning to life that is 'personally authentic'. Much as in the Greek *polis*, this view of politics rests on the belief that it is only through interaction with others in political activity and civic action that individuals will fully realise their humanity. This contradicts classical liberalism (and modern neoliberalism or New Rightism) which sees the individual in isolation, not in community.

It helps to explain why the objective of socialists should be to create not simply participation in government but also a participatory economy and participatory *society*. Politics, as the Italian socialist Antonio Gramsci stressed, is not confined to parliament or town hall but extends throughout 'civil society': the local communities, groups and institutions which are the foundations of active citizenship. Participatory democracy should therefore extend not simply to government but throughout society: in industry, the neighbourhood or any arrangement by which people organise their lives. Politics also extends to the personal. It is not simply a vehicle through which people govern themselves. It springs from the way citizens behave privately towards each other, by showing mutual respect and tolerance for individual diversity.

But the focus on state power was allowed to sideline or negate the spirit of collectivism and community which ought to be the essence of socialism.

As a result of non-participatory centralised public provision, individuals' obligations to the state tend to increase and they can lose their obligations to their neighbours. They become individual clients of the state rather than autonomous citizens, passive recipients and sometimes dependants rather than active cooperators with each other, taking responsibility for their own lives. Although public provision remains a vital priority for socialism, historically its centralised character and delivery made people dependent upon the state, in the process jettisoning reliance upon individual initiative, communal identity, collective organisation and personal relationships, which are the foundations of citizenship and a good society. Housing cooperatives, autonomous local anti-poverty projects, sustainability initiatives, credit unions – these are grassroots examples of a participatory society in action.

State socialism did achieve very important social objectives in European democracies after the Second World War, transforming the lives of working people and opening up new educational, health and economic opportunities to all. But its incapacity to transform itself led to bureaucratic, centralised and insensitive systems which simply opened the way to the New Right. A classic was when council house tenants were not allowed to paint their own front doors the colour they chose: they had to make do with the standard colour. *Their* house was not *theirs*. As people became less deferential and more aspirational they wanted more control which only council house ownership seemed to offer.

In 1994 Ralph Miliband wrote: 'I think of socialism as a new social order, whose realisation is a process stretching over many generations, and which may never be fully "achieved". Socialism, that is to say, involves a permanent striving to advance the goals that define it.'[27] There will be no sudden point at which a socialist society 'arrives'. It will be a gradual process of achievement, building from the present. Whether or not this process is successful will depend upon the extent to which a more socialist society of the future can be 'prefigured' under contemporary capitalism. That is why, for example, even limited forms of worker participation or employee share ownership are desirable as staging posts towards greater industrial democracy and more popular forms of ownership.

The lesson for Labour in future is that legislative change is obviously necessary but not sufficient. But in government it must also do something not previously attempted. It must generate support through popular mobilisation and campaigning for socialist ideas. Because the problem is that in liberal-capitalist democracies like Britain's, Labour has found itself in office but not necessarily in power. Any Labour government is considerably constrained by 'extra-parliamentary' forces in the City and the financial markets, hostility from a predominantly right-wing media and the dead weight of the state apparatus. It needs to work and negotiate with these forces; but, to strengthen its hand, it also needs to reach out to the electorate, highlighting the constraints it faces and encouraging its supporters to back it. Where Margaret Thatcher was adroit at presenting herself as a battler against the establishment of which she was in reality a creature, Labour Prime Ministers from Harold Wilson and Jim Callaghan to Tony Blair and Gordon Brown behaved in a more orthodox way.

Markets

There is a compelling case for government intervention to ensure the economy works both efficiently and fairly. But although such strategic intervention or, where appropriate, planning, is needed at a national level, it too cannot succeed without decentralisation. As Geoff Hodgson showed:

> it is necessary to create localised planning structures which can relate to their sphere of influence on a more direct and informed basis. In addition, it is necessary to give each enterprise considerable autonomy to plan its production and work out its requirements. Some degree of centralisation and coordination is necessary under

socialism. But central planning cannot function without considerable decentralisation at the same time.[28]

A market mechanism is also necessary because not only is it entirely compatible with decentralisation, it is also essential for decentralisation. Indeed, Geoff Hodgson argues of state socialists that none of them 'understood that effective and long-lasting devolution of power away from the state requires the preservation of significant private ownership of property and of the means of production, and the major use of markets for goods and services (in investment and consumption)'.[29] Those on the left who have argued that markets equal capitalism and the absence of markets equals socialism are both wrong and utterly simplistic. This is both because capitalism cannot in practice be equated with markets and because, at their best, markets can enable consumers to exercise choice, act as spurs to innovation and efficiency, and empower citizens.

But unfettered capitalism has never operated solely according to market theory. It has always existed within a governmental framework which has allowed capital the freedom to distort markets according to the demands of the financial elite, or the dominance of large corporations. The way in which the global economy operates in favour of the ultra-rich confirms that capitalism has a tendency for a small group or class to control or even rig markets. People do not always get the goods and services they want, and which in theory a perfectly functioning market mechanism might deliver. On the contrary, they frequently get thrust upon them – through monopolistic distribution or centralised determination of choice – the products which suit the interests of private capital. The New Right notion that free, unregulated markets automatically deliver some optimal equilibrium is nonsense, as Will Hutton demonstrates:

> Markets turn out to be unstable, irrational and quite capable of producing perverse results ... Yet they are also quite capable of producing great wealth, productivity and sponsoring innovation. The problem is to tease out why they go wrong and how they can be corrected. The answer is not to let them do what they like.[30]

In its anger at inequality and its understandable impatience to establish collective provision to overcome this, state socialism neglected the importance of individual choice and individuality which markets can help to be exercised. But for choice and individual aspiration to be real for the many and not simply for the privileged few, people must have not simply the *right to choose* but the *power to choose*. In a socialist society, egalitarianism should be promoted and market forces positively channelled through regulation, democratic control and popular ownership in favour of strategic or social interests.

The free market mantras wreaked upon Britain under Margaret Thatcher from 1979, and taken up with even greater gusto by David Cameron and Nick Clegg from 2010, proved devastating both socially and economically. Market forces are essential, indeed economically necessary – provided they are properly regulated. They have an important role, but as the servants not the bosses of society, as a key ingredient of socialism. As Bryan Gould wrote in 1989, 'Where market provision is the preferred alternative, this requires a conscious effort to empower and enable each citizen so that market power is fairly distributed and choice becomes a practical reality rather than a chimera.'[31] This can be done through progressive, redistributive taxation and by tighter regulation of monopoly power and anti-competitive practices, for instance.

This is not to concede the case for New Labour's 'market socialism' which saw markets as the predominant mode and was sceptical about social ownership or public intervention. A key objective of socialism is to create an economy which is democratically accountable to its citizens. As Michael Meacher wrote in 1992: 'state versus markets is not so much an irreconcilable antithesis as a continuum where different trade-offs are possible ... between ... a much more flexible state regulation, and ... a much more constrained market system.'[32] Where markets offer the best way, they should operate. The extent to which they are regulated or influenced by strategic government intervention should not be a matter of ideological dogma, but a practical matter to be judged on its merits. For instance, we regulate the water companies more closely than the bread producers: there is an Ofwat but no Ofloaf. We employ private sector companies to build hospitals, but the NHS is a public service.

Regulation and ownership

However, casting the state as an 'enabler' rather than a domineering 'enforcer' does not mean a passive role in the economy. On the contrary, government should be highly active, intervening in partnership with industry to train the workforce and create high-quality infrastructure. It should intervene in markets to steer economic activity towards social or strategic objectives, as has been the case, for example, in Japan and the successful 'tiger economies' of the Pacific Rim. It should ensure delivery of long-term goals for the good of society and shape incentives to achieve those, for instance in renewable energy, housing and infrastructure – which, if merely left to sometimes parochial interests, would never be achieved.

Moreover the state is the only vehicle through which long-term change can be strategically implemented. Neither local cooperatives nor profiteering capitalists are capable of setting the kind of goals needed for society to change and succeed, though both may play a part. Leadership at a state level is needed, for instance, in tackling climate change, or promoting new forms of green energy, or coping with an increasing proportion of elderly citizens.

The state should also promote industrial democracy and popular ownership of industry. Public ownership is still appropriate for strategic reasons, to kick-start growth and innovation, or to maintain activity which would otherwise be closed down – as with the banks in the financial crisis or when the state-owned East Coast rail company took over rail services between London, the North East and Scotland in 2009 when the private sector train-operating company National Express Group walked away from its franchise. So is a combination of regulation and or 'golden share' stakes by government. But Old Left fundamentalism which insists upon blanket nationalisation is just as absurd as neoliberal fundamentalism which insists on privatisation of all enterprises.

This argument is not confined to the national level. There is a strong case for regional – or Welsh, Scottish and Northern Irish – public ownership, regulation and intervention. As there is for municipal ownership, regulation and intervention, not rigidly preordained according to some socialist master-plan, but locally, organically and democratically driven. For example, after being privatised, Welsh Water hit problems and transformed itself in 2000 into a self-financing not-for-dividends company with a board determined to serve the interests of Wales. As a private company limited by guarantee, it has been able comfortably to raise investment capital through its own profits, indeed able to borrow on the money markets at a significantly cheaper rate than private water utilities across England because lenders know it is not subject to the usual speculator-driven merry-go-round requiring a higher margin to safeguard investors. The website of Welsh Water describes how it has operated since 2000: 'A single purpose company with no shareholders and that is run solely for the benefit of customers.'

In parallel with such a strategic approach, popular ownership should be spread and deepened through promoting cooperatives, employee share ownership, profit sharing, and 'wise earner' ownership whereby (as with the Swedish model) workers' pension funds gradually assume ownership of their industries.

Similarly, as we saw in the last chapter, industrial democracy is a key plank of a socialist economic strategy: not merely as an agency for socialising industry in a popular way, which centralised nationalisation could never be, but as one more likely to produce the high productivity, investment and wealth needed for economic success, as various studies have confirmed. The experience of works councils in Germany suggests they lead to high standards and productivity by generating greater teamworking and commitment, which is such an important requirement of complex modern production systems.

Conclusion

The failure of neoliberalism has created a vacuum which needs filling – but not by some 'third way' between capitalism and socialism, between markets and intervention.

Western European social democracy – whereby private capital and the market economy are regulated and welfare services provided by a democratically elected state – was successful in the era after the Second World War, when it was the product of a particular settlement between capital and labour, between the market and representative government. And certainly it *was* successful compared with prewar stagnation: it delivered three decades of welfare services, economic stability and relatively fast growth which seemed a godsend, and was consequently extolled by Tony Crosland. In Sweden, extensive government interventionism without nationalisation and a high-quality welfare state was perhaps the model for this social democracy.

But, instead of taking that forward and transforming it in the way that this chapter has argued, Europe (with Britain in the vanguard) has put austerity before growth. The social democratic parties (some calling themselves 'socialist') which have followed this path across Western Europe have lost their way, with their working-class base dangerously alienated and vulnerable to racist and fascist appeals, or in Britain to UKIP's right-wing populism.[33] We always knew we had plenty to fear from the likes of the BNP. But until 2008 we never realised how much damage could be done by the likes of BNP Paribas.

Some in the Labour Party became timid over macro-economic policy – spurning demand management for growth in favour of public spending cuts. An anxiety to demonstrate at all costs that Labour is not against entrepreneurial innovation and enterprise has led to excessive emphasis upon the virtues of a 'dynamic market economy' while neglecting its downsides: large income inequalities, instability, job insecurity, underemployment, mounting household debt and underinvestment, together with the social problems created by poverty and inequality.

The future for socialism requires a new synthesis. Modern socialism will only succeed by projecting with confidence an alternative vision: democratic, pluralist and libertarian.

CHAPTER 8

A new internationalism

Tony Crosland's *The Future of Socialism* appeared in 1956, just before the Suez debacle sounded the death knell on unilateral adventurism in Britain's foreign affairs. That insane episode came to a sudden stop when the White House obliged Prime Minister Anthony Eden to call off his misbegotten military action for fear of financial consequences for the UK economy. The lesson should have been crystal clear: the 'Age of Empire' was over and Britain could no longer get far internationally without a strong economy and the support, or at least the understanding, of key friends, partners and allies.

But that lesson had been only partially learned by the time that Tony Crosland became British Foreign Secretary in 1976, when the UK economy was again struggling with problems provoked by the consequences of Suez: a great hike in the world oil price by the Organization of the Petroleum Exporting Countries (OPEC). British diplomacy was still very much about national interests, and the Foreign Office applied its craft in the same way as it had done for generations. But that became increasingly unsustainable as the globalised economy developed. Freight containers, bulk carriers and satellite communications transformed international trade. Jumbo jets supplanted ocean liners and made mass overseas travel affordable. The internet facilitated unimagined new connections. But in parallel came new threats: climate change, cross-border crime, unprecedented levels of migration, population growth, global poverty, pandemics, international terrorism and cyber-attacks. To that lengthening list has now been added the growing threats of food and water shortages. Together there are all the ingredients for a 'perfect storm' to hit humankind.

The days of go-it-alone have gone. Welcome to the world of ambiguity and compromise where the art of coalition building is a key skill. Where ministers search for partners in European Council meetings at the Justus Lipsius building in Brussels, the slowest speed-dating club in Europe. Where every balanced package sends out a mixed message and where, when you reach your final destination, it feels like a halfway house. Where a dual-sourced, twin-track, copper-bottomed guarantee could contain a get-out clause in the small print, making it worth its weight in mould. Where an ability to combine a straight face with a white lie could get you noticed. Where dinosaurs and dodos died out but diplomats survived: so many shades of grey in today's Foreign Office colouring book.

When Tony Crosland died in 1977, Britain was still a relatively new member of what was then a comparatively young European Common Market, having overcome its initial hesitancy over joining. Today the Common Market's successor, the European Union, is the largest single market in the world and plays a significant role in international affairs. In Crosland's time Britain was one of the major world powers supporting the US as the only genuine superpower. Today we are a medium-sized nation state in a multipolar world.

The emerging economies of the BRICS countries (Brazil, Russia, India, China and South Africa), with their growing economic wealth, and middle classes numbering hundreds of millions of people, represent a shift of economic and global power towards Asia and the South, and away from the US and the old European colonial nations like Britain in the North. By 2050 the developing countries could constitute 85 per cent of the world's population, 12 times Europe's at 7 per cent, according to a 2012 United Nations report.

When Crosland became Foreign Secretary Mao Zedong was still the leader of China (although he died the same year) and the country was technologically backward and poor, languishing far behind Western powers like Britain. It had hardly changed when I visited in 1980, but by 2013 it was as if China had reached a different planet. It had become

> the second biggest economy in the world, the number
> one trading partner for 128 countries, the biggest

holder of foreign reserves, the world's biggest polluter, the biggest consumer of Middle Eastern oil and gas, the country with the fastest growing defence budget and the biggest contributor to United Nations peace-keeping missions among the [Permanent Five] members of the Security Council. And over the next decade and a half, it is likely to be transformed not just in relative power to the West but in the structure of its economy, politics and foreign policy. Its economy could grow to twice the size of America's. Rather than being an exporter of cheap products it could have the world's biggest consumer market and the largest spending on R&D ... And rather than having the passive foreign policy of recent years, it will become active in defence of its global interests.[1]

Not simply the momentous rise of China but that of the whole of Asia will necessitate Europe, Britain included, while not turning away from Atlantic alliances, recognising that Pacific alliances will become at least as important.

The economies with which Britain now competes are themselves increasingly influenced by varied forms of state capitalism, because markets alone do not provide them with the tools they need for the large-scale restructuring and technological development necessary to remain competitive. State controlled or influenced sovereign wealth funds are increasingly important to both domestic and foreign investment. Even the US, seen as the doyen of free-market capitalism, has not hesitated to use state funds to rescue the giant car-maker General Motors or to bail out the insurance giant AIG and shore up the balance sheets of America's big banks. Britain's free market Conservative-led coalition government had to seek investment in a new generation of nuclear reactors from EDF, a largely state-owned French utility, and Chinese state-owned nuclear operators ultimately answerable to its Communist Party.

The progressive left's belief in internationalism not isolationism, in multilateralism not unilateralism, in transparency and accountability of power, and in protecting the interests of the many not the few offers a much better way of meeting the challenges of globalisation.

And new mixed-economy models based on government intervention, state ownership stakes, and policy-driven regulation offer a much better alternative to the neoliberalist orthodoxy pervading the West's economic governance.

Just as the modern global financial system needs to be tamed and regulated through international intervention and collaboration by governments, and the neoliberal orthodoxy of recent decades rejected, so governments need to collaborate to avoid increasing and indiscriminate threats to the whole planet. And not simply for the obvious reasons that have traditionally encouraged governments to cooperate – to tackle disasters, avoid war, thwart terrorism and prevent proliferation of weapons of mass destruction.

Today all the big and fundamental global challenges require new and global solutions, because the old nation-state solutions simply will not work. The new threats could be overwhelming if not combated by governments working together. When global warming and climate change, food and water insecurity, threaten the future of humankind, there is no escape for any country that either acts alone or leaves these problems to be resolved by market forces.

International institutions will therefore be even more necessary in the future than in the past. Which brings us directly to the need for Britain to be a leading player in the European Union and not simply the United Nations, the International Monetary Fund and the World Bank. Increasingly, we will have limited impact if we try to act alone. Gordon Brown gave a masterclass in how Britain can play a leading role by galvanising agreement at the April 2009 G20 meeting to tackle the threat of global recession, with his European Union allies playing a weighty and crucial support role.

The 'little Englander' isolationism of the British right – from Tories and UKIP to the BNP – simply cannot deal with the scale and scope of the big challenges of our era. It is not only wrong for all the old reasons that have long encouraged socialists to reject nationalism in favour of internationalism – that we are one humanity. It postures unilateral stances on issues which require multilateral solutions. In seeking British withdrawal from the European Union it would also marginalise British influence and leave the country trailing behind, frantically waving a Union Jack instead of joining with other leading nations near the head of the pack – an eccentric posture in an era when global threats are growing all the time. For much the same reasons, nationalist pressures for break-aways from nation states – whether in Scotland or Catalonia – are eccentric: opting for small solutions to big global problems is a route to irrelevance, a passport to diminished influence.

Food and water shortages

Take the very basics of life. Food and water supplies are under acute pressure from a booming global population, estimated to be approaching 7.2 billion but growing by 200,000 people a day to an estimated 9 billion by 2050 and more than 10 billion by the end of the century.

Rocketing food prices and an exponential increase in the demand for food, especially in China and India, mean food security is a major problem – not simply for the near billion people undernourished or starving,[2] but for us all, Britain included. Food reserves are at a 50-year low, hindered by climate extremes, and rising demand seems insatiable.

In China, for instance, urbanisation and a rapidly growing middle class have brought a radical change in dietary preferences, with a fall in traditional staples such as rice and corn and a massive rise in meat consumption. Consumption of fruit and vegetables, now the largest part of the average Chinese diet, has more than quadrupled since the early 1960s. Meat, fruit and vegetables require much more land and water to produce than cereal crops. Over 12 times the quantity of water is required to produce the equivalent amount of beef as rice and wheat.

Consequently food and water security are inextricably linked. In sub-Saharan Africa alone, 40 per cent of the population, or 330 million people, have no accessible decent water, a plight affecting nearly 900 million people across the world. To get access to water, more than 1 billion people make a three-hour journey on foot, and over a third of the world's population live in a water-scarce region. As societies urbanise and industrialise, modern lifestyles require huge additional amounts of water, which is in turn a potential source of conflict: it would not be a surprise to see 'water wars' in future.

Indeed Egypt's presidents, Hosni Mubarak in 2011 and Mohamed Morsi in 2013, both made thinly veiled threats to use military force against Ethiopia to uphold Egypt's historic access to the waters of the Nile, the world's longest river, upon which its 84 million people totally depend for their water, along with many African countries. The dispute arose over the construction of the $4.8 billion hydroelectric Grand Renaissance Dam, the largest in Africa. Trying to fend off these threats, the Ethiopian Prime Minister observed in February 2014 that there was no international court specialising in arbitrating water disputes.

Water also became a weapon in the Iraq civil war in 2014, with rivers, canals, dams, sewage and desalination plants all military targets. The climate of Iraq's semi-arid region produces regular and extreme water shortages, and, as Michael Stephens, of the Royal United Services Institute in Qatar, explained:

> Control of water supplies gives strategic control over both cities and countryside. We are seeing a battle for control of water. Water is now the major strategic objective of all groups in Iraq. It's life or death. If you control water in Iraq you have a grip on Baghdad, and you can cause major problems. Water is essential in this conflict.[3]

Control of water in the Levant around the Red Sea could equally cause more tensions between Syria, Lebanon and Israel. One of the problems at the heart of the Israel–Palestine conflict is access to water, which is in scarce supply and over which Israelis have assumed de facto control, even in so-called Palestinian 'territory'.

The world will require fully 50 per cent more food and water by 2030 and the same amount of extra energy – in part to source the extra food and water. And acute energy shortages coupled with extreme volatility in fuel costs – oil prices very high and forecast to remain very high – are another source of potential civil unrest, triggering mass migration northwards from the South and directly impacting upon Britain, where migration has already become politically problematic.

International problems, international solutions

These problems are all internationally interconnected. For instance, how have we allowed vast tracts of rainforests, the 'lungs of the earth', to be destroyed? The answer is in order to satisfy rising, market-driven, global consumption – most of it initiated in the West and now being emulated almost everywhere, especially in China and India. Yet we know that the destruction of rainforests deprives the planet of a key means of absorbing carbon dioxide and generates hugely destructive climate change.

Another example: the global banking crisis of 2007–08, which was triggered by worldwide contagion from 'subprime' mortgages in America. It gridlocked private sector credit and investment. The initial response was a widespread rise in government spending on welfare benefits as unemployment rose, and in public sector investment, to try to stem the threat of recession. But a combination of budgetary pressures and neoliberal orthodoxies meant that this soon gave way to massive cuts in Western government spending and investment, not just domestically but on overseas aid and development, triggering a crisis in recipient countries with no direct link at all to the poor US householders who could not maintain their loan repayments. As a consequence the United Nations estimated there was a financing gap of up to $200 billion needed from developed countries to achieve its anti-poverty Millennium Development Goals in 2015.

And rich countries like Britain are just as vulnerable, blurring the distinction between 'foreign' policy and 'domestic' policy. A domestic government campaign against HIV/AIDS faced the fact that in 2000 three quarters of British victims were infected while travelling in Africa; British funding for HIV/AIDS programmes on that continent helps tackle the problem at source.

Both the resilience and the encroachment into personal life of the global communications infrastructure are now major questions. No single country could prevent a handful of students in the Philippines in 2000 from sending out a virus disabling 10 million computers worldwide. Over the succeeding years, protection against cyber-attacks became a preoccupation of government security agencies. Meanwhile there was a global backlash against the threat to privacy from those very same agencies when their seemingly ubiquitous surveillance was revealed in 2013 by US national security whistleblower Edward Snowden.

Global warming and drug trafficking are not caused by some hostile power's ambition or greed, but by millions of individual decisions made mainly by Western consumers. These challenges require multilateral, intergovernmental responses, the 'foreign' being now inextricably intertwined with the 'domestic'.

Over the coming decades the main threats and changes to our economy, our security, our health and our general well-being will not be domestic but global in both origin and impact. A major global flu pandemic could cause global economic losses of $1 trillion due to knock-on macro-economic effects. Migration – with 200 million people (the size of Brazil's population) now on the move globally every year – places huge strains on the entire domestic agenda from jobs to housing to race relations. Furthermore, the pensions of European workers are likely to depend in part on investments made in fast-growing economies such as China and India.

The problems are joined up, so governments must be joined up. Previously, responsibility for foreign policy resided in an elite group of specialist diplomats. But tensions arising from declining water tables and rising populations in the Middle East, collapsing fish stocks in the Atlantic and persistent drought in East Africa cannot be solved at a summit. The task requires the specialised skills of all government departments in the countries trying to address the problems – and the committed and innovative involvement of non-government actors in business and civil society.

Successful international policy will in future centre on 'convergent' policy solutions by joined-up governments forming new partnerships both domestically and globally. Partnerships in which we discover best practice by learning from each other and where our common aim is the achievement of world-class standards. As the concept of 'foreign' becomes ever harder to define, we should re-badge the British Foreign Office the Global Affairs Office, and give it both a larger budget and a Treasury-type reach into every Whitehall department, with each required to agree its own 'convergence programme' (Treasury-speak for government departments to comply with overall budgetary requirements). We need to evolve a new foreign policy based upon global linkages and embracing global responsibility; a foreign policy for a world in which there is no longer any such place as 'abroad'.[4]

Globalisation and interdependency

Our growing interdependency is surely self-evident, and our response cannot be either that of those on the left who advocate a Canute posture, trying to defy the rising tide of globalisation, or that of those on the right who are happy to take its economic benefits, but not the social responsibility that goes with them. As on the economy, the right – with its prejudice for nationalism, protectionism and unilateralism – offers only simple responses to complex problems when in truth reliance on free markets and national self-interest is incapable of producing the necessary responses to threats that are global and universal.

The refusal of neoconservatives like George W. Bush to grasp this undermined even his major obsession: global support for the fight against international terrorism. In clear contrast to the Bush administration's approach, there was a bipartisan US project on national security published in autumn 2006 – chaired by President Clinton's former national security adviser, Tony Lake, and President Reagan's former Secretary of State, George Shultz. It rightly acknowledged: 'power cannot be wielded unilaterally, and in the pursuit of a narrowly drawn definition of the national interest, because such actions breed growing resentment, fear, and resistance.'[5]

Labour needs to draw upon the rich internationalist tradition that it shares with colleagues in centre-left parties abroad: the passionate Europeanism of Tony Crosland, Roy Hattersley, John Smith, Jacques Delors, Gerhard Schröder and Robin Cook; the unflinching Atlanticism of Ernie Bevin, Denis Healey and Willy Brandt; the anti-apartheid zeal of Neil Kinnock, Barbara Castle, Olaf Palme and Helen Clark; the green leadership of Al Gore and Gro Harlem Brundtland; the crusading anti-poverty zeal of Clare Short and Anna Lindh; the unyielding support of anti-colonial struggles by Fenner Brockway and Michael Foot; the courage of Jack Jones and George Orwell travelling out to fight fascism in the Spanish Civil War.

In our increasingly interdependent world, marrying that internationalist heritage to the progressive goals of the future is more important than ever: recognising that common interests and common problems can only be solved by collective action; that global stability depends upon global justice; and that we must maintain the left's historic duty to defend human rights and promote democracy and sustainable development around the world.

Stronger international institutions in a multipolar world

Because the challenges presented by globalisation will frequently come from beyond our own borders, so too will the solutions. That's why international institutions and respect for common international rules are more crucial than ever.

Britain is well placed to lead the imperative for effective, global multilateralism because of its membership of all the key international institutions: the United Nations Security Council, the European Union, the G7/G20, NATO, the Commonwealth, IMF, World Bank and the World Trade Organization. Yet these traditional bodies are mostly Western dominated and need reform, especially the IMF, the World Bank and the UN Security Council. The Archbishop of Canterbury, Justin Welby, was right to call for the IMF to be reshaped in line with its original purpose in a new Bretton Woods-style agreement on global stability. (Bretton Woods was the 1944 conference that wrote the post-war rules governing commercial and financial relations between the world's major powers and set up international institutions to promote stability.) Sadly, in Welby's view, the IMF 'tends to look like a police officer when it should look like the fire brigade'. The membership of the UN Security Council should reflect the world as it is now, not as it was in the colonial age of 1945. It is absurd that Germany, Japan and India are not permanent members like the US, Russia, China, Britain and France. It is also ludicrous that neither Africa nor Latin America has a permanent member: adding South Africa and Brazil would remedy that.

Not that UN reform will of itself be a cure-all for global problems. The old adage remains valid: that the UN is only as strong as its most powerful members will allow it to be. What reform means is that UN leadership will become more representative and that countries now able only to carp from the sidelines will have to take responsibility for solving conflicts and tackling human rights abuses – or face the consequences of failing to do so. Nevertheless, in the 70 years since the UN was established there have been no wars between the major powers, a sign of success unequalled in previous history. Cyber-attacks maybe, proxy conflicts and trade wars certainly, but no world wars comparable to the past. As the former UN Secretary-General Dag Hammarskjöld memorably put it: 'the UN is not here to take us to heaven, but to prevent us from going to hell'.

At the same time the international bodies are no longer as powerful as they once were, and are coping uneasily with a new world. There is an increasing 'diffusion of power – both from the West to the Rest … and from the nation state to an array of non-governmental organisations ranging from Oxfam to al-Qaida', all which requires of Britain an 'extended multilateralism' rather than a focus upon US or EU alliances alone.[6] At the same time there is a 'crisis of legitimacy' for the Old Order, with challenges from the Tea Party on the right to Occupy Wall Street on the left; from the Arab Spring to the people protests against elected governments in Turkey and South Africa.

Europe

Yet, just when the world is in flux, there are those who wish to sideline Britain internationally by isolating us within Europe. Despite the enduring euro crisis and a failure to deliver strong, collective leadership on foreign and defence policy and on economic reform, Europe's progress over the past 60 years has been massive: the creation of once unimaginable peace and stability across a continent where more wars were fought in recent centuries than on any other; the promotion of democracy and human rights, especially in the former dictatorships of southern and eastern Europe; and the development of a competitive single market in which social justice and environmental standards have all been enhanced.

The European experience is a remarkable story of how, by sharing sovereignty but still retaining national identity, states can work together to confront common challenges, promote mutual interests and achieve shared aims, and thereby each become stronger together. For the first 50 years of its existence the European Union delivered faster economic growth as trade among member states multiplied faster than trade with the rest of the world. Then came the 2008 global financial crisis triggering a sharper initial drop in world trade than even at the start of the 1930s Great Depression. The growth initiatives agreed at the April 2009 G20 summit in London were due in part to backing from the four EU sovereign states of Britain, France, Germany and Italy, and Spain as a permanent guest member, *plus* the 20th member, the EU itself, led by the President of the European Council and the President of the European Commission.

That is why Labour's willingness to show leadership on Europe will become ever more vital in future; Labour leading at home by unrelentingly making the case that our membership of the European Union makes Britain stronger, safer, wealthier and greener; and Labour leading in Europe, ensuring that together we look outwards to the challenges of the 21st century, building a world in which social justice, democracy and human rights are spread ever more widely as the key to sustainable development.

But this means Europe must shape, not just react to, international affairs. Although in recent years the European Union has indeed played an increasing role, it has been less influential than it ought to have been as still the world's richest single market. A stronger EU foreign policy would bolster all its members' influence in world affairs, not weaken them, by advancing each of our interests in ways that we cannot do alone.

With China already an economic and geopolitical superpower and the emergence of the BRICS group of countries, US global dominance is being superseded. Britain is still big enough to stand up for itself; we still count for something. The UK economy still ranks in the world's top ten in terms of GDP and in the top 25 in terms of GDP per capita. But by acting in concert with our EU partners we can move up several gears, increasing our effectiveness and getting more punch from every ounce of effort we put in.

That was confirmed by President Obama's horrified reaction in 2013 to the Conservative push for Britain to withdraw from the EU. Washington's view is that Britain alone would no longer merit the influence it currently enjoys in the 'special relationship' with America because, quite simply, it would have less clout and therefore be of less value as a 'close friend'. That is not on its own a reason for the UK to stay within the EU but it is an important supporting argument – especially for those on the right who yearn nostalgically for the glories of an Atlantic rather than a European alliance.

The frustration is that Europe could play an even more powerful global role. The European Union already contributes over half the world's overseas aid. It negotiates as equals with the US over international trade. But EU foreign and security policy has been largely ineffectual. At European Foreign Ministers' Councils various countries' representatives tend to read out their points, then rush outside to repeat them with a self-serving gloss to the waiting microphones, telling domestic audiences what they want to hear, but too often afterwards nothing happens. For Europe to be able to punch its weight in global diplomacy will require a mind shift by member states and their ministers from '*resolutionary*' diplomacy to *serious* diplomacy. The 2013–14 negotiations led with great skill by Catherine Ashton, the EU High Representative for Foreign Affairs and Security Policy, with the new Iranian regime of President Rouhani is an exemplary case in point. On Iran's nuclear capabilities, she was the lead diplomat, ahead even of the US Secretary of State John Kerry.

The full-time President of the European Council and single Foreign Representative agreed in the Lisbon Treaty was a big step forward, and could in future position Europe to be a serious global force: not so much a rival for the US as a force to be reckoned with by the US and the emerging powers in the emerging multipolar world. But that will only happen if member states are prepared to elect substantial, powerful figures to be President and Foreign Representative. Coupled with a willingness by the smaller countries to permit nations like Britain and France which have serious defence capabilities to play a bigger role, and a readiness by bigger countries like Germany to shoulder more serious defence responsibilities, that could enable Europe to play a crucial and potentially pivotal role as a force for progressive internationalism. Never again should Europe have to beg for US air-force intervention, as – led by Tony Blair – it did over Kosovo to fill vital gaps in European capabilities. Without Washington's help, European demands for an end to Serbian ethnic cleansing would have remained wishful thinking, and the killing would have continued.

Yet European military capabilities are weak and it may require more money to put this right. But the primary goal should be to ensure greater efficiency in existing national military spending, where together we obtain only 15 per cent of US capabilities for 50 per cent of US spending. That is why we should support measures to improve capabilities by working constructively in the intergovernmental European Defence Agency.

Social justice and global stability

Lawrence Korb and Max Hoffman have pointed out that since 1950 global economic output is up fivefold and per capita incomes have increased by 350 per cent; and since the early 1980s, 660 million Chinese have been lifted out of poverty; indeed Asians living in extreme poverty have dropped to a sixth of their former number.[7] Nevertheless, stronger international institutions still have to be driven by a progressive purpose: although globalisation has brought with it great opportunities for the 'Starbucks generation', that is not the case for the 1.3 billion people living on less than a dollar a day; for the 30,000 children who die every day due to extreme poverty; or for the 90 per cent of sub-Saharan Africans outside South Africa who have no access to electricity. In January 2014 an Oxfam report highlighted the appalling global inequality which helps perpetuate world poverty: the richest 85 people in the world have the same amount of wealth – $1.7 trillion – as the entire bottom half of the earth's population, 3.5 billion people.[8] For far, far too many people, at best the promise of globalisation is totally hollow; at worst globalisation appears to stack already poor odds ever more heavily against them.

Furthermore, much greater prosperity, mobility, and access to information in a digital age have all contributed to rising expectations of, and demands upon, governments worldwide. Assertiveness has replaced deference, especially among those who feel left behind by globalisation and are bombarded daily by television or the internet with inviting images of materialism and opulence.

All of which demands a new 'globalisation of responsibility' as the cornerstone of promoting social justice and sustainable development around the world, based upon equal opportunities regardless of race, gender, religion, nationality, sexual orientation or disability. This imperative is not only the right course, it is based upon self-interest: injustice and inequality breed despair, social division and conflict which in turn can affect the powerful, indeed us all.

Women: a global injustice

For instance, the exclusion of women from economic development is a central reason for the endurance of world poverty. Sixty per cent of the poorest people in the world are women and while gender inequality continues, climate change and food and water insecurity will have a disproportionate impact on women.

Where the state is weak to non-existent in developing economies, women play an even greater role because they have primary responsibility for the health and education of their children. Women know intimately their families' needs and the resources they have available to meet those needs. Therefore it is not just women but their families and the societies they live in who suffer from only 10–20 per cent of women possessing land rights in the developing world; this seriously hampers their ability to make decisions over the allocation of resources. Or, indeed, when women are denied the basic right to plan their pregnancies, taking them out of the labour force and preventing them from playing an active role in society.

The empowerment of women has become crucial to combating climate change and creating a sustainable future for our planet, whether through sustainable agricultural practices, reducing greenhouse gas emissions or overcoming food and water insecurity. Targeted investment in modern, safe and renewable energy production for every household means women will no longer have to spend their time collecting firewood or struggling with primitive and dangerous domestic fuels which cause greenhouse gas emissions.

To realise the true potential of sustainable development, economic investment must therefore be accompanied by a radical change in the place and status of women in society. The empowerment of women is a crucial cure for poverty and is now inseparable from the struggle against climate change, not least because both climate change and the subjection of women are manmade. For instance, despite India's enormous and successful economic expansion, a quarter of girls aged 15 to 24 remain illiterate and only 1.3 per cent of GDP is directed towards tackling gender issues.

Throughout the developing world women are disproportionately deprived of the fruits of economic growth and prosperity. Although they make up 40 per cent of the global workforce, women possess a miniscule 1 per cent of the world's wealth. The World Bank estimates that in some countries, the full participation of women in the workforce could on its own lead to a 25 per cent increase in labour productivity.

Girls must therefore have the same opportunities as their brothers to learn to read and receive a formal education, providing an invaluable boost to the economies of developing nations.

The urgent challenges we face as a planet cry out for creativity and ingenuity. To deprive future generations of the full potential and talent of half the population is not simply a global injustice but a global tragedy.

Human rights, liberty and democracy

But apart from a commitment to social justice, the values that British democratic socialists have long cherished – liberty, pluralist democracy, the rule of law, freedom and human rights – are not unique to us; they are not solely 'Western' or 'Judaeo-Christian' values. They are universal, enshrined in the UN Charter and the Universal Declaration of Human Rights. It is not, as critics have alleged, a question of seeking to 'impose' them on other religions or other regions – for they already share them, as the Arab Spring demonstrated. Rather it is a question of defending these values against assault by those who embrace hatred and violence, tyranny and terrorism.

For some on the left, promoting democracy across the world became indelibly associated with the neoconservative agenda and, by extension, with the war in Iraq. Some deride the notion of extending democracy as the ideology of 'American imperialism', imposing alien ideas on societies with different values and traditions. But just because some neoconservatives have appropriated the language of democracy, that does not mean that socialists should abandon our values.

Equally, however, the Arabic word *democratiy* is often viewed in Arab countries as an alien, English word implicitly linked with US policy and therefore to be treated with suspicion. For example, some noted that the July 2013 military coup against Mohamed Morsi, the democratically elected President of Egypt, and leader of the Muslim Brotherhood, was either openly or covertly welcomed by Western democracies like Britain, inviting accusations of hypocrisy – and they also noted that the new regime soon attacked human rights. (However, many Egyptian pro-democracy protesters who had ousted Mubarak in 2011 also backed the 2013 coup because of Morsi's lurch into sectarianism and authoritarianism.) For democratic socialists, there needs to be a clear set of principles which inform policy and engage hard-headedly with the realpolitik of global affairs, so that we, and our interlocutors, know where we stand. We need to be honest about national interest and global interest (especially in relation to aid). For the West, there is, of course, an interest in supporting democratic change in fragile states because it is easier to do business with stable democracies, and is likely to benefit the economies of countries like Britain. But there is also an international benefit, in that democracies tend not to go to war with each other, tend not to experience famines, and it is far easier (and cheaper) to support a fragile state than it is to fix a failed one.

'Use your liberty to promote ours,' said Burma's freedom warrior Aung San Suu Kyi. How can we say to a girl wanting schooling in Kabul, or women wanting to vote in the Gulf, or an Iraqi citizen ignoring the bomb threats and queuing to vote in the early hours, that democracy is for us, not you? Exactly such specious arguments were deployed by racists preserving apartheid in South Africa. It is odd to see them advanced by those on the British left who joined in the fight against apartheid. Similarly Cuba's admirable social agenda in the face of an aggressive US siege should not have blinded the left to its human rights record: not all the political prisoners in Cuba are confined to Guantanamo.

Nevertheless democracy, freedom and human rights cannot simply be imposed by military might, as the British government was disastrously on the verge of attempting over the Syrian civil war in 2013, before a vote in Parliament by MPs opposed to being dragged into the Syrian quagmire blocked it.[9] Yes, in Sierra Leone in 2000 and Kosovo in 1999, Britain with the international community, and with the support of the House of Commons but without the formal backing of a UN resolution, had to resort to force in the face of ethnic cleansing, gross abuses of human rights, mass murder, and aggressive threats to peaceful neighbouring nations. But there must be international support for such action, meaning a coalition of willing participants rather than one nation acting independently – ideally backed by an explicit UN resolution.

Climate change

Perhaps the most pressing case for coordinated global action springs from climate change. As the 2006 Stern Report made clear,[10] 'business as usual' could see global temperatures rise by 5 degrees Celsius above pre-industrial levels, leading to massive costs – far outweighing those required to invest and place the world on a sustainable agenda – and a 5 to 20 per cent cut in global living standards. Ominously, Lord Stern announced in 2013 that his earlier prognosis on climate change had been wrong; the situation was much worse than he had anticipated only seven years earlier.

Climate change won't just dramatically affect temperatures, or sea levels, or weather. Stern laid out the links to increases both in mosquito-borne diseases like malaria, and major incidences of flooding: and each tonne of carbon dioxide released into the atmosphere costs approximately $85 in mitigation measures.

The costs are already hitting hardest and earliest in the developing world despite the fact that much of the climate damage has been done by industrialised nations. Stern's report predicted a decline in crop yields in parts of Africa already scarred by famine, affecting hundreds of millions of people, and some of the world's poorest countries, which are likely to lose 10 per cent of their economic output. According to the *Lancet*, 2.1 million people a year are dying prematurely from air pollution in the cities of Asia.[11]

In September 2013, the Intergovernmental Panel on Climate Change stated that human-related activities would alone raise global temperatures by more than 2 degrees Celsius from pre-industrial levels, which could trigger plumes of methane gas from the thawing Arctic tundra, while the polar ice caps, which reflect solar radiation back into space, could disappear and sea levels could rise by a metre by 2100 and 3 metres by 2200, inundating many coastal cities worldwide. Each of the past three decades has been warmer than any previous decade on record. Increased land surface and sea temperatures have already reversed the previous 5,000 years of cooling across the Northern Hemisphere. In March 2014 the UN Panel of scientists went further, finding evidence of climate change far beyond thawing Arctic permafrost and crumbling coral reefs 'on all continents and across the oceans'. Importantly the UN Panel showed that climate change was certainly damaging food availability, including the staple crop wheat and fish.

Most scientists maintain that the primary issue is that the earth is in radiative imbalance, with more energy from the sun entering the top of the atmosphere than exiting it since about 1970, because of 'greenhouse' gases. Since the start of the industrial revolution, carbon emissions from fossil fuel combustion and cement production are estimated to have released 365 billion tonnes of carbon dioxide, and deforestation a further 180 billion tonnes, at a rate that increases year on year. Humanity is responsible for creating the 'greenhouse' phenomenon, which is slowly suffocating the planet, and only radical changes in human behaviour can reverse this and dramatically cut our carbon dioxide emissions.

Extreme weather means that wetter regions get wetter and dryer areas dryer, causing more and worse monsoons, typhoons, hurricanes, flooding, droughts, wildfires and famine. According to Jeffrey Mazo, by 2009 such climate change was causing 300,000 deaths, economic losses of $125 billion and 'seriously affecting 325 million people every year'. He also argues that the huge spike in global food prices in 2010–11 – in turn triggered by climate change-induced droughts – was an important (albeit by no means the sole) trigger in the Arab Spring uprisings.[12] The UN Panel report of March 2014 also found evidence that 'climate change can indirectly increase risks of violent conflict in the form of civil war and inter-group violence', for example riots triggered by food shortages and spiralling prices. This was the first time the UN scientists had linked climate change to food insecurity.

Western nations have failed to accept that we are, in the large part, responsible for these problems and we should therefore bear the larger part of the burden of finding and implementing solutions. That is why it was never acceptable for the United States, with 5 per cent of the world's population and 25 per cent of the world's emissions, to opt out of international curbs. Equally, however, China and India are now major and fast-expanding polluters, Brazil is pursuing development often at the expense of its environment, and South Africa is also a significant polluter for its size because of coal. Only agreement among the major powers, North and South, East and West, will resolve the gridlock over effective global action to combat climate change.[13]

Sustainable development is not about the avoidance of tough choices; it is about making different choices. Sustainable development is not about zero growth; it's about smarter growth and greener growth, about exploiting the massive economic and job opportunities which arise from the need to restore and maintain our environment.

Renewable energy in Africa

Take, for example, the need for energy in Africa, where the scale of the challenge is daunting: 17 of the 20 countries with the lowest electricity access on the planet are in sub-Saharan Africa, where 585 million people are without any electricity. (That is, over 80 million more people than live in all the countries of the European Union.) Quite apart from the resulting misery and poverty, a huge number of Africans are therefore without the essential prerequisite for a stable modern society.

The solution lies in harnessing Africa's abundance of renewable energy sources; in providing communities not only with light and power, but also with opportunities to generate sustainable and self-sufficient wealth and employment, reducing emissions and thereby reducing serious African food and water shortages.

Without energy, health and social services are non-existent to primitive; educational opportunities extremely limited; and getting online impossible. Without radical change, the people of sub-Saharan Africa will be trapped in this vicious cycle.

Yet Africa has the potential to go its own way with stand-free renewable energy and leapfrog costly grid-based generation as it has done so effectively in telecommunications through mobile telephony. With the help of EU investment, Africa – instead of being a continent falling behind – could be a world leader in renewable energy, something which foreign private investors have yet to recognise. There is a huge investment opportunity in Africa, for instance in hydroelectricity, where only 7 per cent of the potential energy resource is being utilised, and in geothermal energy, where only 1 per cent is being exploited.

Policy makers meeting in Brussels have already considered covering parts of the deserts, mainly the Sahara, with solar panels. Remarkably, more energy falls from the sun on the planet's deserts in six hours than the world consumes in a year. As well as serving Africa's needs, the Sahara, being close to Europe, could one day realistically deliver 15 per cent of Europe's electricity. A significant part of Europe's huge aid and development budget should be allocated to funding a substantial renewable energy investment programme in partnership with private companies. Although the EU–Africa relationship has been one-sided for centuries, global climate change is binding our fates together.

For there is no such thing as 'foreign policy' any more. The 'national' and the 'international' are inextricably interlinked. The problems the world faces can only be solved by the multilateral action of many states. And Britain is only powerful as a strong voice in the European Union.

Any sensible reading of world politics gives the lie to the British right's view that we can retreat into our island shell, and either protect ourselves from the buffeting of global forces, or enjoy the same sort of influence. For Britain to thrive, and for its citizens to be assured of a reasonable standard of living, it has to engage with the world in a different way that recognises and welcomes the challenges that come with being a modern, international and cosmopolitan nation. What has made Britain influential is our ability to go out into the world, not to hide away from it. Yet the right has demonstrably failed to wrestle with these challenges, its whole mindset at odds with the realities of the modern world. Only democratic socialists offer the vision and insight to give Britain what it needs in the decades to come.

We all need each other more than ever before in the global search for a 'perfect solution' to the gathering 'perfect storm'.

CHAPTER 9

Britain in Europe

Tony Crosland was a passionate European: one of only 20 Labour MPs who defied the party's three-line whip by abstaining in the key vote in October 1971 approving UK entry to the Common Market. But he did not join the 69 other Labour rebels led by Roy Jenkins and John Smith who voted in favour and therefore against Labour's then policy to oppose British entry. His abstention was due to balancing party unity with his principles, not to any lack of courage. His first foray into continental Europe had been in wartime with the Parachute Regiment, and he played his part in winning the Labour government's 1975 referendum when the British people voted for a European future.

Although Crosland made plain that *The Future of Socialism* was about the British domestic scene, his horizons did not stop at Dover. He recognised that 1950s Britain had lots to learn from Scandinavia with its greater social equality, and noted with approval how differently industrial relations and capital markets worked in Sweden and West Germany from the UK.

He lost his South Gloucestershire parliamentary seat at the end of May 1955 and may have missed the significance of the Messina conference, held only days later, when the foreign ministers of the six member states of the European Coal and Steel Community gave fresh impetus to the idea of European integration. Their call for a customs union and a common market led to the Treaty of Rome in 1957 and the creation of the European Union – but, sadly, without Britain.

Since those founding years – albeit more by accident than design – Europe has become the world's leading multilateral force. It kept alive the Kyoto protocol on climate change and the Comprehensive

Nuclear-Test-Ban Treaty. It helped to establish the International Criminal Court. And in supporting Labour government initiatives at the time, the European Union was also projecting its own values onto the global stage – values which involve nations working together and pooling their sovereignty in order to deliver a better world both at home and abroad for our citizens.

Europe's place in the world

The immediate challenge is for Britain to decide once and for all whether it really wants to become a true 'insider' and leader in Europe. For that will be impossible so long as our deeply ingrained scepticism always seems to triumph. Even Tony Blair's government – the most pro-European ever – was in a constant battle with the media and with a large section of the public, which sometimes led Downing Street (or more often the Treasury) to adopt sceptical anti-Brussels public postures under pressure from Rupert Murdoch, the *Daily Mail* and the *Telegraph*. And the government wasn't assisted at all by the frustratingly slow and difficult negotiations to reconfigure the EU institutions to cater for enlargement, which focused attention on institutional questions rather than policies, giving an impression of a 'Brussels bubble' indulging in seemingly permanent navel contemplation, obsessed with integrating rather than delivering, and in the process opening up a gulf with citizens and undermining Labour's pro-Europeanism.

Partly because of this there has been increasing disillusionment with the EU – and not simply in Britain. Over the 30 years since they were first staged, Europe-wide turnout in successive elections to the European Parliament fell from 63 per cent in 1979 to 43 per cent in 2009. The euro crisis precipitated a further decline in popular legitimacy, including in countries previously seen as pro-Europe. In France and Italy three quarters of citizens believed that economic integration was bad for their country, and the same proportion of Spaniards did not trust the EU.[1] It is salutary to recall that when the leaders of Europe went too far ahead of their citizens and proposed a new constitution, the treaty to enact it was rejected in 2005 referenda by the founding countries of France and the Netherlands, meaning it could not be ratified and fell.

Rapid EU expansion – from just six members in 1957 to 12 by 1986, 27 by 2007 and 28 by 2013 – was not matched by the pace of progress towards the Treaty of Rome's declared aim of 'ever closer union'. Lack of agreement between member states, such as on the EU budget, frustrated progress and delayed reform; qualified majority voting took 30 years to arrive and then only greased the wheels on specified issues; and the tendency of the European Commission to take the EU into new territory by triggering fresh initiatives before existing ones had delivered results only undermined the credibility of the European project, one that had long been spiced by lurid British press stories of an unaccountable Brussels gravy train. The eurozone's struggle to create a viable single currency testifies to what can happen when ambition runs too far ahead of accomplishment. All this has encouraged an upswell of xenophobia, Islamophobia, racism and fascist parties like Greece's Golden Dawn.

However, if at the end of the Second World War modern Europe's founders, Jean Monnet and others, had concluded that 80 years of bitter Franco-German hatred would make European unity impossible, then the following 60 years of Franco-German reconciliation and EU achievement would never have occurred. It is incumbent on our generation to find the means to take Europe forward.

Growth and power may be shifting fast to the East and the South from Europe and indeed the US. The EU may have become economically sluggish. It may have structural problems – including over-regulation, an ageing population and high unemployment. But it remains the biggest, richest economy in the world: 'The EU's GDP per capita in purchasing-power terms is still nearly four times that of China, three times Brazil's, and nearly nine times India's.'[2] It also spends the second largest amount on defence after the US. The leading European economy, Germany, is the strongest, most socially fair and economically efficient in the world. By 2014 there was also evidence of a reversal of Western decline and a shift back in jobs and investment, mainly because of structural problems in China and India together with their rising wage costs. So the fashion in Britain for writing off Europe is badly misjudged.

Europe's evolution

But how is greater European purpose to be achieved? The nation state rightly remains the bedrock of today's EU – its main challengers are separatists who want to create new breakaway states (Scotland, Catalonia, for instance) – and no other form of governance yet enjoys such legitimacy. But at the same time, capital has gone global. So we have to manage a complicated set of problems and deliver solutions through new partnerships. Europe's forefathers created the instrument. Pooling of national sovereignty for over 60 years in order to meet specific challenges has been the principle on which European unity has been built.

Step-by-step economic integration was the chosen route. So was building the habit of working together on the basis of shared goals, supranational institutions and common rules. The purpose was always to build greater political union from the bottom up, not one imposed from Brussels, which is why unanimity is rightly required for constitutional change. And why qualified majority voting – to prevent recalcitrant member states from blocking sensible reform – is limited to areas which Britain has agreed to, such as economic reform, which might otherwise be blocked out of self-interest.

Europe's first achievement was to remove the internal tariff barriers that held back growth and prosperity. Britain accepted that, especially with globalisation, our interests were best served by bringing down barriers. Britain, a trading nation, which itself has markets open to foreign competition, has everything to gain from the European Commission's work in safeguarding and extending the single market, thus giving British companies access to over 500 million customers and 21 million companies on our own doorstep generating £11 trillion in economic activity.

To many on the left, the emphasis on first creating a common market – dubbed a 'businessman's Europe' – originally seemed alien. However Europe's success in reconciling once bitter foes established the EU as a progressive force that consolidated peace, democracy and civil rights. The EU's successful enlargement in the 1980s to include Greece, Spain and Portugal – countries earlier under fascist dictatorships – and since 2004 to former Communist states of Central and Eastern Europe, have amply shown the EU's democratic strength.

What's more, as the EU's drive for a common market, then single market, brought with it 'flanking' policies to extend social, environmental and consumer rights, the its commitment to a distinctive European social model became evident. For all its faults – notably a slowness to embrace necessary economic reforms – Europe has proudly proclaimed a politics of building a 'market economy', but emphatically not a 'market society'. High-quality public services and social standards are Europe's benchmarks, not neoliberal free marketization. The common market brought common rules aimed at fairness and the protection of workers, consumers and the environment.

The core mission of the European Union is to ensure that we and our neighbouring countries work together in our common interests. We need access to the European market (the world's largest and richest, vital for our exports and jobs) and a voice at the table where the rules for that market are decided. We need those rules to provide for fairness, equal opportunities, consumer protection, respect for the environment and fair trade – not an unregulated free-for-all, dominated by the most powerful.

Growth not austerity

However, after the banking crisis the austerity agenda pressed by northern EU leaders upon Europe and especially the southern Mediterranean countries has been just as disastrous as the one in Britain.[3]

EU unemployment is very high – in 2013 standing at over 20 million, including 5 million young people – with its southern nations especially badly hit. Yet full employment and security for working people are realisable objectives within a more dynamic European economy. This means sharing best practice on raising rates of employment and participation, increasing skills, targeting investment on new technology and low-carbon enterprises to drive growth, reforming tax and welfare systems, promoting employability rather than protectionism and tackling social inclusion: that is the task for a new European social agenda.

Europe has its faults – but the remedy is to get in there, and argue for a reformed, stronger Europe, not for Britain to turn its back, or worse, walk away. Although it has become fashionable to criticise Euroland, its productivity per hour worked is far higher than Britain's; the workforce is more highly skilled; and public services like health and transport are frequently far superior.

The Continentals may have something to learn from Britain's better record on employability and its more flexible labour market. But we in Britain need to acknowledge that our employees are far less protected and share with Irish workers the highest sense of job insecurity in Europe[4] – and that brings with it not only injustice but also high social costs over the long term. We also have far more to learn from Europe's record of social infrastructure investment than we do from America, if we want all our people to succeed in a knowledge economy. American-style free-marketisation may have delivered higher productivity and growth in the US but at a cost of poor public services, crumbling infrastructure, low social standards, weak communities, endemic violence, a huge prison population and high poverty levels. That's not an agenda for a fair or successful Europe.

Nor should we shy away from changing EU policies that are wrong. The Common Agricultural Policy, which is both internally wasteful and works against the interests of the world's poor, is a prime example, even if recent reforms have made significant progress. But a Britain on the margins of Europe would not be in a strong position to change the CAP further and create more sustainable agriculture and rural communities. Without a full commitment to the EU, we will have less influence in determining the EU's position in the World Trade Organization negotiations; less ability to challenge the rigid intellectual property rules that favour multinationals against the people of the world's poorest countries; less clout to insist that the cause of world development should prevail over narrow vested interests. The long-term interests of our agriculture and industry will suffer as a result. The EU's leverage in trade talks to prise open markets in Asia and the Americas helps British exports. Leaving the EU would not only jeopardise Britain's access to the European market on our doorstep, it would require us to negotiate new trade agreements with every country in the world to replace the ones we currently have via the EU – and we would be doing so with far less weight.

Without a continuation of the concerted European approach on the question of the environment, Britain on its own will be unable to guarantee a sustainable future for our citizens. Because we are so close to the continent, clear skies, pure water, clean beaches and a healthy environment can only be delivered by cooperation at a European level.

Britain in Europe

Of all Europe's social democrats, the British Labour Party was the slowest to recognise the EU as a bulwark of the values it stands for. It is not just that around 3.5 million jobs and much of our present prosperity depend on the 50 per cent of our trade we conduct with Europe. Nor only that the jobs that depend on Europe are good jobs, for the most part offering decent pay and conditions in key manufacturing and service companies. It is not simply that almost half of all overseas investment in the UK comes from within the EU. Nor that Britain's prosperity depends upon our assured position in Europe's single market, underpinned by a successful euro and a growing European economy. Europe benefits British citizens much more than that. In the last 25 years, the greatest promoters of workers' rights, women's rights, rights for all against discrimination on grounds of race, gender, sexual orientation, age and disability, have been European directives and the judgments of the European Court of Justice, often forced on reluctant British governments. Tory 'reform' of Britain's terms of membership of the EU, and their threat to withdraw altogether, could cost working people all such rights as well as undermine our anti-discrimination rules. Europe has done at least as much to advance the principles of fair and equal treatment as any Labour government in Britain. It was the trade union movement which first recognised this in the 1980s and helped shift the Labour Party towards the pro-European stance it should always have adopted.

Throughout the long Thatcher/Major years of public spending restraint and cuts in the 1980s and 1990s, it was the EU that provided hope for devastated industrial communities and the former mighty cities of Britain's regions and nations, through the availability of Structural Funds.

Furthermore, without an effective European common policy on asylum and immigration, Britain on its own will fail to deliver on the dual imperatives of firm control at our borders and fair and equal treatment of all those properly entitled to settle here.

But there is nothing wrong in celebrating national achievement, a common national culture and a sense of national pride and identity, including on the sports field. On the contrary, we should all be proud to be British – and proud to celebrate British successes, just as we revel in Europe's victories over the US in golf's Ryder Cup and welcome the opening up of awards like the Man Booker Prize to authors writing in English from anywhere in the world. For patriotism is a noble value, not a narrow one. True patriots are also internationalists because they respect others' patriotism too. And patriotism should not be confused with the jingoism and national chauvinism – the narrow, reactionary, parochial and backward-looking British nationalism – of the Conservative right, UKIP and the BNP. Prejudice and intolerance are the Achilles heel of such nationalism, promoting the fantasy that Britain can pull up the drawbridge and declare 'ourselves alone' in such an interdependent world.

The best of British values are very different: community, mutual aid and mutual cooperation. And these values that democratic socialists share with the British people are also fundamentally European values: community, solidarity, social justice and cohesion, a fair chance in life for all. It is time we acknowledged that these British values are best realised with Britain at Europe's heart.

Some anti-EU Tories call for withdrawal and joining the North Atlantic Free Trade Agreement. Yet British trade with the EU is three times that with North America. We do over twice the trade with Holland that we do with major South East Asian economies. The rest of the EU buys three times the value of UK exports compared with the UK's next most important export partner, the US, equivalent to 15 per cent of UK GDP. The EU accounts for 48 per cent of the

UK's world trade (imports plus exports) despite having just 6 per cent of the world's population. Indeed UK exports to the EU have grown six times faster over the past ten years than UK exports to China.

The withdrawal fallacy

Those advocating British withdrawal suggest that we can have our cake and eat it by staying within the European single market to retain the great bulk of our trade which is with EU countries. This they see as avoiding, first, the costs of membership they denounce as too high, second, EU regulations which they insist make our economy uncompetitive, and third, the loss of sovereignty they allege comes with EU political union.

Inconveniently the facts are rather different. First, the 'price' of Britain's EU membership is rather more modest than the anti-Europeans would have us believe. The government contributed £7 billion to the EU in 2012, around 1 per cent of total UK public expenditure and equivalent to 0.4 per cent of GDP. (This was net of receipts from Brussels under the Common Agricultural Policy, EU regional funding, and the budget rebate.) And, although leaving the EU and rejoining the single market would cost Britain less, it would not be that much less. We would have to negotiate the kind of relationship enjoyed by Norway, the largest of the nations in the European Economic Area (EEA) we would presumably join. And entry to the EEA would cost Britain around £6 billion – £1 billion or 17 per cent less than for the EU,[5] but still high by comparison; and assuming our former EU partners, sore at our departure, would be in a generous frame of mind.

But, second, we would still be bound by the very regulations the EU-antis denounce. In return for access to the single market, Norway and other countries like Switzerland and Iceland must adopt nearly all EU legislation relevant to the free movement of goods, services, capital and people, together with laws in areas such as employment, consumer protection, environmental policy and competition. In practice, this means that the vast majority of the EU regulations identified by critics as the most burdensome to businesses, including the Working Time Directive, would still exist if the UK left the EU but remained a member of the EEA.

Britain would also be bound by *future EU law* in these areas. Crucially, however, because we would be outside the much reviled political union, we would have absolutely no say over the content of these regulations. In order to save under a fifth of the cost, we would be abandoning the voice Britain enjoys as a large, powerful EU member. That doesn't seem much of a bargain.

Nor, to pick on the third part of the withdrawal argument, does it mean an increase in UK 'sovereignty'. On the contrary, it would mean a loss. Having abandoned our seat at the negotiating table, the EU would be able to impose upon us pretty well whatever trading and single market rules it chose to. Indeed, because we would no longer have a voice the 'integrationist' tendency in the EU would strengthen, risking still more of the regulations EU critics maintain are so intrusive.

As a CBI report, *Our global future: The business vision for a reformed EU*, argued in 2013:

> 'One step removed' – the 'Norway option' of leaving the EU but remaining in the European Economic Area (EEA) – would reduce the UK to a 'standards taker' on the fringes of influence. Leaving the EU and opting for the Norway model of membership of the EEA would not solve many of the challenges some see with the UK's current relationship with the EU. Businesses would still have to follow EU rules – thereby leaving the regulatory burden in place – but the UK's ability to influence those rules would be removed by relinquishing the UK's seat at the table in Brussels.

The CBI report added that what it called 'Pick and choose' – the 'Swiss option' of bilateral agreements – might provide greater flexibility but it would certainly reduce market access and influence. The time it would take for the UK to renegotiate an agreement similar to the Swiss would mean a significant period of dislocation and uncertainty as negotiation took place. More importantly, however, there is no guarantee that the UK would achieve agreements on all its prioritised areas and, where it did, it would be likely to have to accept a package of EU-designed rules related to the single market in order to get market access.

The CBI report also dismissed a customs union – the 'Turkey option' – as the worst of the 'half-way' alternatives, leaving the UK with very limited EU market access and zero influence over trade deals. Retaining membership only of the customs union would be an inappropriate economic stance for the UK in the modern global economy. With non-tariff barriers often replacing tariffs as the major obstacle to trade, a customs union would not be sufficient to support Britain's trading ambitions in the modern global economy with its complex supply chains, and it could limit UK access to EU markets in areas such as services.

An advanced UK–EU Free Trade Agreement, while addressing some of the costs of EU membership, would fail to secure vital benefits for business. Although it is likely that, on exit, the UK could secure some form of bespoke trade deal with the EU, given the relative interdependence of the two economies, there is a large degree of uncertainty around the willingness of the EU to offer favourable terms to the UK that would fully support British business in its global ambitions. The EU's clout – offering a market of 445 million people to the UK's 64 million, with an economy around six times the size – gives it a stronger negotiating hand than the UK. Moreover, the UK is more dependent on the EU for its trade than the EU is on the UK – around half of the UK's total trade is with the EU while just 8 per cent of EU trade is with the UK.

Trade

Britain's trade with countries outside the EU is all conducted under the auspices of trading agreements negotiated centrally by Brussels, because the EU has exclusive competence to negotiate trade agreements with other countries. Although it means no EU member state can have its 'own' separate bilateral trade agreements, it gives each country, Britain included, much greater influence than on their own and prevents others applying measures in a way that discriminates against one particular country. Trade embargoes between countries do exist, but they are considered to be exceptional diplomatic measures, rather than a natural state of affairs. But the trade agreements negotiated by the EU, which provide for preferential access to other overseas markets, would no longer apply to the UK. Thus UK companies might face higher tariffs (and other trade barriers) when exporting to these countries.

Without a negotiated arrangement, the UK would become subject to tariffs that the EU imposes on goods entering from outside the Union. It might also face higher tariffs levied by other countries with which the EU has preferential trade agreements.

As the CBI report argued: 'going it alone' on the basis solely of membership of the World Trade Organization would reduce market access through increased tariffs on UK goods and services. Refraining from entering any formal relationship with the EU and simply relying on WTO rules is not a model that would assist Britain in achieving the global trading role to which it aspires.

Foreign direct investment

Although UK trade with Europe did rise before we entered the Common Market in January 1973, from 23 per cent of total UK trade in 1948 to 41 per cent in 1972, it had rocketed to 52 per cent by the end of the 1970s, and peaked at 59 per cent in the early 1990s. The rise of emerging markets has seen the EU's share decline but, even so, the EU currently remains the UK's most significant market by some distance: it was the destination for 45 per cent of all exports in 2012, and the establishment of the single market helped trade between the UK and the rest of the EU grow by 74 per cent in real terms from 1997 until 2006, the year before the financial crisis began.

But the benefit is not simply a UK-to-EU one. Many foreign direct investors locate in the UK mainly because it places them within the EU as well. For example, the UK is the preferred European destination for Japanese investments, and its government highlighted the UK's membership of the EU as a major reason why Japanese companies choose to invest in the UK. More than 1,300 Japanese companies have invested in the UK, as part of the EU single market, creating 130,000 jobs, more than anywhere else in Europe. This fact demonstrates that the advantage of the UK as a gateway to the European market has attracted Japanese investment. The government of Japan expects the UK to maintain this favourable role. Indeed the Chief Executive of Nissan told the BBC in November 2013 that if Britain left the EU, his company would have to 'reconsider' whether to maintain its huge factory in Sunderland, employing 6,500 people. Unilever warned in January 2014 that it would review its UK investment and the 7,000 jobs involved if Britain left the EU.

All in all, the 2013 CBI report estimated, every British household is £3,000 better off from membership. In 2013 a survey by the CBI of its own member businesses showed eight out of ten – including roughly the same proportion of their small and medium-sized enterprise members – wished the UK to remain a member of the EU; nearly three quarters reported that the UK's membership of the EU had had a positive overall impact on their business. Despite frustrations, over half of CBI member companies (52 per cent) said that they had directly benefited from the introduction of common European standards, with only 15 per cent suggesting this had had a negative impact. Indeed they believed that UK influence had helped maximise the openness of the EU; 72 per cent of British businesses believed that the UK currently had a significant influence on EU policies that affected their business. The City took much the same view: an Ipsos-MORI survey of 101 of Britain's financial sector executives published in October 2013 by City UK showed 84 per cent in favour of Britain staying at the centre of the EU.

British Europeans

But how did Britain get into the position where passions and politics about Europe are so polarised? We always were Europeans. Our monarchs interbred. Our people mixed and traded and travelled and lived across Europe. But when it came to the reconstruction of Western Europe after the Nazis were defeated, we half forgot we were Europeans. We did help devise the new German constitution. We did help set up the Council of Europe. We did help draft the European Convention on Human Rights. But we stood aside on the crucial

Monnet plan for a new European union. We imagined we could still cling onto the remnants of our empire, as if a rapidly changing Commonwealth could somehow be an alternative trading bloc for us to Europe. And so we missed out on the post-war reconstruction of continental Europe, in the process falling behind economically: victorious on the battlefield but defeated in the market.

Then came our belated, long and painful journey into modern Europe, until Conservative Prime Minister Edward Heath showed visionary leadership over Britain's 1973 entry. The idea that Europe's future lay in a loose, free-trade area was the British illusion of the 1950s: one that we had to admit would not work when we eventually (albeit unsuccessfully) applied for membership of the Common Market in 1961. Britain's other great historic mistake was not to help fill the vacuum left by the vanquishing of Stalinism. When the Berlin Wall fell and Europe faced the historic prospect of reunification and modernisation in the early 1990s, where was our government? Sulking, sidelined and irrelevant. When leadership was desperately needed, Britain was whingeing about Europe, throwing tantrums and threatening vetoes, not shaping it.[6] In the course of the last 30 years, Europe has moved beyond mere free-trade zones, to a customs union, then to a common market – with Britain resisting at first and then reluctantly agreeing. Next it moved to a single market with the advantages of free trade, across-the-board free movement of capital and labour, common safety and employment standards and a common competition policy.

No other European country would for a moment consider throwing away the benefits of a single market and the institutions that make it work. No other European people would for a moment consider giving up the clout that a 500 million-strong trading area gives Britain in world negotiations. Only a dogmatist would claim that overseas investment comes to Britain in spite of Europe rather than because of it.

British anti-Europeans have a mistaken view of British history harking back to the 19th century. They believe that Britain does best when detached in 'splendid isolation'. Not only is theirs a selective reading of Britain's role in Europe – our history shows that we have always been a European power – but in today's globalised world 'splendid isolation' looks more like 'ignominious irrelevance'.

Practical Europeanism

However, this is not to pretend that the other extreme is any better. Of course the nation state will remain the focus of our British identity and our loyalty. It is entirely right that the test of whether we want to be part of any future European venture is whether it is good for Britain: the same national interest test applied for themselves by every other member state.

Not everything emanating from Brussels is desirable. Much is unintelligible to the general public. We need plain language, not Eurobabble. At European Union summits, politicians and journalists are trapped in a security-cordoned bubble talking to each other. Then they talk the same 'summit speak' to a perplexed and alienated outside world:

> The Antici Group considers that agreement at the next GAC is crucial for the following IGC, so the troika and PSC must be consulted to get consensus amongst the Presidencies, especially over any extension of QMV in the second or third pillars, but then again ESDP could also be affected by action in the first pillar if the Commission intervenes through conciliation given the Parliament's right to co-decision with the Council.

OK – that is actually made up. But it's uncomfortably close to the real thing. The odd Eurovisionary may have dreamt of the day when there would be a single language across the continent. If this is it, we'd be better off with the Tower of Babel. We need a new popular language if we are to reconnect the European Union to its citizens, to show that we are in fact talking about the things that really matter – jobs and living standards, peace and security, social justice and the environment.

Despite this, young people are instinctively pro-European. They travel to Paris, Brussels and Berlin just as easily as to London,

Edinburgh and Cardiff, and to any and all European capitals of culture. They get by with the language, gaze at the galleries and gulp the wine. Millions of our football fans love the European Champions League. Yet our education system fails to inform our citizens about the supranational level of political representation, namely the European Union, of which they are a part. Ask them about the Council or the Commission or the Parliament and they are either barely familiar with them or reflect the generally hostile coverage in the British media. The very low turnout right across Europe in European elections underlines the big gap between the EU and the majority of its citizens. Perhaps people also grasp something about the significance of European institutions when they see top British Members of the European Parliament (MEPs) preferring to pursue political careers at Westminster instead, like Nick Clegg, Chris Huhne, Caroline Lucas, Wayne David, Geoff Hoon, or Ann Clwyd.

If it can actually be graced with the title 'debate', then the British debate on Europe is dominated by caricatures. There is no Brussels machine 'monstering' our lives. EU institutions are relatively small: they employ 47,500 people, 11 per cent of the size of the UK civil service. EU spending is 1 per cent of EU output, or less than a 40th of total EU member states' public spending.

Then there is the myth of being seduced into a European 'superstate'. A 'superstate' would have an elected central government. A parliament with the power to tax and determine public spending. A standing army. A foreign policy independent of its constituent states. The power to declare war. The kind of relationship with the nation states of Europe which the British government has with Wales, Scotland and England's regions.

None of this exists today and none of these changes could happen without the agreement of every member state. Britain shows no sign of wanting it. So we could veto it if we had to. But, more importantly, although some European leaders seem to advocate a 'superstate', other key ones don't want it either. More important still, the people of Europe don't want it. So we can win the argument for the right kind of Europe.

Let us also be more confident – and get more real – about our 'sovereignty'. Does getting more involved in Europe mean we will 'give up our sovereignty'? No, because there is a difference between 'giving up' and choosing to 'pool' sovereignty because this promotes British interests.

We have already 'given up' our right to do what we like in defending Britain because we are members of NATO – we already pool sovereignty with the US and others because by doing that Britain has stronger defences. Anybody attacking us invites retaliation by all the NATO nations. NATO shows that pooling sovereignty in appropriate policy areas can make nations stronger. So does the European Union.

So also does the United Nations. Just seventy years ago we 'gave up' our right to do simply what we liked over foreign policy by agreeing to establish the UN Security Council. Its resolutions have the force of international law. Everyone, including Britain has to respect them. However, as a permanent member of the Security Council, we get to make the laws. We pool sovereignty in the World Trade Organization and the International Monetary Fund and in international treaties which, for example, ban anti-personnel landmines. By pooling sovereignty, the British people have greater influence in building a safer, more stable world.

Pooling sovereignty can mean compromises. This is sometimes hard for some commentators and politicians to understand. But real people know that in real life we cannot always get exactly what we want. Nor can other countries in these international bodies. We can better advance British interests by being right at the centre of NATO or the UN – and indeed the EU.

This doesn't take away our sovereignty. It strengthens it. In today's global village, power shared means power regained. For instance, on foreign policy: Britain alone can do a lot, but Britain and the rest of Europe can do much more. On trade we live in a global marketplace. Opening it up further depends on our clout in world trade negotiations: only the EU collectively has that clout. And only the EU has the clout to protect Britain's own interests when our exporters meet unfair competition.

If we left the European single market, we could have total power over our own market. But we would have less power to export to other EU member states – or to help shape the world's biggest single market of over 500 million people. Switzerland out of the EU has had to adjust its laws and finances to conform to EU norms. Being outside the EU would mean abiding by EU rules with no say in making them. Acid rain and pollution cannot be stopped by immigration officers at Dover. If we really want power over our environment, we need to share decision making with our EU partners.

But to reject Euroscepticism doesn't mean embracing Europhilism. More of Europe isn't always the right answer. There are areas where more European action is desirable: tougher efforts to fight cross-border crime and people trafficking, for example. There are plenty of other areas such as taxation where decisions must be taken in London by our Parliament, not in Brussels.

Trying to drive the EU from the top down on a cocktail of high-octane Europhilia would soon leave us running on empty. Europhiles are often too Eurocentric, forgetting that the EU isn't the world – for example, that it is just as important to have an open trading relationship with the rest of the globe as it is within the EU; that the US is simultaneously a trading partner, a commercial competitor, a technological rival and a military ally but not a security threat; that while ever more institutional tinkering may be fascinating to those within the 'Brussels bubble', there are much bigger challenges out there: like remaining competitive against Asia, eradicating world poverty, or stopping global warming destroying our planet.

The Eurosceptics are not living in the real world either. Many say we should not be in Europe at all; others that we shouldn't be in this kind of Europe. We are in Europe. Look at a map. Read a history book. We can either influence Europe or simply be influenced by it. Inside the EU we do the first. Outside, we'd do the second. Inside the EU all partners' views are heard before decisions are reached. Outside, our neighbours could turn a deaf ear to British concerns. It's a choice between a two-way street or a no through road, not between life in the slow lane in a congested Brussels Boulevard and full speed ahead on a British open road. It's a Europe in which all the key Western European nations are already members of the EU. An EU which our eastern and southern neighbours have either all joined or cannot wait to do so. A club that everyone else wants to join cannot be that bad.

Of course the EU is very far from perfect. It would have been better had we joined at the start and helped shape it then. But it is the only one we have got. If you want to reform it, you have to be in it, putting the case, winning the argument.

Like David Cameron's posturings, Margaret Thatcher's rantings were ignored in Brussels and Paris and Bonn. She and her sceptics failed to influence any other government's thinking on Europe and failed to reform the Commission and the other institutions. Perhaps we should also remember that it was she who signed the Single European Act, in February 1986, which created a single European market – one of the biggest acts of European integration – and extended qualified majority voting. Her Conservative successor, John Major, signed the Maastricht Treaty – another huge act of integration – which created the European Union and led to the single European currency, the euro. But his 'empty chair' policy failed to prevent the ban on British beef imposed in 1996 amid concern over BSE, the human form of mad cow disease. It took Tony Blair, with his policy of positive engagement, to get it lifted.

In government between 1997 and 2010, Labour demonstrated that being pro-EU and pro-reform is a strategy that works. Britain may not always have got its way – nor did any other member state. But Labour's approach of 'practical Europeanism' consistently won the day over those European leaders obsessed about ever-intrusive integration.

Moreover, as Richard Corbett pointed out in 2014, there is not so much a two-tier Europe of British folklore, more a multi-tier, variable Europe to accommodate different member states' particular interests.[7] Ten member states are not (or not yet) in the eurozone. The UK and Czech Republic are outside the Stability Treaty, that is to say, outside the fiscal compact governing almost all EU members. The UK, Ireland, Cyprus and (so far) Romania and Bulgaria are outside the Schengen zone with its absence of internal EU border controls. The UK, Ireland and Denmark do not participate in all areas of the Area of Freedom, Security and Justice (AFSJ). The UK and Poland have a protocol to the Charter of Fundamental Rights restricting its impact upon their domestic law. Denmark is not in defence cooperation and has an exemption from the single market affecting residencies. Spain and Italy lie outside the unified EU patent system and 12 states are outside divorce law cooperation. All this demonstrates the EU's practical, give-and-take approach – a far cry from the rigid monolith of Eurosceptic nightmares.

European reform

The substantial reform the EU needs is more likely to be delivered from a pro-EU Labour stance than an anti-EU Tory position.[8] Agriculture and fisheries policy needs major reform. We also need some very discernible safeguards to reassure our citizens that we will not countenance – and nor is it in the EU's interest to create – a centralised superstate. It is in Britain's national interest to remain in the EU and support its constant reform. Ours should be a hard-headed, patriotic case, founded both on Britain's national interest and on the wider European interest, for positive change in Europe.

For instance, Labour helped improve national parliamentary scrutiny of European affairs by securing a treaty requiring that EU proposals have to go first to national parliaments, giving them eight weeks to instruct their ministers before they go to Brussels to negotiate. We could do what the Scandinavian countries do, and require any minister going to an EU meeting to come beforehand to Parliament for big issues, either in the Chamber or to specialist Parliamentary Select Committees like the Danes do, and to the European Scrutiny Committee for routine issues, to explain what is at stake and any 'red lines', so that there is accountability for broad policy, even if the detail would inevitably be subject to negotiation.

Of course, a common market needs some common rules in order to work properly and indeed fairly, not least over consumer protection and basic workplace rights to prevent a race to the bottom on employment conditions or health and safety. That was why in May 1997 the incoming Labour government sent Minister for Europe Doug Henderson to Brussels on his first full day in office 'to sign the social chapter'. But EU regulations are too often excessive and over-prescriptive and Labour subsequently negotiated a protocol to limit the application in the UK of various economic and social rights in the EU Charter of Fundamental Rights, part of the Lisbon Treaty.

When Labour was in power we strengthened safeguards against such intrusiveness. We managed to establish a procedure to prevent the EU straying beyond its remit, by building in a test for 'subsidiarity' in the treaties. National parliaments (even if their government does not agree) can object to European Commission proposals that go beyond the remit of the EU (known as the 'yellow card' procedure).

The Lisbon Treaty Labour helped negotiate specifies explicitly that the EU only has those competences conferred upon it by the member states. And it ensures that EU competences can flow two ways, not just to the centre, but can be devolved back to national governments. EU legislation now needs approval by the European Parliament as well as by national government ministers in the European Council – a double-check on anything the EU adopts. The Council must now discuss legislation and vote in public and the results of its votes must be published. There is now a 'freedom of information' right of access to EU documents. And the EU can now be challenged in the courts if it fails to respect fundamental rights.

All these safeguards were pressed for by Labour and secured – and they should be built upon. For example, the 'yellow card' procedure was triggered for the first time only in 2012, and the Commission immediately withdrew its proposal. But the second time – over a proposal for a European Public Prosecutor in late 2013 – the Commission decided to ignore the yellow card. Therefore why not get the Commission to recognise that it is in practice normally a 'red card' procedure? After all, if a third of national parliaments oppose a measure, it is unlikely to get past the ministers, representing those same parliaments, in the Council, where at least 74 per cent of the votes are needed (and in sensitive cases unanimity) for approval.[9]

Other new safeguards are needed. It should be made easier to repeal EU legislation that is out of date or has not worked as intended. If a simple majority of member states in the Council or of MEPs in the European Parliament request it, then the Commission should automatically bring forward a proposal for repeal. When the EU is legislating for the first time in a new field, there should be a prior discussion of a Green Paper in national parliaments ahead of the Commission drafting any specific proposals. Proposals for new legislation should be withdrawn if no agreement is reached on them after a reasonable period of time. Legislation should more frequently have either a review clause or a sunset clause. The requirement for impact assessments for any new EU legislative proposal, introduced under Labour, must be applied vigorously. The 'yellow card' procedure should cover 'proportionality' – that is to say: 'Is it too intrusive?' – and not simply 'subsidiarity', 'Should it be at the EU or national level?'. The European Parliament should hold public hearings and questioning of candidates for key EU posts: it already does for the Commission, so why not do the same for other key appointments? We should not take on trust the nominees from each country (for example Special Representatives) without checking their qualifications, because there can be a 'Buggins' turn' element here or member state leaders can use these appointments for patronage or reward.

Sometimes less, sometimes more Europe

Where EU cooperation impedes our interests we should support bringing powers back to Britain. But where it could take them forward, the EU should do more, for instance through cooperation on tackling climate change or on fighting transnational crime and tax evasion.[10]

The EU should focus on where it brings added value, not try to intrude everywhere. For instance, Labour should be proud to have negotiated the setting up of the European Arrest Warrant, enabling Britain to secure the speedy return of fugitive criminal and terrorist suspects who attempt to flee our justice.

The European single market needs deepening in the areas where obstacles still hinder cross-border competition, such as in service industries, especially digital. Labour helped negotiate the Services Directive to deal with this, but it has not been fully implemented. Britain should do more to back British businesses by pressing for full implementation of this directive across Europe, instead of seeking to undermine the single market by allowing countries to ignore or opt out of its rules.

Everyone claims to want to fight tax fraud, tax evasion and tax avoidance. They are not only grossly unfair to honest citizens who pay their taxes, they are also now of such a magnitude that they dramatically impact upon government budget deficits. But, because of the high volume of cross-border transactions, fighting them requires international action. This is an area where more effective action by the EU could save us billions of pounds, especially if it were coupled with support from the UK and Germany for a 'Robin Hood tax' on financial transactions at EU level. Common rules on transparency, automatic exchange of information between national tax authorities, police cooperation on international frauds and scams, action on tax havens, plugging the loopholes in the EU Savings Taxation directive by extending it to cover investment funds and innovative financial instruments, developing the Quick Reaction Mechanism to fight cross-border VAT fraud, and other collaborative mechanisms could pay huge dividends to Britain and our EU partners.

EU spending should be cut where it doesn't give value for money. In government, Labour managed to reduce spending on the Common Agricultural Policy from half of the budget to one third, but negotiations in 2013 backed away from a proposal for a further significant reduction. For the future, the CAP should be co-financed with the recipient member states – like every other area of EU spending: why should agriculture alone be fully financed from the EU and not from beneficiary countries? Why should the biggest landowners get a subsidy based simply on the size of their land? Why should the EU budget be loaded in favour of agriculture when it would be better spent on encouraging economic growth through investment in infrastructure, energy and innovation? The EU budget should also be used for items where spending at EU level can save money at national level, for instance by avoiding duplications on research and development programmes, or where pooling resources can make them more effective through economies of scale.

The critical area of energy supply is where European countries share common problems of external dependency, high costs, and environmental challenges. Deepening the EU's single market in gas and electricity would cut costs and encourage more efficient use of resources. Energy security would be enhanced through developing trans-European connections.

Of course, Britain and its EU partners should not be the only countries taking tough measures to fight climate change: action at world level is needed. Here, the EU can be of double importance: through its collective leverage in international negotiations and in setting standards through its own rules as the world's largest market.

There is no point in denying that for Britain, internal European migration has become highly controversial, undermining popular backing for the EU. Significant numbers of people come from other EU countries to work in Britain – like over 26,000 NHS workers, including over 13,000 doctors[11] – and over 2 million Britons work or live in other EU countries. All enjoy certain rights, but also obligations. For this to work, it is important to ensure that the public can see that the system is fair, is not subject to abuse, and does not place burdens on local communities without the means to deal with these burdens. That is why proper enforcement of British laws (including employment law and the minimum wage, to prevent unscrupulous employers exploiting migrants and undercutting British workers) is essential. That is also why it is right to reform the rules enabling EU citizens easily to obtain benefits on coming to Britain – although to do so without infringing the basic principle of free movement of labour.

With more countries joining the EU, it is important to prevent its institutions and bureaucracy getting bigger and bigger. In government, Labour successfully negotiated a ceiling on the size of the European Parliament and of various advisory bodies like the Committee of Regions. With more countries joining, still more could be done. The proliferation of specialist agencies should be looked at with a view to reducing their number through mergers, and cutting the size of their supervisory bodies.

There is still much more to do and much more that is wrong with the EU. And the way to get the changes Britain wants is not to rant from the terraces – it is to be on the pitch, mid-field, shaping the play: right in there, helping to run Europe, not outside running away from Europe.

Always remembering, however, that, as Roger Liddle so cogently argued:

The British case for Europe is normally made in terms of a narrow economic calculus of our national interests in the single market. These arguments remain valid, but they do not stir the soul. Rather the argument for Europe should be an integral part of the argument for a progressive alternative for Britain. As part of making a historic break with over three decades of neo-liberal political economy, Britain should take a decisive 'European Turn'.[12]

CHAPTER 10

Refounding Labour

It was a world so different that it's hard to comprehend today how politics once was. No telephones let alone smart ones and the internet. No radios let alone television. No cars to speak of. Networks meant the telegraph, connections meant the railways, and communications meant newspapers or the postal service. No Humphrys, no Dimblebys and no Paxman, and definitely no Warks, Montagues or Husains, to interrogate politicians on air. Politics was communicated face to face, mainly by mass meeting or small local gathering, and by letter or pamphlet, not text or email. Although these were the days before the sound bite, rhetoric mattered, and politicians had to campaign and to speak in the community or go unheard.

Nevertheless, the basic structures and constitutions of political parties in Britain and elsewhere in the democratic world were formed in that very age a century ago – and still survive in their fundamentals. So in the case of the Labour Party at least, reminding ourselves about the context in which these fundamentals were established in 1918 could provide some understanding as to how Labour should be forging its future.

That year was a cathartic moment for the party because it needed to change, to reach out to an electorate that had nearly trebled since the 1910 general election and now included 6 million women voters. And it did so by adopting a new constitution and a fresh policy programme.

The 1918 constitution aimed to transform what had hitherto been a narrow sectional group into a broad national party with deep local roots. Henceforth, instead of being just a federation of trade unions plus a few socialist and cooperative societies, it would also include individual members organised in constituency parties. As well as taking Labour's message to voters, these local parties were intended to become Labour's link with local communities. It was hoped that recruiting large numbers of individual members would keep constituency parties in touch with the concerns and ambitions of their local electorates and ensure that Labour remained representative of the people whom it sought to serve and whose support it needed to win elections.

By the time that Tony Crosland became an MP in the 1950s, first for South Gloucestershire, then for Grimsby, local Labour parties looked like their electorates. You could refer to Labour's 'massed ranks' with good cause. Some local parties had huge memberships. The biggest were Woolwich and Faversham, each with several thousand individual members plus active affiliated trade union branches, successful fund-raising schemes, a full-time organiser, and local halls where political meetings, fish and chip suppers, jumble sales and kids' Christmas parties could be held.

Although some up-and-coming Labour MPs had a colourful wartime background – Denis Healey and Tony Crosland had fought in Italy, Dick Crossman had served in the Political Warfare Executive, and Roy Jenkins had been a code-breaker at Bletchley Park – at grassroots level Labour looked like Oliver Cromwell's 'plain russet-coated captains'. It was a mainly working-class party, since working-class voters far exceeded the professional middle class. Plenty of Labour MPs had been manual workers in the mines and factories and kept their authentic accents, attitudes and concerns. They brought working-class experience and aspiration to the House of Commons – unlike today, when a more common complaint is about the spectatorship of the proletariat in the Parliamentary Labour Party, with working-class people on the outside looking in.

These were the days when it mattered which way a Labour Party Conference vote went and when the trade union block vote counted, though it was usually cast in support of the party leader after deals had been done in literally smoke-filled rooms. The party was run by the elected National Executive Committee, not the party leader's office. Most of the party's funds came from union affiliation fees and donations, not from rich donors, and decisions were usually made openly and collectively in committee rooms – sometimes on the floor of conferences – not fixed behind the scenes.

A hundred years after Britain's Labour Party adopted a new constitution and new structures in 1918 another renewal is required because in Britain the manner in which politics has changed poses a fundamental challenge for Labour (and for that matter *all* our parties). Right across Europe, '*both* extreme lows in turnout *and* extreme peaks in volatility have been recorded since 1990 in almost all of the long-established European democracies', and 'membership levels in absolute numbers have been nearly halved since 1980.'[1]

A worryingly compelling analysis by the political scientist Peter Mair should be a wake-up call for all concerned to sustain a healthy democracy. Mair concludes:

> Parties ... might well be accepted by citizens as necessary for the good functioning of politics and the state, but they are neither liked nor trusted ... although the trappings of party government may persist, the conditions for its maintenance as a functioning governmental mode are now at serious risk.

He adds:

> state subventions to political parties have compensated for the inability of parties to raise sufficient resources from their own members and supporters ...At the same time, citizens withdraw from parties and a conventional politics that no longer seem to be part of their own world: traditional politics is seen less and less as something that belongs to the citizens or to the society, more and more as something done by politicians ... Citizens change from participants into spectators, while the elites win more and more space in which to pursue their own particular interests. The result is the beginning of a new form of democracy, one in which the citizens stay at home while the parties get on with governing.'[2]

Recent trends in Britain

All that has ominous lessons for Labour. To begin with, the two-party model, for generations dominated by a Labour–Conservative duopoly, is bust. Fundamental changes in British politics mean Labour must change radically in order to lead progressive opinion and win consistently in the future.

Fewer voters are wedded to one of the main parties these days. In the 1950s and 1960s Labour and the Tories regularly took 90 per cent of the vote. That dropped to 75 per cent in the mid-1970s. And it dropped further at each of the four general elections to 2010: by then only 67 per cent voted for the main parties.

The marked decline of the traditional 'core voter' attached to a particular party is reflected in volatile opinion polls. For Labour, as for the Conservatives, the solid group of core supporters who will always vote – provided of course that the party can persuade them to go to the polls – has been getting smaller.

This crisis of confidence in British politics is demonstrated most vividly by the dramatic decline in voter *turnout*. In the 1951 general election over 80 per cent of the electorate voted, plummeting to a mere 65 per cent in 2010.

The pervasive public disaffection with politics is also evident in the decline in the proportion of the *electorate* voting for the majority parties. In 1951 the Tories won most seats (though with fewer votes than Labour), receiving 40 per cent of the electorate's votes. In 1964 Labour won with 34 per cent of the electorate, and the trend continued even in the momentous landslide elections of 1979 and 1997, with the Tories on 33 per cent in 1979 and Labour on 31 per cent in 1997. By 2010, the Tories, as the largest party, could claim to have the support of only 23.5 per cent of the electorate; just over half of what they had in 1951.

This mass withdrawal from elective politics, by large swathes of the population, has serious implications for the legitimacy and credibility of government in the United Kingdom. A new model of party politics is required to reconnect our political institutions to the people they are established to serve.

There has been a common pattern, first with the serious Conservative defeat in 1997 and then the equally serious Labour defeat of 2010, both after long periods in government.

After 1979 – and despite winning general elections – the Tories initially lost their local councillors, then their members and then finally their voters at the election of 1997. This haemorrhaging of support left them so hollowed out by 2010 that the Tories took office on a historically low base for a governing party. Their vote had been stuck for nearly two decades, inching up painfully slowly from a dreadful low of 30.7 per cent of the votes cast in 1997 to 31.7 per cent in 2001, then to 32.4 per cent in 2005 and finally to just 36.1 per cent in 2010.

In other words – despite facing Gordon Brown, an unpopular Prime Minister, and a Labour Party that had lost the public's trust, mainly by virtue of being in office during the worst banking crisis for 80 years – not only did the Tories fail to win, they managed to gain a mere 5 per cent over 13 years following their landslide defeat in 1997.

Apart from when the Tories nosedived under Tony Blair's leadership of Labour, David Cameron achieved the third lowest number of Tory votes since 1931 – and that despite a significant population rise in the meantime. He also polled the lowest Tory percentage of the electorate since 1918.

Intelligent Conservative commentators, such as Lord Ashcroft, or Tim Montgomerie in *The Times*, have acknowledged this and demanded root-and-branch change in their own party. Labour's task is to deliver our version of that change, because Labour's recent story has been similarly ominous. Despite impressive achievements of the last Labour government during at least the decade before the banking crisis, the party lost thousands of councillors, over 200,000 members and 5 million voters – heavily losing the general election. By May 2010 the party activist base had been seriously depleted and many members were deeply disillusioned with what they felt had been turned by New Labour into an ideology-free zone, a party dominated by careerist professional politicians with the same narrow university and MP's assistant background. Only tenacious or transformative campaigns, particularly in the key seats, and the abject lack of Conservative Party credibility, masked a dismal 29.7 per cent share of the votes cast.

Defying the millions poured into marginal constituencies by Lord Ashcroft, many Labour Party activists performed heroically. In the bitter battle of Barking, the British National Party leader was trounced by an enthusiastic Labour campaign led by the sitting MP Margaret Hodge and supported by hundreds of Unite Against Fascism activists. In a dozen other constituencies Labour MPs were also re-elected against the odds, suggesting that in the new politics it is possible to defy even a big *national* swing with different *local* campaigns.

The hallmarks of these campaigns, be they Oxford East, Islington South or Bethnal Green and Bow, Edinburgh South or Birmingham Edgbaston, were twofold: first a large activist base drawn not just from party members but usually representing more supporters than members in their volunteer ranks. Second, a professionally organised, ruthlessly focused campaigning effort on a mix of local issues that demonstrated differentiation not just with the national party but with the broader anti-politics mood of voters at large. Taken together this allowed local campaigns to buck national forces.[3]

Changing political culture

The whole political culture of Britain has been changing massively. While the two major parties, Labour and Conservative, saw declines in both support and membership from the early 1950s, other parties grew. Until they joined the Tories in a coalition government after 2010, the Liberal Democrats were the overwhelming beneficiaries of the decline of the Tories and Labour.

Additionally, the Greens performed strongly in the 1989 European elections, gaining 2 million votes and a 15 per cent share of the vote, and by 2013 they had 141 local councillors and their first Member of Parliament.

The British National Party gained two European MPs in the 2009 European elections, and had for a time 55 councillors and two London Assembly members. UKIP, the United Kingdom Independence Party, surged in the 2009 European elections, polling more individual votes (2,498,226) than Labour (2,381,760) and winning the same number of seats (13). After falling back in the 2010 general election, UKIP surged even higher as it won the 2014 European elections, winning more MEPs than any other party (24 to Labour's 20) and receiving 4,375,635 individual votes to Labour's 4,020,646, with the Tories trailing behind in third place and the Liberal Democrats almost wiped out.

The 2014 elections, both European and for local councils, revealed a 'plague on all your houses' stance by the electorate, with UKIP able to capitalise on that anti-politics mood very effectively. So for three decades did the Lib Dems – before they sold their souls in government with the Tories.

Leaving aside UKIP's reactionary politics and plain bigotry, the writing should have been on the wall for the main parties and the pundits. Tory defectors to UKIP expressed a visceral, ideological distrust of their former party and its leadership – a deep sense of betrayal. White working-class Labour defectors were protesting against the political establishment which for the last couple of decades they felt had let them down, especially on secure, decently paid jobs and the lack of affordable housing, many viewing the culprits as immigrants taking cut-price jobs and crowding out housing.

The high point of the Tory/Labour ascendancy in British politics was in 1951, when 97 per cent of the votes cast were for Tory or Labour, but that had collapsed to two thirds by 2010: its lowest since 1922 when Labour first emerged as the main opposition to the Tories.

There is no evidence that this will easily be reversed and there are several reasons for that, not least the increasing number and frequency of elections. In the past people voted every four years or so in a general election and for their local council, often on the same day. Now there are five-yearly European elections, annual elections for multiple layers of local government in many parts of England, and elections every four or five years for devolved institutions in Wales, Scotland, London and Northern Ireland – with mayoral elections to boot. And, to compound voter fatigue, there were in 2012 elections for new Police Commissioners too (albeit on a miserable turnout in the low twenties).

The more opportunities people had to vote for different bodies or posts, the more politically promiscuous they became. The Lib Dems were for decades the first main beneficiaries, but UKIP, the Greens, the BNP, Plaid Cymru and the Scottish National Party also enjoyed increased votes. Once people broke the habit of a lifetime by voting neither Labour nor Tory, they were more likely to look elsewhere again and it became much harder to win them back, even at a general election.

The decline of the 'core voter', wedded to one particular party, shows up in opinion polls. Labour, like the two other main parties, can no longer depend on a solid group of firm supporters who will always vote loyally providing the party can convince them to go to the polling station. Past voting patterns count for less and less. People need a reason to place their cross against the Labour candidate's name.

Furthermore, some people started to vote for different parties at different elections. In Wales, for example, significant numbers voted Labour in a general election, Plaid for the Welsh Assembly and Lib Dem or Independent for their local councillor. People started to mix and match, enjoying greater choice and seemingly liking the idea of politicians having to work together.

Compounding the decline in core voter numbers is a decline in the number of *swing voters* – those voters choosing between the two main parties. For as the number of voters loyal to each party diminishes those voters that remain with the main parties tend to be more ideologically committed to them. This means that the incentives to appeal to voters of another party persuasion en masse is less in the 2010s then it was in the 1990s. But the mathematical need to convert such voters to win seats remains – which means that, even more important than broad-based appeals to voters of the other party through mass media, there is a need to convert such voters through direct voter contact. Community campaigns around local issues can be an excellent means of achieving such conversion in spite of the national political environment – Birmingham Edgbaston in the run-up to 2010 being a prime example; it was won for Labour in the face of a national swing that should ordinarily have installed a Tory MP.

The introduction of individual voter registration, rather than a member of the household registering all eligible within it, will almost certainly widen the gaping gulf between voters and parties. The experience of Northern Ireland, where turnout fell by 10 per cent after the introduction of individual registration, and of Canada where there was also a decline in turnout after the adoption of the policy, suggests that public participation in political life is set to decline. The Electoral Commission is concerned that it will particularly disenfranchise those whose first language is not English or who live in private rented accommodation; namely ethnic minorities, the young and those living on the minimum wage or less – Labour's natural constituency. A high percentage of these groups are already not registered to vote. A case study published by the Electoral Commission in 2010 found that 49 per cent of private sector tenants, 56 per cent of 17–24-year-olds and 31 per cent of black and minority ethnic citizens were not registered. Due to individual registration this is likely to decline by a further 10 per cent; 10 per cent, including the most disadvantaged people in our country, removed from the register.

A December 2011 report by the Commission found that at least 6 million people in Great Britain were not registered to vote after the yearly household canvass in autumn 2010, compared to an estimate of 3.9 million after the 2000 canvass. It also found that 56 per cent of 19–24-year-olds were registered compared with 94 per cent of those aged over 65, that 77 per cent of people from black and minority ethnic communities were registered compared with 86 per cent of white people, and that 56 per cent of people living in private rented homes were registered compared with 88 per cent for homeowners.[4]

Chris Ruane MP fears that we may end up with overall registration rates as low as 65 per cent: 'like Alabama in the 1950s', he says, when black Americans were prevented from voting. This would be a moral outrage as well as a looming political catastrophe for the Labour Party. Furthermore the efforts of local authorities to militate against this effect may well be hindered by the astronomical cost of canvassing individuals to sign up, instead of households: an increased cost of nearly 50 per cent has been estimated by one authority.

It should also be remembered, of course, that a depleted electoral register has wider consequences beyond reduced turnout. The non-registered are not summoned for jury service. Incomplete registers also skew the drawing of constituency boundaries and the calculations for government grants to local councils.

When life is tough and hectic, registering to vote – that fundamental democratic right and responsibility – needs to be made as easy as possible. The Tory/Lib Dem government's approach, which included a proposal to drop the threat of a £1,000 penalty for not registering, makes voting just another choice in a consumer society which is easier to make the better-off you are. Paradoxically, a policy with the stated purpose of restoring credibility to our electoral system is likely to further discredit it.[5] It is in this light that the failure of Labour to live up to Ed Miliband's 2012 promise of 'the largest voter registration drive in a generation' is particularly acute.[6]

Multiparty government

All this points to majority single-party government becoming the exception rather than the norm in future, or at least until there is another sea change. That in turn means Labour needs to fight harder than ever for every vote in order to win elections.

But it also means the party must accept that coalition politics may become a semi-permanent fixture in British parliamentary democracy, just as it has in local government.

In which case, it is essential that coalition politics be enacted a lot better than under the Cameron/Clegg government, which made it a byword for broken promises, unpopularity and incompetence. If it is the will of the people that no party should govern alone, they deserve a more mature approach to coalition government, and that means Labour radically rethinking the way the party does politics.

By joining the Conservatives on an agenda that repudiated all their long-held claims to progressive credentials, the Liberal Democrats gave up, if not forever then for at least a generation, their niche as the 'anti-politics' party – and thus their ability to tap the growing reservoir of disaffected British voters. By promising to abolish and then instead trebling student fees they also lost the youth vote – rather as Labour did after Iraq. So the Lib Dems face a difficult future.

Nevertheless there is no reason to suppose that the two main parties will bounce back to their previous hegemony. Some of the anti-politics vote the Lib Dems attracted has been going elsewhere, in particular to UKIP and the Greens. The crisis in Europe and the fault line in the Tories also means opportunities for UKIP. As highly rated political scientist John Curtice has persuasively argued, 'the hung parliament brought about by the 2010 election was no accident. It was a consequence of long-term changes in the pattern of party support that mean it is now persistently more difficult for either Labour or the Conservatives to win an overall majority.'[7]

To achieve a more grown-up approach to this new politics, Labour should learn from the lessons of the 2010 talks where the party was ill prepared.[8] Back channels with potential partners, preparatory research on areas of policy crossover and clarity on 'red lines' in advance of general election campaigns will become a necessity. Labour should also learn from the success of the German SPD's 'festival of internal democracy' in 2013, and debate and vote on any coalition agreement so as to ensure maximum party legitimacy for any deal.

Councillors and communities

Labour's 2010 general election defeat followed years of poor local election results. For instance, in local government elections between 2006 and 2009, Labour lost over 1,400 local council seats in England and Wales and 161 in Scotland. The Tories gained over 1,700 council seats and 69 councils to hold nearly half of all council seats, with Labour holding less than a quarter: a total of some 4,500 Labour councillors in the UK facing well over 9,000 Tories.

Losing council seats weakens any party's ability to keep in touch with communities, undermines its contact networks, and deprives it of a platform from which to promote the party's cause. Critically, it weakens local party organisation, on which all effective election campaigns depend: each councillor has a network of friends, relatives and community contacts beyond their local ward members – 'supporters' if you like. Once a councillor loses an election, that network invariably goes and is replaced by a rival one.

It is notable that through their 'community politics' strategy adopted in the early 1970s,[9] the Liberals first won local council ward seats, then advanced into neighbouring wards and finally took parliamentary seats, their meagre total of six MPs in 1970 rising ten times to a high of 62 in 2005 followed by 57 in 2010.

Meanwhile 20 years of European elections saw Labour's share of the vote fall by nearly two thirds: from 43 per cent in 1994 to 26 per cent in 1999, 22 per cent in 2004, reaching a pitiful 16 per cent in 2009. This was from a party that claimed in government to be 'a leading partner in the European Union' and which Bill Clinton once described as the most formidable political fighting force in Europe.

The record shows that the worse Labour did in *all* elections the weaker the party organisation became and the more daunting the subsequent electoral challenge.

General elections, which used to be two-horse races, gave way to kaleidoscopic contests where Labour took on Tories, Lib Dems, Welsh and Scottish nationalists, UKIP and the BNP, plus Greens – and of course 'Independents' in local government elections. Elections have become much more complicated affairs in which Labour has to work harder to win every vote.

Supporters not joiners

Since the 1950s membership of political parties has been in decline across Europe's established democracies. Nevertheless the UK has one of the lowest rates of party membership of all. The 1.5 per cent of the electorate who belonged to parties in the UK in 2001 compared to nearly 5 per cent elsewhere in Europe in the late 1990s.

By 2005 only 1.3 per cent of UK voters were members of any of the three main political parties, plummeting from nearly 4 per cent in 1983. Labour's individual membership fell steadily throughout the postwar era: from 900,000 in 1951, 800,000 in 1964, 670,000 in 1979, 300,000 in 1983, 400,000 in 1997, to a low of just 150,000 in 2010 – a huge percentage fall of 80 per cent. The collapse of Tory membership over the same period was no less catastrophic: from 2.6 million in 1951, 1.7 million in 1964, 1.1 million in 1979, 1 million in 1983, 0.5 million in 1997 to just 0.25 million in 2010 – an even bigger percentage fall of 90 per cent. The Liberal fall over the same period was from a high of 250,000 in 1964 to 50,000.

Perhaps the way all parties defined membership before 1980 exaggerated their figures; that is certainly the view of the House of Commons Library. Maybe higher subscription fees caused all parties to lose members. Or maybe more people find that party political participation is simply not for them these days.

In any event, in order to succeed in future Labour has to find new ways to reach out to people who remain supporters even though they won't join as they might well have done in past generations – the thinking behind the Refounding Labour project which in 2011 created a new category of 'registered supporters': people happy to be linked into, but not ready to join, the party.

This new category is absolutely fundamental to re-energising Labour's base and therefore an essential component of winning elections. However, the party has yet to embrace anything like its full potential. Whether it does so will be crucial in determining whether it will be a successful electoral force in the future.

The principle of both enrolling and enfranchising supporters of Labour was further extended to trade unionists by Ed Miliband and endorsed at the special conference of the Labour Party on 1 March 2014. This was in the spirit of the Refounding Labour agenda and could deepen and strengthen Labour's political and electoral base. A new category of affiliated supporters was created among members of trade unions affiliated to the party. Instead of retaining their long-standing right to opt out of being an individual member of Labour they will be asked to opt in and be accorded new rights in the process: principally to become directly linked to local Labour constituency parties and to be granted a direct individual vote in the election of the party leader and deputy. This would open the potential for Labour to once again enjoy the kind of close organic relationship with hundreds of thousands of trade unionists which existed in past generations, albeit through the old delegate-based structures which have hollowed out. Instead of millions of paper members associated to Labour in name alone, the party could recruit workplace activists in huge numbers, helping embed Labour in work and communities better than at any point in decades.

For if people are not 'joiners' any longer they remain 'supporters' – and in large numbers, potentially hundreds of thousands in Labour's case. There is enormous potential for the party to enlist active backing from a network of sympathisers who share the party's ideals or support particular campaigns but fight shy of formal membership.

There are lessons from the campaigns of President Barack Obama, who mobilised masses of supporters to win in 2008 and 2012, twice succeeding in presenting his centre-left policy agenda as congruent with both the general interests and ideology of the United States. This was in part accomplished by his sweeping rhetoric; situating his hopeful message of 'change' within a Whiggish historical narrative of continuity in progress. The technocratic discourse of the social democratic policy-wonk, so familiar in European politics, was rejected for a more universalistic appeal to the values, principles and institutions which bring the United States together. The election was fundamentally a battle to reimagine the 'nation' in the wake of two wars and a devastating financial crisis. Obama's pledge to represent 'Main Street' and not 'Wall Street' proved a simple but winning message. He politicised the 'nation' and nationalised his politics.

Obama was occupied from day one by the task of reconstituting the Democratic core vote: shifting away from a narrow focus on the base voters of the 1960s and 1970s and to what the Center for American Progress called 'the coalition of the ascendant', namely college-educated whites, ethnic minorities, unmarried women and strategically important blue-collar workers.

During his primary campaign Obama posted the pertinent question on Yahoo Answers: 'How can we engage more people in the democratic process?' Seventeen thousand people responded: ordinary voters with their own anxieties and hopes about the future. A serious and productive discussion was facilitated which engaged a diverse range of perspectives from across the country. In a sense, therefore, Obama's question answered itself; he found his own salvation.

Obama's fresh idealism influenced the character of the campaign's strategic operations. Direct contact with voters was prioritised over traditional 'airwave war' campaigning methods and new social media were utilised to powerful effect. The campaign website, for instance, had a tool which enabled grassroots supporters to flag up neighbours who they thought might be potential backers. Combined with a sophisticated analytics programme identifying voters in battleground states, organisers were therefore able to unobtrusively obtain the most local and intimate of political knowledge and adapt their canvassing efforts accordingly. The 2012 innovation of 'targeted sharing' allowed the campaign the means to connect with 95 per cent of all voters on Facebook via those voters who had 'friended' the President. This in turn allowed organisers to encourage existing identified supporters to contact target voters they were friends with and thus win them over via known acquaintances, not just unknown canvassers.

'Respect, empower and include' was the idea that the very act of campaigning could have an immediate and tangible impact on the local community. This appealed to those who had perhaps become disillusioned with party politics but wanted nonetheless to bring about change on a certain local issue, albeit with a national dimension, which was important to them.

This mammoth political campaign, conducted under the gaze of the world's media, and costing $750 million in 2008 and over $1 billion in 2012, thereby remained sensitive and responsive to the concerns of individual voters: a remarkable achievement.

There are lessons here for the Labour Party in its efforts to tackle the pervasive apathy, even antipathy, towards politics and politicians, among its traditional base. This widespread disengagement from mainstream party politics can partly be explained by the rise of the consumer society and competing pressures on people's time from work and study, obligations to friends and family, and other sport and leisure interests. People have also preferred to back non-party groups. The National Trust and Oxfam, for instance, have experienced substantial increases in membership and committed donors, and organisations such as Mumsnet have pioneered a new model of grassroots participation.

Especially with the limited reach into workplaces which our affiliated trade unions now offer Labour, and the growth of civil society groups both locally and nationally, we need to find new ways of engaging with wider society. We need to grant 'recognised consultee' rights to groups who would not choose to affiliate to the party at national or constituency level, but who would value formal access and the opportunity to put their points of view. Additionally, those of their members who chose to register as Labour supporters could thereby participate in party decisions, albeit in a way that does not undermine or discourage fully fledged members and activists – for example, by being involved in party policy discussions even if the final decisions are made by party members. This would broaden and strengthen Labour's base in the localities in the way that used to be the case at the height of the trade union movement.

People are engaging in politics in entirely new ways from when I first became active in the anti-apartheid movement in the late 1960s or joined the Labour Party in the late 1970s. Politics and political engagement are even radically different from what they were during Labour's landslide wins in 1997 and 2001. The pieces of the political jigsaw puzzle have been shaken up and it is far from clear what pattern they will form as they settle.

There is another, increasingly important factor. Just as politics has become more global it has also become more local. So what matters more than ever is how Labour engages with people in their neighbourhoods on local issues. The national swing that swept away so many Labour MPs in 2010 did not include our MPs in Edgbaston or Oxford East or Tooting, for example – all seats Labour should have lost. Despite their vulnerability they and their constituency parties did something quite different. They were able to mobilise whole layers of people outside traditional Labour loyalties. These examples need to be replicated to build a new type of party capable of winning in the contemporary era.

Labour's challenge

Over the past three decades, local Labour parties have been hollowed out, with an ageing and declining membership, just like other traditional organisations in the UK – from churches to social clubs. This has left the party with a weak base from which to develop contacts in the community and build popular support. In too many constituencies where Labour's vote is small, the party barely functions. In heartland 'safe' seats complacency is widespread.

Activism among Labour members has diminished as members spend less time on party activities. The proportion of members who canvass voters by phone and who donate money has risen slightly. But members nowadays get involved less often in canvassing on doorsteps, delivering leaflets, attending meetings, signing petitions, or even displaying election posters. Declining individual and affiliated membership has narrowed the range of voices heard within the party's discussions and reduced the chances of a voter hearing the party's policies advocated in the course of everyday life.

Worryingly, we are experiencing this trend just at the point when Labour needs to be more visible in the community than ever before. As Margaret Hodge came to realise in her campaign to defeat the BNP in Barking, Labour can't shirk making the political argument and fighting our corner with the voters. Ignoring anger and discontent in our traditional base, however repellent some of its prejudices may be, won't endear us to those who feel left behind by the party. For too long the Labour council in Barking was distant from the community; pathologically introspective and closed off. It took the terrifying success of the BNP in the 2006 local elections, when they won 12 seats, to galvanise this complacent party into a proactive campaigning force.

In her attempts to reconnect with her constituency Margaret abandoned tired party-politicking and ribbon-cutting ceremonialism for a candid and receptive approach to being an MP. Stale and fruitless town-hall meetings were replaced by coffee afternoons during which she chatted individually with constituents. This gave her an opportunity to challenge racism and ignorance face-to-face with its proponents, but equally it forced her to confront the concerns of local people, many of whom felt ignored by Labour. Nobody could accuse Margaret of ducking the difficult issues.

As some constituency Labour parties have been able to demonstrate, much closer and organic links with local community groups can also help provide valuable sources of extra volunteers at election time – even hundreds extra, as in Edgbaston, where they outnumbered members. Inspired by Obama's success in 2008, Edgbaston Labour Party embarked on a daring and ambitious campaign led by MP Gisela Stuart and brilliant organiser Caroline Badley in which it devoted its time and resources in the run-up to the election to recruiting volunteers and building a network of supporters. This required postponing canvassing until a healthy and organised volunteer corps had been established to do the job properly. The community took ownership of the campaign and the party forged new relationships with local people that will survive the fluctuations in Labour's political fortunes.

Other local parties that innovated and expanded did exceptionally well, with double-digit percentage increases in Labour's share of the poll in some cases. Oxford East, for instance, boosted their share of the vote by 6 per cent on the basis of a strong and active membership. Andrew Smith focused all his time and resources on being a visible and responsive MP, harnessing the extraordinary energy and commitment of the University of Oxford Labour Club to pound the pavements twice a week all year round. Again, the winning formula was a large, well-trained and organised volunteer team to take the argument to the doorstep. Having nearly lost the seat to the Liberal Democrats in 2005, clinging on by less than 1,000 votes, Andrew achieved a 4.1 per cent swing in 2010, defying national trends.

Affiliated trade union members

Additionally trade union membership has shrunk and changed shape, falling from over 13 million in 1979 to about 7 million today. Having lost nearly half their members, not even the rise in UK employment under Labour to record levels before the global financial crisis, and the strengthening of unions' right to organise, could generate a recovery: union membership simply stabilised. Meanwhile the number of local union shop stewards fell by two thirds from over 300,000 in 1980 to only 100,000 by 2004.

Today unions represent just a quarter of people in employment – a tiny 4 per cent in the private sector and 57 per cent in the public sector. In the mid-1990s just over half of all union members worked in the public sector. Today over 60 per cent do. If unions could rebuild their membership, especially in the private sector, they would speak with a stronger voice in society. Despite improved recognition rights under Labour, they have been unable to do so. Where they have done well is in recruiting half a million more women members: most trade union members today are women.

All this has had significant implications for Labour, undermining the party's traditionally strong base in the workplaces up and down the country. Compounding the problem, the affiliated membership among unions linked to Labour has also gone down, from a peak of 6.5 million in 1979 to 4.6 million in 1992, and just 2.7 million in 2010, of whom only about 10 per cent actually voted in the Labour leadership election of 2010. Where once there were numerous union activists in almost all constituency parties, now they are few and far between.

But, although the potential for engagement and support from Labour's wider membership in affiliated unions has not been realised for many years, trade unions still provide an invaluable link to working people that no other party has, and both the party and the unions must together either find a way of regenerating this link or see declining influence and a dwindling relationship – ominous for both.

Importance of local campaigning

In 2010 nearly 40 per cent of voters only decided which way to vote during the four-week election campaign, a proportion that has been steadily increasing over the years. This contains two immediate lessons: first that most voters still make their mind up months and sometimes years before polling day – which is why Labour needs to build long-term relationships both with individual voters and a wide range of community organisations. Second, that an intensive and effective campaign in the final few weeks can hold the key to victory, especially if it involves supporters in the community and in workplaces as well as local party volunteers.

In today's cynical political climate Labour policies and promises may command more credibility if they are promoted enthusiastically by volunteer party members on the doorstep, backed by a local network of Labour supporters with whom a strong relationship has been built, and endorsed by independent community activists who have worked closely with local party representatives on common campaigns. In some cases in 2010, people only voted for their Labour MPs because they identified with them through their constituency party's vibrant relationship with their local community.

This approach can also help combat the saturation the average voter feels as a result of endless direct mail, email spam and pizza-advert style political leaflets. Local volunteers knocking on doors and speaking face to face with voters can achieve that fabled political cut-through factor and actually shift people to the polls.[10]

Local campaigns can make a tremendous difference to election results and there is no substitute for bodies on the ground – maximising the Labour vote using techniques developed in the 1990s like voter identification through doorstep canvassing and get-out-the-vote work by volunteers, some or many of whom may not have been members. They made a decisive difference in 2010.

Well-run campaigns by local parties with deep roots in their local communities are as vital as national campaigns fought through the media. Indeed, throughout the 2008 Obama campaign, local groups were given unprecedented organisational autonomy. Not only did this abolish the need for an inefficient and hierarchical bureaucracy. It also served to motivate the volunteers, making them feel like trusted and valued colleagues, rather than expendable door-knocking fodder.

Interestingly when Greg Schultz, Obama's campaign director for the key swing state of Ohio in 2012 spoke to Labour MPs in January 2013, he confirmed that – despite all the immense value of social media campaigning through Facebook and Twitter, through email, texting and telephone canvassing – there was in the end no substitute for face-to-face contact on the doorstep. Indeed, the danger of voter saturation and fatigue through online campaigning meant such work was essential.

Community organising

Maybe half a million people are members of a political party, including most of the UK's 22,000 elected councillors. But millions more make a massive contribution to civil society in other ways, like the 300,000 who volunteer as school governors, the 150,000 community service volunteers, the 200,000 Women's Institute members, the 100,000 trade union stewards, the 29,000 lay magistrates and the 1.4 million registered blood donors. None do so for financial reward. Energy is also harnessed by social enterprises and not-for-profit groups, usually in areas where market failure occurs, where markets don't or can't work well, if at all.

Millions of volunteers are independently doing lots of little things that make a big difference to society. They often do it initially to support their children, later for fun, or simply because somebody has got to do it or it won't get done. Like Labour Party activists they do it in all weathers and despite a dozen setbacks.

To become genuinely embedded in the new and evolving political culture, local Labour parties must work more closely with such civic activists and social entrepreneurs, building local alliances with community groups which share a common sense of purpose. That means genuinely reaching out to them, for they can spot an insincere initiative a mile off and can be quick to resent what they see as outside interference, even if it is well meant. However, achieving their objectives almost always requires engaging with politics, so there is a common agenda to explore if Labour representatives have earned the trust to do so.

A few Labour Party veterans remember the days when they joined friends from across the community on cross-country cycle rides. Many are active members of local Labour clubs that still provide excellent links for the party with the local community. But like the demise of miners' lodges which built community halls, libraries and swimming pools in coalfield areas, such traditional roots in the community have been eclipsed by the passage of time and by dramatic lifestyle changes away from collectivism towards individualism, away from socialising in the community to socialising at home, away from the cinema to the television. So constituency parties still structured for an age long gone are struggling to stay in touch with the very people Labour wants to serve and whose support we solicit at election time.

Activism is thriving and mass movements still exist, mainly in support of single-issue campaigns. Millions backed the Stop the War protests, especially over Iraq. Hundreds of thousands turned out to show their support for Make Poverty History or Unite Against Fascism or to oppose increases in university tuition fees, the scrapping of education maintenance allowances or to save forests and libraries.

Cooperating more closely with long-term single-issue campaigns and community groups poses different challenges from working with one-off campaigns. Persuading members of the former to broaden their involvement in choices across the policy spectrum is one thing.

They tend to have well-established organisational structures with which Labour can pursue relationships, and the task is to extend their focus. The latter tend to be more informal networks or loosely linked associations that gain much of their energy and support from events. Building relationships with them needs a different approach.

However, what some of Labour's companions and critics in single-issue campaigns sometimes overlook was summed up by an Edinburgh activist who told the BBC News website: 'Single issue groups are avoiding difficult decisions. If you only care about one thing then you don't have to worry about the impact of dealing with that on everything else.' Nye Bevan's declaration that 'Socialism is the language of priorities' still prevails. Politics and government are indispensable to the necessity for difficult choices and establishing priorities. Civil society groups need Labour just as we need them, but we need to work hard to persuade them of this; the problem is proving our worth.

Here is where Arnie Graf, who in 1986 ran a ten-day seminar course on community organising attended by a young Barack Obama, comes in. He was solicited by Labour in 2011 to conduct a 'root and branch review' of the party and made an important contribution. Through his extensive experience as a 'community organiser' in some of the poorest neighbourhoods in the US, Graf appreciates that if the social democratic political party is to survive as a powerful political force, it must be more open and 'relational' in its conduct. It must reach out beyond its membership; not just at election time but all-year-round. We can't duck difficult challenges for the sake of short-term political expediency; we must fight aggressively for social justice in our local communities, however tough it gets and however likely failure may be.

Graf explained in 2013:

> My understanding of the Labour Party's origins was that it started rooted in community. Its politics reflected the concerns of working people at the time. Since there was no mass media then, it grew from a large amount of conversations and meetings in various neighbourhoods. My effort, along with many others, is to see a party that

is deeply rooted in communities throughout the country. It is an effort to build a Party that believes in devolving power, as much as possible, to the local authorities so that local people are entrusted and given the responsibility and authority to make decisions that affect their own communities.

It is an attempt to treat people as citizens as opposed to either consumers and/or observers. This can be done by building local Parties throughout the country that spend time meeting and listening to people through conducting thousands of conversations with people. From these conversations, plans for local actions can be formulated on the best ways to change, improve, or develop new initiatives. Organising is a deep process of listening, discerning and developing campaigns by a cross-section of a community. This challenges and frees up the local talent of so many people that I have met throughout the country.

Graf more than most understands that the dejected and disillusioned don't only want to be talked at by candidates chasing their votes, once every five years. After all, the damaging and pervasive perception that politicians make promises they have no intention of keeping will not be tackled by yet more promises. To reconnect with those we left behind, Labour must be seen to be working within the local community, day in day out, whether opposing the closure of a factory, fighting for a hospital accident and emergency unit to be kept open or resisting the reduction in public transport provision. This way Labour can effect real change for the '99 per cent, before a single vote is cast', he argues.

But operationalising this approach means picking the right campaigns for the right purposes. In this it is important to understand what different community campaigns can and can't achieve. For instance, a campaign on low pay for the living wage may rev up the activist base and win back disillusioned supporters but is unlikely to change the minds of voters who switched to Cameron in 2010. They may require a campaign based more around local speeding or litter picks for example, to demonstrate Labour's community value to their neighbourhood. As a result, campaigners should choose their type of campaign not just with their community goal in mind but also with their political objective in mind: volunteer capacity building, voter persuasion or rebuilding local trust.

London Citizens has been leading the way in bringing together different sections of an infinitely diverse city, from faith groups to trade unions, to campaign around issues of common concern. When disparate progressive opinion is harnessed and organised in this way, even a right-wing mayor can be convinced of the need for a 'living wage'.

There is a lesson here for Labour: that those sections of society who may not be diehard Labour loyalists may still share with us ambitions for our community and country. Historical demographic allegiances to Labour have declined, if not vanished, but there remains a progressive base – that vast decent majority in the United Kingdom – whose support can be won if the party finds new ways of reaching out to them.

Party organisation

Society has moved on radically since 1918 and so has politics. In the 60 years since Tony Crosland's *The Future of Socialism* was published, politics arguably changed more radically than it did over the previous 60 years.

But Labour's institutions and practices haven't kept up. Numbers of party and trade union activists from whom delegates can be selected for the governing bodies of constituency parties, General Committees (GCs), have plummeted. As a result GC membership has not only fallen but narrowed.

Furthermore the delegate structure enabled two-way communication through physical report-back and feedback in an era when telephones hardly existed and transport was limited. Today's culture of mass car ownership, mobile phones, email, Facebook and Twitter is a world away from when the party's structures were designed around delegates and their personal interaction to and fro with members.

While the introduction of all-member meetings in place of GCs in some constituencies has increased attendance, it has not on the whole broadened the range of those attending constituency meetings. GCs can become over-focused on short-term winning of votes at the expense of forging closer links across their community that could enhance their electoral potency in the longer term. They can become bogged down in procedural detail instead of tackling the big issues or pressing local concerns that attract people to politics in the first place. This can frustrate party members and put off potential recruits, leading to poorly attended local party meetings. As membership participation falls off, chances to develop contacts with local community groups can be missed and the burden falls on the shoulders of ever fewer party activists, with newly enthusiastic members often joining up, pitching in and burning out.

To embrace change properly, Labour should allow members to join, based not just on geography but also on occupation or area of political interest. The party should conduct a skills audit of its entire membership and supporter base to identify the talent at its disposal and then channel that expertise effectively. And the party must be willing to allow for a culture based less on the 'command and control' style of New Labour with its attendant demands for 'strict message discipline' and embrace the more progressive approach of Obama's 'Respect, empower, include' creed.

New media and new technology

In 2010 Labour made three times the number of contacts with voters than in 2005 by effective use of new technology, social networks and community-organising techniques in local campaigns. These included house parties, virtual phone banks, texts, Twitter messages, YouTube videos, issue-specific websites, email lists and online fund-raising. However, the party only achieved an inconsistent link between online mobilisation and offline activity.

Like most political parties, Labour was slow to respond to the campaigning opportunities the internet offers. The real value to political parties of the digital revolution, which is still too often overlooked, is the opportunity it affords to break out of the

Westminster bubble and engage more directly with voters both on a national scale and increasingly across interest groups with hyper-local and targeted messages. This is where so much untapped potential lies and where Labour could realise the real electoral value of the internet, not in Twitter spats with journalists or right-wing bloggers.

The internet makes it easy to participate in civic and political affairs, whether by accessing websites, signing an e-petition or responding to a government e-consultation. Frustrations arise over email due to too much one-way communication and lack of responses from elected representatives, with MPs on the other hand sometimes submerged under bombardment by email. But the potential is clear. New technology and fresh techniques could also help to revive the party's internal democracy by closing the gap between the leaders and the led. Genuinely two-way communication could ensure that the authentic voice of the grass roots is heard and cannot be ignored. Citizens are looking for more than the traditional broadcast-only relationship with their MPs. In Mumsnet, for example, members have an online network configured to enable them to feed views upwards and to each other onto 'message boards' where they get attention by the office leadership, especially if they get critical mass. Something similar could be utilised by Labour's leadership.

When it comes to how Labour campaigns and organises online, some clarity and sharpness is required: improving content, accessibility and design; sometimes doing less but doing it better and being nimble and flexible. Although a strong digital team is needed at party headquarters, the leadership needs to let go because it cannot and should not try to produce, manage and control every Labour online campaign centrally. The internet is essentially bottom up, not top down – though, of course, it does afford quick and powerful messaging from the centre. For instance, although the Obama campaign was able to remove from its central website any disruptive or malign supporter group, it did not try to control what local volunteer networks – for instance, Joggers for Obama – did: instead the leadership encouraged them to self-organise and self-mobilise. The potential of digital politics will not be fully realised if it is simply seen as an add-on to traditional party structures and modes of organising. Its capacity to be transformative needs to be fully understood and absorbed right across Labour: from party staff right through to volunteers and stakeholders, sharing best practice and building capacity. Digital needs to be integral to everything Labour does as a party.

Less a party, more a movement

The old political order is over. No Labour member can assume that there is a 'natural' constituency materially bound to the party which just has to be triggered into action at election time. Some members might pine for those days, but they're gone. The challenge now is how to reorganise Labour to reconnect with progressive opinion in all its varied manifestations. The party is at a crossroads. It can trundle along with the other major political parties, rooted to the old model of political organisation, and continue to decline as a social and political force. Or be bold and courageous; rebuilding into a formidable fighting force fit for the 21st century – to 'mend our broken politics', as Ed Miliband expressed it in an impassioned speech on 1 March 2014 at the special party conference which agreed a second stage of Refounding Labour reforms. "Politics," he said, "is like a match being played while the stands are emptying. Fewer people are watching. We won't turn that round by saying we're right and they're wrong. We won't do it by singing the old songs even louder." And he continued:

> As Prime Minister, I want to change this country, but I can only do it with a movement behind me. It has always been this way. Workers' rights at the beginning of the 20th century. The National Health Service after 1945. The principle of equal pay for women in the 1970s. The minimum wage in the 1990s. Gay rights at the 20th century's end. All of these things happened, not because leaders made them happen, but because people and movements made them happen. Today if you vote for these reforms you will be voting for Labour to be a movement again.

Although the conference carried the reforms overwhelmingly, what remained was the hard part: transforming Labour from a traditional *party* to a modern *movement*.

CHAPTER 11

Faster, sustainable growth

Like developers and councils addicted to building on flood plains, Britain has yet to heed the wake-up call sounded by the banking crisis. Our transient prosperity rests precariously upon flimsy foundations. Whatever state Britain's financial sector is in when the recession is long gone, banking will never provide the bedrock on which this country can build an internationally competitive economy. Nor can we pay our way in the world selling properties in central London at grotesquely inflated prices to mega-rich foreigners. Nor – however competitive they become and whatever contribution they make – can we prosper simply by supplying fashion accessories to customers abroad and by attracting overseas students to universities and colleges here.

How is Britain going to pay our way in the world without changing the whole trajectory of economic policy? Our share of world trade fell by a fifth between 1998 and 2010, and is forecast to fall by a further tenth by 2019. By August 2014 UK foreign trade performance had been the worst in the G7 over the previous 20 years: a terrible predicament for a country whose Tory Prime Minister was then regularly trumpeting as being world beating. And sadly there seems no end in sight to this decline. In March 2014 the Office for Budget Responsibility reported that 'net trade is expected to make little contribution to growth over the remainder of the forecast period, reflecting the weakness of export market growth and a gradual decline in export market share'. Yet the 2014 Tory/Lib Dem budget did not address that at all and Britain's trade figures in June 2014 were some of the worst in recent history. Unless there is a change of export culture – which means a new industrial policy driven by our government in the way Germany's is – there will be no export-led recovery, and Britain's relative international decline will continue.

The lesson of Germany is a salutary one for those who think otherwise. For it is the one European economy to have emerged from the financial crisis in reasonable shape – and why? Primarily because it has a strong, advanced and internationally competitive manufacturing sector which, despite relatively high social and labour costs, has underpinned a vigorous economy. Manufacturing accounts for 21 per cent of German GDP but only 11 per cent of the UK's. Germany is the world's third biggest exporter after China and the US, selling three times as much abroad as Britain, which comes tenth in the exporting league table. German industry benefits from a business-supportive banking system, whereas Britain has a business-averse banking system. Where Germany has vocational skills in abundance, Britain has a long-term deficiency. Germany has a government culture that believes in backing business, not a UK Treasury one of leaving business to survive or sink on its own.

Germany's triumph in the 2014 football World Cup symbolises the contrasting approach that our two countries tend to adopt, not just in sport. The British Premier League has seen our biggest clubs bought up by foreign families, unlike Bundesliga clubs. They have to be majority-owned by club members, which discourages control by a single financial interest, either foreign or domestic. This helps promote loyalty and repeat business from each club's key customers, its local fans: Bundesliga matches are the best attended in the world. It also raises standards of service and product quality, with all clubs required to run a youth academy to boost the stream of local talent. By contrast, Premier League clubs prioritise the quick fix by buying in foreign stars rather than developing indigenous talent, to the obvious detriment of the national team. England's 2014 World Cup campaign turned into a six-day war which they lost, without even one short-term triumph. Germany went on all the way to win the tournament in style for the fourth time, having built a sustainable basis for national performance.

Britain shares few of Germany's strengths. Our banks are anti-business in the sense that – if they lend at all – they are obsessed with the short term, whereas German financial institutions expect a long-term return rather than a quick profit. The keys to German competitiveness include its education and training system. Without an equally skilled workforce, the UK cannot hope to run the high-tech production processes and flexible manufacturing systems on which high-quality products and demanding standards of customer service depend, and in which Germany's *Mittelstand* of medium-sized businesses excel. By comparison, Britain's skills base is second-class and too many of our small and medium-sized firms are laggards not leaders.

Austerity or bust?

You might have been forgiven for thinking otherwise if you had listened to Britain's Chancellor of the Exchequer George Osborne giving his annual budget speech in March 2014. It was typical of the genre. He claimed credit for finally getting the British economy growing again and said that 'we're now growing faster than Germany'.

What he didn't say was that his policies had delayed Britain's recovery from recession, which had taken *twice as long* as Germany's; or that the two economies were therefore at different stages in the business cycle, with Britain enjoying an initial burst of 'catch-up' growth that usually follows recession; or that the British economy has shown an in-built tendency to grow for the past 150 years, albeit at a slower rate than that enjoyed by Germany and our other key competitors. This growth momentum has normally been at about 2 per cent per year, only falling short when a budget squeeze or high interest rates or some external shock like a big rise in world oil prices or the banking crisis has suppressed the economy's growth propensity.

Sooner or later economies in recession show signs of recovery and start growing again. Most economies possess reserves of what British football manager Mick McCarthy prized most in his teams when the game was going badly: 'bounce-back-ability'. NIESR analysis shows that the UK 1990–93 recession ended quite quickly, with GDP hitting the bottom of the trough and beginning to grow again after only 15 months, and passing its previous peak after 30 months. The 1973–76 recession hit bottom after 24 months, and GDP got back to square one after 33 months, tempting Jim Callaghan to think about an early election before deciding to soldier on. The front page of the *Financial Times* of Monday, 8 May 1979 reported that 'Sir Geoffrey Howe, the new Chancellor of the Exchequer, will start his first full day at the Treasury today faced with growing evidence of an upturn in the level of economic activity.' Economic recovery had not rescued Labour at the polls. Nor did it stop Howe pitching the UK economy into the 1979–83 downturn which lasted as long but thankfully did not sink so deep as the 1930–34 Great Depression, taking 48 months before GDP passed its previous peak.

The downturn that began in 2008 lasted even longer. The wait for real recovery persisted because Tory/Lib Dem government policy prolonged the pain. As we have seen, the economy had begun growing again under Labour early in 2010 but recovery was choked off by George Osborne's June 2010 budget cuts. Liberal Democrat David Laws, briefly Chief Secretary to the Treasury, claimed in January 2011 that the coalition cuts package had been too small to hit growth and that 2011 would be the year when the coalition would be proved right on economic policy. He said: 'A recovery is under way and is likely to be sustained ... This is likely to be the year that recovery is entrenched.'[1] But events proved Laws completely wrong. He celebrated too soon.

His government's fiscal squeeze meant that GDP had still not regained its previous peak by the beginning of 2014, six long years after the economy sank into recession. What a contrast with the US and German economies where GDP rose above pre-crisis levels in 2011. The UK recovery lagged three years behind America's and Germany's, during which time there was colossal human cost and economic waste, and with real wages still below pre-2008 levels by early 2014.

When recovery finally resumed in 2013, it provided a pretext for the government to claim their 'policy was working'. But the encouraging signs were really a response to the fact that the severe squeeze of 2010–12 eased off a little in 2012–13. The pace of public spending cuts slowed temporarily and the reduction in the budget deficit levelled off, causing the OBR Chair Robert Chote to note: 'deficit reduction appears to have stalled'.[2] It was easing the squeeze in 2012 that allowed the growth tendency to show through in

2013.[3] Yet there remained no end in sight to the Tory/Lib Dems' overarching targets – which drove their whole policy – of cuts in the deficit, borrowing and debt. Despite massive spending reductions, they were nowhere near eliminating the deficit by the conclusion of the 2010–15 Parliament. But instead of learning from that abject failure, they promised more of the same: the budget tightening resumed in 2014, with five more years of planned austerity due to bite especially hard again from 2016, calling into question the sustainability of the Tory/Lib Dems' much trumpeted 'success', which nevertheless struck chords in gullible markets and a subservient media gripped by neoliberal propaganda.[4]

By autumn 2014 the UK recovery was already losing momentum, with the IMF, the Bank of England and the CBI all expecting slower growth. With his self-trumpeted 'economic recovery' past its peak George Osborne, as usual, blamed the eurozone slowdown rather than his own austerity policy and failure to address the fundamental weaknesses of the economy. The truth was that both the pace and durability of UK recovery was once again being inhibited by the prospect of a double dose of the same Tory austerity: austerity which would no more eliminate the budget deficit in the next Parliament than it did in the one elected in 2010.

George Osborne's June 2010 budget undertook to eliminate the deficit, where Labour promised to halve it. Specifically, he pledged to cut government borrowing in 2014–15 to exactly half what Labour's March 2010 budget had planned, £37 billion instead of £74 billion. But by March 2014 the Office for Budget Responsibility (OBR) expected borrowing in 2014–15 to exceed £95 billion – not only wildly over his targeted pledge, but actually exceeding Labour's much more realistic one which he had so strongly condemned. The Tory/Lib Dems justified their savage cuts as essential to deliver on their key deficit-elimination commitment. Yet this failed – and failed spectacularly because that austerity policy curbed economic growth. Even deeper Tory spending cuts in the next Parliament would do the same.

Labour's whole argument since 2010 had been that easing the squeeze would allow the economy to grow again. Once recovery had been firmly established and steady growth in excess of 3 per cent a year achieved, the budget deficit would largely, though not totally, have taken care of itself. There would have had to have been rebalancing of the public finances – of course. But Tory/Lib Dem plans for further big spending cuts in 2016–17, and announced Tory intentions for even further cuts beyond that, are exactly the opposite of what the UK economy needs. The fundamental argument remains: sustainable growth requires investment, public and private, not a further fiscal squeeze.

The prospects for public spending: aspiration and anxiety

Which brings us to public spending. Getting right essential balancing of public finances, on the one hand, and investment for growth and high-quality public services, on the other, is not easy. But the right's shibboleth that Labour governments always 'spend more than they earn' is perfidious propaganda. For instance, back in May 1975 on the back of a huge hike in world oil prices, Labour faced raging inflation and a rapidly rising budget deficit forecast to reach 5 per cent of GDP in 1975–76, equivalent to £75 billion today. In response, Tony Crosland issued his own warning against lax limits on public spending. He told local government leaders that 'for the time being at least, the party's over ... We are not calling for a headlong retreat. But we are calling for a standstill.'

A three-year standstill on total public spending in 2011–14 was what the Labour government planned in 2009, with current spending rising slowly as capital expenditure dropped back from its 30-year peak. That standstill was forecast to halve public borrowing by 2014 and eliminate it by 2017–18 thanks to renewed economic growth. Instead, growth collapsed under the Tory/Liberal Democratic coalition, which slashed spending programmes, squeezed the economy hard and delayed UK recovery, causing their timetable for cutting the deficit to disintegrate. Yet, although their policy failed, they carried it off with bravado, blaming Labour and seemingly escaping any responsibility as they ploughed on – to plaudits from media as compliant as they had been for similar policies in the 1930s.

If Crosland was adroitly prudent about public finances, he maintained a sensible and wholly justifiable resistance to the neoliberal default stance of the British Treasury of which Keynes had been so devastatingly contemptuous in the 1930s. In November 1976 Crosland argued in Cabinet that any further public spending cuts agreed with the IMF should be modest, to limit the deflationary effect of lower government borrowing in 1977–78 to £1 billion, as higher economic activity would help to shrink the budget deficit further.[5] He foreshadowed Labour's argument after the 2008 financial crisis that higher government borrowing today can mean lower borrowing tomorrow by getting the economy growing again and keeping the engine of growth in gear.

In the event, in December 1976 the Cabinet rejected his case and agreed more substantial cuts, which meant slower growth and higher unemployment. History shows that the cash limits system,[6] which had been introduced in 1975, led to under-spending of departmental budgets and the actual cuts *exceeded* those agreed with the IMF. The cyclically adjusted public sector deficit fell by over 3 per cent of GDP between 1975–76 and 1977–78, which delivered exactly what Crosland had warned against: 'a further and needless sacrifice'. However, this two-year Labour squeeze in the mid-1970s was less tight than the first years of George Osborne's squeeze, and in his case the squeeze was ongoing with no end in sight.

The publication during the depths of recession in September 1992 of Giles Radice's influential Fabian pamphlet *Southern Discomfort* (analysing why the Labour Party was weak in southern England) coincided almost exactly with 'Black Wednesday', when sterling was devalued and dropped out of the European exchange rate mechanism, causing the Tories' claim to be competent economic managers to collapse. That was when voters began to listen to Labour again. Radice's findings, especially what they showed about the importance of aspiration and ambition among potential Labour voters, played a big part in shaping Labour's response – encouraging Labour's subsequent 1997 landslide.

But getting a hearing from voters became a much tougher task after the 2010 defeat. Patrick Diamond and Giles Radice's 2011 findings, *Southern Discomfort: One Year On*, showed that after the 2008 financial crisis most voters doubted the ability of either major party to run the economy well, viewing Labour and the Tories with almost equal distrust. Labour's claim up until 2007 to 'have abolished boom and bust' counted against the party, understandably so.

Diamond and Radice's survey confirmed that developments since the global credit crunch had changed people's priorities. Recession and a frustrating wait for recovery reminded voters of their vulnerability to economic events beyond their control, made them pessimistic about their prospects and, above all, led insecurity to overtake aspiration as their key concern. By turning Labour's modest 2010 recovery into renewed recession and bringing growth to a stop in 2011–12, the Tory/Lib Dems ensured that insecurity and worry about what the future might bring would prevail among voters. They caused public concern about the economy to rise, especially among the middle classes and people living in the South East of England. By September 2013 the number of people feeling insecure at work had almost doubled since 2010 and 40 per cent of working people were worried that their job would become more insecure in the future.

That new age of anxiety meant Labour faced a stiff challenge in convincing voters that the state has a key role to play in meeting their insecurity concerns. Everyone knew that tight budgets and tough choices would remain the order of the day for some years, whichever party was in power. But at the same time there remained majority support for a fair and a civilised society.

And that still required ongoing state support, since there are some vital services that only government can supply. Markets, after all, only provide services to customers who can afford to pay and are willing purchasers. Left to themselves, commercial concerns cherry-pick the most profitable market segments and ignore the rest. When markets fail, as financial markets periodically do in an inherently unstable capitalist system, even paying customers can be left high and dry.

But government exists to provide more than just a safety net in troubled times to citizens who have lost out in the lottery of life. It also delivers the ongoing public services and much of the essential infrastructure on which we all depend: the very social fabric that forms the common foundation of personal and financial security which we share with family friends and neighbours, that binds us together in a cohesive society and that supplies a springboard for individual achievement.

We can see where so-called 'compassionate conservatism' and a shrunken state leads by looking at the American example: long lines of unemployed, desperately poor people queuing at charity soup kitchens or visiting food banks, while others, some previously with professional careers, face compulsory redundancy and the prospect of losing their home and the possible break-up of their household. Or people turned away from hospital because they cannot afford private health insurance premiums. Any idea that the American model saves money is contradicted by the huge level of additional private spending required to fill the gaps in state provision. US private spending on social needs, notably medical insurance and private pensions, exceeds 10 per cent of GDP and brings total US social spending up to 29.4 per cent, almost as high as Finland with 30.7 per cent. And the fastest rising costs in America are in their private healthcare system, driven by over-treatment of patients, rising insurance premiums and increasing legal costs.[7]

Above all, countering insecurity means policies to encourage economic growth since growth is the key to jobs, to incomes and to restoring financial stability in both the public and the private sectors. That means taking active steps – vigorous fiscal steps – to ensure that growth is not again interrupted, and the economy caused to stall, as it did between 2010 and 2013. Simply relying on the Bank of England to keep interest rates low, and hoping that quantitative easing would boost bank lending by enough to offset a continuing fiscal squeeze, proved a poor recipe for recovery. Yet that is what Tory/Lib Dem economic policy amounted to. All it did was delay the turnaround. Their 2010 monetary measures, including near-zero nominal interest rates and negative real rates of interest, could not on their own end the recession because the economy had become caught in what Keynes called 'a liquidity trap', in modern economic parlance 'a zero lower bound'. This is when expanding the supply of money and credit cannot drive interest rates low enough to generate economic recovery, making a fiscal stimulus the key to escaping recession. The UK economic engine simply idled for three years while the American economy, boosted by President Obama's 2009 fiscal stimulus, began growing again.

What Britain needed instead was a growth plan backed by expansionary budget measures to increase total spending (with the key contribution coming initially from public investment), get the economy moving up through the gears as it picked up speed, and enhance its capacity for fast growth in future. That is the way to meet people's concerns about job insecurity in particular, both for themselves and for their children.

The room for expansion

The Tory/Lib Dems had no growth target for the UK economy – only an ambition to shrink the size of the state. Tory Chancellor George Osborne signalled in 2013 a three-point plan aimed at running a budget surplus in 2018–19. Firstly, to cut government spending on goods and services as a share of national income to pre-1948 levels by further cuts in departmental spending programmes. Secondly, to tighten his already crushing squeeze on welfare benefits by even deeper cuts in the support that society provides to those in need, irrespective of the suffering caused. Thirdly, to limit public investment between 2013–14 and 2018–19 to an average of 1.5 per cent of GDP, one third less than the pre-crisis share and way below what the economy requires and could afford.[8]

The clear implication is that, if allowed by the voters in 2015, Osborne would extend his austerity drive well beyond 2020 by demanding a decade of budget surpluses in order to bring Britain's debt burden back to pre-crisis proportions of 40 per cent of GDP by 2030 or earlier. Although he failed to reduce the budget deficit as quickly as he had planned in 2010, by March 2014 Osborne hoped to be back in surplus by 2018–19 and, by sticking to his austerity stance, to halve debt as a share of GDP from its peak of nearly 80 per cent in 2015 to 40 per cent by about 2030. This would be an echo of Tory economic policy in the 1920s when the Geddes Axe was applied to public expenditure and social spending was slashed by nearly 10 per cent in an effort to achieve a budget surplus and reduce national debt.

It would mean yet more and even deeper cuts to public services, welfare benefits and public investment – far beyond anything witnessed between 2010 and 2015. And all to restore the ability of the state to rescue failing banks once again, by taking the economy back to 2008 when national debt was around 40 per cent of GDP. (We can be confident that Osborne has considered a target of 40 per cent debt by 2030 because the Treasury's March 2014 Budget Report even included a scenario showing how running a £15 billion annual budget surplus could cut debt to *30 per cent of GDP* by the mid-2030s.[9]) Surprisingly, a Fabian Society commission came close to endorsing the idea of a 40 per cent target for debt/GDP by the early 2030s.[10] The neoliberal rot had indeed seeped into Labour.

There is a better alternative. That is for Labour to cut government borrowing more slowly, take longer to bring debt down, and allow faster economic growth to bear more of the burden of deficit reduction. In November 2010 the IMF examined the implications for advanced economies like the UK of reducing their national debt/GDP ratio to *60 per cent* by 2030. At that time George Osborne was planning to cut Britain's budget deficit far faster than required to hit such a target. Sixty per cent by 2030 remains a better medium-term debt target for advanced economies than Osborne's secret 40 per cent one.

Output gap

The scope for faster growth is actually much greater than George Osborne or the OBR accepted. The OBR consistently erred on the side of caution in assuming that Britain's output gap – the amount of slack or spare capacity in the economy due to plant and equipment operating at less than full tilt and some labour being unemployed or underemployed, as shown by the difference between actual national output and the maximum possible that the economy could produce if it were working at full capacity – was very small, as Chapter 4 noted. Although UK output by the beginning of 2014 was some 15 per cent below where it would have been on the pre-crisis trend, the OBR believed that almost all of that potential output had been lost forever and was irrecoverable.

If a company's plant and machinery is left lying idle for part of the week due to insufficient orders from customers, and if its workforce has to work short hours or is laid off because there is nothing for them to do, then the firm has spare capacity. If business picks up again and orders increase, the firm can quickly raise its rate of production by operating its plant more intensively, by extending working hours through overtime or by putting on extra shifts and by re-hiring workers it previously laid off. Similarly, total output in the economy as a whole can grow abnormally quickly for a while by bringing previously underused resources into production.

This relatively fast growth rate – 'catch-up' growth – can continue until the economy reaches full employment, when growth normally slows to its long-term trend rate. So, how fast the economy can grow as it recovers from recession depends in part on how much capital equipment and labour is being underemployed. The TUC estimated that in early 2014 the level of under-employment (i.e. people working part-time because they cannot get a full-time job or wanting more hours in their current job) exceeded fully 3 million. The greater the amount of spare production capacity, the faster the economy can grow in the recovery phase. In 2013 and 2014 the OBR reckoned there was very little such spare capacity, much less than other forecasting groups estimated on average. Therefore the scope for fast growth was very limited in the OBR's view, providing convenient cover for continued government cuts.

In December 2013 the OBR reckoned that the amount of output lost due to capital equipment and labour being left idle would shrink to 1.8 per cent in 2014, and by Budget Day 2014 this estimate had shrunk to only 1.4 per cent of GDP – meaning that the economy was already producing at close to its maximum capacity; indeed that it expected growth to slow down in 2015, not to continue or to speed up. Yet the average forecast of the 2014 UK output gap or unused productive capacity among a range of independent bodies at that time was 2.7 per cent – half as much again as the OBR figure – and by the time of the February 2014 Green Budget from the Institute for Fiscal Studies the Oxford Economics team (which provided the estimate of the output gap that IFS adopted) put it at 4.3 per cent of GDP.

Defying such authoritative estimates, the OBR consequently saw no scope for fast catch-up growth of the kind that the UK experienced as it recovered from depression between 1933 and 1936, growth in excess of 4 per cent per year.[11] But, as the former BBC economics editor Stephanie Flanders pointed out, that degree of caution was equivalent to assuming that the financial crisis did more permanent damage to the UK's long-term potential than the Great Depression of the 1930s, the 1970s oil price crises, or either of the great World Wars.[12]

In his November 2013 Wincott memorial lecture, Martin Wolf, the chief economics commentator of the *Financial Times*, challenged the idea that Britain has permanently lost much of its productive potential, on three grounds.[13] First, the pre-crisis build-up of debt was overwhelmingly used to buy existing assets rather than to finance consumption or investment, and there was no big surge in UK construction, unlike in the US, Spain or Ireland. Second, Britain's banks were lending overwhelmingly to each other and to finance investment in property, with lending to manufacturing forming only 1.4 per cent of the assets of our leading financial institutions, so finance for productive innovation wouldn't have been greatly improved. Third, much lost ground can be recouped as UK output and productivity pick up again. Wolf noted that for Britain to get back to the 1980–2007 growth trend over ten years would require the economy to grow at an annual rate of 5.6 per cent. 'Catch-up' growth of that order should be our ambitious but feasible aim, not some plodding 2 per cent. It is the output gap that makes such an aim feasible.

A bigger output gap also means that more of the budget deficit is cyclical and less structural than the OBR calculated, meaning that a larger proportion of the deficit would disappear as the economy grew, leaving less pressure for budget cuts to eliminate the remaining structural deficit and more time for them to do so. The urgency of the need to bring down government borrowing is much less pressing than George Osborne wanted everyone to believe – his motivation was always a neoliberal one first and a fiscal one second.

Two-year public investment plan for faster sustainable growth

Which raises the question: what should Labour's policy be in the 2015–20 Parliament? Labour's leadership made a commitment to tough fiscal rules to ensure the *current* budget was brought back into balance through what its front-bench Treasury team called 'no more borrowing for day-to-day spending in 2015–16' – which meant accepting the reality that Tory/Lib Dem spending plans would already have been set for the year by the time a new government was formed.

That made unpalatable choices inescapable while allowing scope for increased public investment in infrastructure, housing and other capital projects. It meant Labour would not be able to take the waiting out of wanting for expanded public services simply by paying for them by borrowing more. From the start, better public services, or services that Labour saved either by scrapping planned Tory cuts like cutting welfare by a further £12 billion between 2016 and 2018, or by reinstating spending that the coalition had already cut, would have to be paid for either from taxation – fairer taxation – or from charges where appropriate, or from what the party's zero-based review called 'cost savings which at the same time improve services'. Projects and services that could not be afforded would have to be postponed until economic growth provided the resources to pay for them. But successfully convincing voters of that strategy remained critical to regaining their trust. Otherwise voters would have to live with their insecurities and Labour supporters with their frustrations – all in the name of 'economic credibility' demanded by the neoliberal political orthodoxy of the time.

The Tory/Lib Dem plan to tighten the fiscal squeeze again in 2016 provides no long-term or sustainable future. Its public investment commitment is pitifully inadequate: only 1.3 per cent of GDP in 2018. Yet in 2013 there were mainstream calls for significant extra UK public investment – for £10 billion, from the IMF, for at least £20 billion over two years, from Professor John Van Reenen of the LSE Growth Commission,[14] and for £30 billion, from both Jonathan Portes of NIESR[15] and the Trades Union Congress.[16] In March 2014, when Britain's unemployment rate was higher than that in the US but both economies were growing at the same annual rate of 2.8

per cent, Paul Krugman called for a boost to the American economy. He suggested increasing US government spending by perhaps 3 per cent of GDP each year for two years, to raise America's growth rate and expand employment.[17] Such a boost to the UK economy might have meant increasing public investment in Britain by £45 billion per year for two years.

A boost to UK public investment of £30 billion per year for two years could be safely financed without jeopardising international market confidence in Britain. It would provide skilled, well-paid jobs. It would also create a much more sustainable basis for long-term low levels of borrowing and debt than the neoliberal cuts agenda, which has simply denuded Britain's economic resilience and damaged our social fabric – while falling well short of its target to eliminate the budget deficit by 2015. Current spending on public services would remain subject to tight discipline and only rise as far as Labour's readiness to raise taxation, increase charges or achieve efficiencies allowed.

This extra £30 billion per year of public investment should be focused upon housing, infrastructure, low-carbon investment, and education and skills, all of which could set the economy firmly on a path of rapid sustainable growth, as part of a ten-year investment programme for two Parliaments. An early start could be made in three ways. First, by giving an immediate go-ahead to increased house-building. Second, by reinstating capital projects that were cancelled by the Tory/Lib Dems when they took office in 2010, such as items from Labour's Building Schools for the Future programme. Third, by learning from the example that Chancellor Alistair Darling set in 2009 when he brought forward £30 billion of capital expenditure scheduled for later years, by accelerating projects in the Treasury's National Infrastructure Plan. Faster economic growth would bring the public finances back into balance sooner than the coalition's 2018 target date and with a fraction (sadly still a significant fraction) of the painful cuts they intend.

American Presidents Bill Clinton and Barack Obama have acknowledged that the key economic weaknesses of the US lie in education, vocational training and the infrastructure network linking American workers to the needs of the international economy.

The similarities with the challenges facing the UK economy are stunning. So are the implications. The sheer scale of the task needed to regenerate Britain is awesome.

Housing

Britain's top priority must be to build more homes because there is a chronic housing shortage which has been pushing up house prices and making rents unaffordable in the private sector, creating long waiting lists for social housing, and putting great pressure on the welfare benefits bill. The Tory/Lib Dems committed to spend only £10 on building new homes for every £100 on housing benefit – virtually a reversal of 30 years ago when, of every £100 we spent on housing, £80 was invested in bricks and mortar and £20 was spent on housing benefit. That is the balance of spending on housing that we have to get back to, and it cannot be achieved by ever more punitive cuts in housing benefit payments, when high levels of total housing benefit spending are a product of a critical housing shortage driving up rent levels.

Even Labour's ambitious and important commitment to raise house building to 200,000 a year by 2020 still leaves a gap, with 2 million or so families on council waiting lists and 3 million adult children staying with their parents because they cannot find or afford a home of their own. The IMF's suggestion of a tax on unused development land, to ensure that more houses are built and that the gains from development are shared with the community whose expansion helps to create them, makes much sense.[18] Also attractive is the proposal by Professor John Muellbauer for central government and local authorities to work together in using public funds to buy development plots, in effect to establish a national land bank, for subsequent sale with planning permission to private developers at a profit to the community. Muellbauer argues that such a radical move could transform housing supply and that similar initiatives have succeeded in South Korea, Singapore, Taiwan and Hong Kong in accelerating urban development and in making housing more affordable.[19] Labour attempted a scheme on similar lines with the 1975 Community Land Act, which Tony Crosland piloted through

Parliament as Environment Secretary but which was scrapped by the Tories in 1980.

As growth accelerates and interest rates begin to rise, the last thing needed is higher mortgage rates putting existing borrowers in peril. Between 1 and 2 million families could face having to spend more than *half* their disposable income on mortgage repayments by 2018, according to estimates by the Resolution Foundation. A partial solution might be to provide a scheme of debt relief based on the American Home Affordable Modification Program whereby the federal government provided help to up to 8 million struggling homeowners at risk of foreclosure, to lower their monthly payments. The aim was to keep them in their homes by cutting their monthly payments to a *third* of household monthly income – still high but considerably better than a *half* without government intervention.

But the priority is to build many more affordable homes, generating much-needed jobs – Labour's 200,000 annual target would create 500,000 new jobs and apprenticeships – and support faster growth. If building regulations for these new homes required them to be zero carbon by designing in renewable energy sources to complement high insulation standards, then that growth would be more ecologically sustainable too.

Infrastructure

Faster sustainable growth will also arise from desperately needed investment to modernise Britain's inadequate infrastructure. What the Tory/Lib Dem government called its annual National Infrastructure Plan was simply a list of projects drawn up by Infrastructure UK, a unit within HM Treasury. The list was not one arising from an evidence-based assessment of long-term UK needs, simply a consolidation of short to medium-term priorities agreed by government.[20]

By December 2013 the plan had identified hundreds of infrastructure projects and programmes worth over £375 billion across the UK, mainly in the energy and transport sectors. To help businesses bid for public sector contracts, the government published details of potential public projects representing 'future government business opportunities' worth more than £177 billion across 19 sectors. Significantly, the 2013 plan also announced further sales of publicly owned assets, including the student loan book, the state-run operator of intercity rail services East Coast Trains, and the government shareholding in Eurostar, as part of a plan to double the target for the sale of state-owned corporate and financial assets from £10 billion to £20 billion between 2014 and 2020.

By beefing up government guarantees and underwriting risk, the Tory/Lib Dem government tried to use the strength of the public sector balance sheet to encourage private sector infrastructure investment. But these are investments that private sector bodies are only prepared to undertake with government assistance, not necessarily investments that the government feels warrant the highest priority. The Tory/Lib Dems also walked into a potential minefield in which the taxpayers' ability to take risks may be transformed into excess profit for the private sector.[21]

Since the start of the 1990s the short-term 'sweat the assets' approach to investment characteristic of City private equity and hedge funds has well and truly infected Britain's public sector. This is hardly surprising in view of the way that public investment has increasingly been financed since then through the Private Finance Initiative (PFI). Much as 'off-balance sheet' jiggery-pokery and other 'creative accounting' allowed banks to get away with false impressions of their true financial position, so private financing of public sector projects via PFI created misleading presentations of the public accounts by understating the true liabilities of the public sector. It did so by artificially excluding from the Public Sector Borrowing Requirement (PSBR) the public sector's obligation to pay back private debt incurred as part of PFI projects. A corresponding obligation to repay public debt would have counted in the PSBR.

Public sector capital projects financed in orthodox ways by issuing public debt ('gilts') would count towards the PSBR. Such projects financed via PFI, whereby a private sector body raises the requisite funds by selling private debt which the contracting public sector body has a contractual obligation to repay over the life of the project, typically do not count towards the PSBR. In this way the government could make debt 'disappear' from its accounts: satisfying neoliberal financial orthodoxy and therefore very convenient, as New Labour found. But the huge drawback is that private finance is massively more expensive than public borrowing. So government could get four or five gilt-funded schools for the price of three funded by PFI.[22]

The 2013 independent Armitt Review on UK infrastructure planning looked at experience abroad. Understandably, it took no account of American practice. In 2008 over 70,000 bridges in the US were graded 'structurally deficient' by the American Society of Civil Engineers, due to inadequate upkeep, reflecting the low priority that the US devotes to infrastructure investment. But it is odd that the Armitt team also turned a blind eye to experience elsewhere in the European Union. As if Britain had nothing to learn from the most crowded country in Europe, the Netherlands; or from the home of the EU's largest motorway and high-speed rail networks, Spain; or from the hosts of some of Europe's most celebrated infrastructure initiatives like the Oresund bridge linking Denmark and Sweden; or from the country ranked best in the EU for the quality of its roads and railway infrastructure, France; or from Europe's most successful economy, Germany.

What Britain should have been doing – and still should be – is grabbing the opportunity, while real interest rates remain at record low levels, to bring our public infrastructure up to 21st-century standards by showing some of the ambition and imagination that the public sector, especially local government, did in Victorian days. That was when many of the foundations of today's social fabric – our rail network, our state schools, our sanitation systems, our public libraries – were laid down. It was when we began to set new social standards for community health and for public holidays, for reading and writing, for health and hygiene, for communications, for sport and for travel – for the essential elements of a civilised society.

The way to do so is to act on the advice of some (surprising) commentators and independent experts. Astonishingly, in February 2013 unnamed *Daily Telegraph* staff called on the Tory/Lib Dems to increase public borrowing in order to finance a £10 billion boost to infrastructure investment.[23] Later that year the *Economist* magazine carried a ringing editorial: 'What better time to invest in urgently needed infrastructure than when the cost of borrowing is at record lows? Greater public investment will boost economic potential in the long term and bolster public spending in the short term.'[24] This is not subversive socialism – more common sense.

Apart from the absolute imperative for new housing, infrastructure spending should focus upon the pressing need to modernise our transport, energy and communications networks. The rebalancing of the UK economy also needs to be more than simply towards investment. London absorbs 45 per cent of all inward foreign direct investment into the UK, according to Ernst & Young, and 27 per cent of all tourism spending in the UK. The worsening balance between the rest of Britain, on the one hand, and London and the South East (which together contributed 37 per cent of the growth in UK output in 1997–2006 and 48 per cent in 2007–2013),[25] on the other, has been aggravating congestion in parts of the country and deprivation elsewhere.

It is extraordinary how quiescent councillors and MPs from around the regions have been about a pattern of infrastructure spending that has so heavily favoured London at the expense of their constituents. The £9 billion invested in the Olympics came on top of £15 billion being spent on the Crossrail east–west route, £6 billion on the Thameslink north–south route, £30 billion upgrading the London Underground network, plus millions more on new London buses and the Thames Tideway Tunnel. New proposals are for a £10–15 billion Crossrail 2 underground rail route running north-east to south-west across London, and more bridges across the Thames in East London. Meanwhile Swansea must wait until 2018 for rail electrification, the South Wales valleys until 2024, and the rest of Wales until 2030. George Osborne's sudden suggestion in June 2014 for a high-speed rail link between Manchester and Leeds caught the headlines. He gave it a title, HS3, and a price tag, £7 billion. What he didn't give it was a timetable, because plans do not even exist on paper for such a project. Osborne said he 'wanted to start a conversation'. It was all spin, nothing more.

A 2013 study of 69 planned transport infrastructure projects in England involving public sector spending (solely or in partnership with the private sector) showed spend per head of population of £2,596 in London, £185 in the West Midlands and £5 in the North East of England.[26] Britain has the most extreme variation in living standards between regions anywhere in the European Union, as shown by the range between the richest UK sub region, Inner London, and the poorest, West Wales and The Valleys.[27] A reform of the Barnett formula for distributing Treasury funds is an imperative to steer a bigger share of resources into developing the infrastructure of Wales, Scotland and the English regions outside London and the South East.

Not only is there an imperative for much greater public investment in infrastructure, it is important to redistribute that right across the UK.

Low-carbon/green growth

Those who thought Britain had lost its sense of community were soon reassured when the floods came to the south and west of England in 2014, a reminder of more widespread 2007 flooding tragedies. The floods showed that when Nature exerts its strength, there is no substitute for the state. Self-help groups can only do so much. The complaint about the Environment Agency was 'too little too late', not 'too much too soon'. Even David Cameron didn't tell the flood victims to 'beware the Big State', as he had told the City just two months earlier. He told them that government was on their side, and quite right too, though his pledge that 'money was no object' proved unreal. The £140 million of new funding to repair recently damaged flood defences that was provided in the March 2014 budget dealt with 'short term recovery rather than long term prevention', according to Steve Bromhead, UK head of infrastructure at the consultancy EC Harris.[28]

Low-carbon investment is both a bulwark against the threat of devastation that climate change poses and the best way to pursue sustainable growth. Indeed in their September 2014 report *New Climate Economy*, the Global Commission on the Economy and Climate, sponsored by the UN, OECD, IMF and the World Bank, showed that growth can be substantially boosted by investment in renewable energy, low carbon fuels and better urban design, including integrated public transport. Changes to water supplies, crop yields, infrastructure needs and public health present all governments with formidably difficult decisions. The UK's growth strategy must take account of the impact of climate change and how its effects can be mitigated. Green investment is an absolute imperative.

For Labour this represents a real opportunity: green investment for growth. The National Federation of Arm's Length Management Organisations set out the first requirement at the end of 2012 – lifting of the borrowing caps set by the coalition government to free up £7 billion for building 15,000 new council homes a year. This one step could create 100,000 jobs and pump £20 billion into the economy as part of a green, low-carbon agenda. It means developing a range of low-carbon technologies and requires the cooperation of researchers, businesses, private investors and the state.

The UK currently ranks sixth in the worldwide low-carbon and environment goods and services market, behind our EU partner Germany, and Britain is among the top ten global destinations for foreign renewable energy investment. We are well placed to forge ahead in the low-carbon industry. We have a competitive edge. But the big roadblock is a lack of political leadership. For all of David Cameron's promise to be 'the greenest government ever', his dismantling of green levies severely set Britain back. His administration halved investment in renewable energy and delayed decisions on the Green Investment Bank. What a contrast with the example set by Ed Miliband, who in 2012 signed up to the 2030 decarbonisation target recommended by the UK government's official advisers, the Committee on Climate Change, recognising that decarbonising Britain's power sector could create 1 million new green jobs. And, with dependency upon gas and oil imports from often uncertain trading partners, the winding down of coal and the decline of North Sea oil, this is even more important for *energy security* reasons. Renewables could provide a passport to the energy security which Britain used to enjoy in the age of coal and North Sea oil but no longer does.

The 2014 floods highlighted how crucial adaptation and technology transfer are in a world where old assumptions, such as about the frequency of extreme events, are being overturned. Planners and developers will have to weigh housing needs against flood risks as well as cut the carbon emissions of individual homes alongside industrial emissions.

The UK Infrastructure Transitions Research Centre has made recommendations for using low-carbon investment in infrastructure to help Britain reach its goal of a reduction in emissions of 80 per cent by 2050. Among them are:

- local generation of electricity from solar power;
- electrifying heat and transport;
- additional liquified natural gas capacity;
- investment in nuclear generation;
- improvement of the West Coast Mainline, Greater London, South Wales and Central Scotland rail networks where the most congestion is expected;
- investment in water supply infrastructure;
- investment in waste and water treatment.

Waste is a case in point. The UK produces 300 million tonnes of waste a year. Recent recycling improvements have halved the amount of waste going to landfill, but saving our countryside from becoming one huge rubbish bin means investing significantly more in carbon-neutral recycling technology and the associated jobs.

Domestic and foreign firms already grasp the profit potential that low-carbon investment can unlock. The state must back them. In January 2013 business leaders – including big carbon producers like Unilever, Skanska, BT, EDF Energy and Shell – talked to the European Commission about the EU 2030 Climate and Energy Package White Paper. It recommends a minimum 40 per cent reduction in emissions by business by 2030.

The Green Alliance estimates that just four clean energy technologies (offshore wind, marine energy, carbon capture and storage, and electricity storage) could contribute £89 billion to UK GDP between now and 2050. So going green would be good for growth. After all the backtracking on the green agenda by the Tory/Lib Dems, Labour must restore confidence in the potential of low-carbon investment and enhance innovation that builds on Britain's advantage in clean technology. The party should also encourage international green markets and trade.

The Severn Barrage

A huge infrastructure investment boost would come from the Severn Barrage, a 'no-brainer', not least because it requires no Treasury funding. The £25 billion construction cost would be financed entirely privately, mainly from sovereign wealth funds and other large-scale institutional investors because they would have a guaranteed revenue stream over a period of 120 years or more. The project would create 20,000 jobs during its nine-year build – and, with multiplier effects, the stimulus amounts to £70 billion and a further 30,000 jobs, making a total of 50,000, many located in communities in South Wales and South West England crying out for such a boost. Eighty per cent of the spend is planned in the UK, unlike wind power where 80 per cent is spent abroad because countries like Germany and Norway have stolen a lead on wind-turbine manufacture.

The scheme would harness one of the world's largest potential sources of renewable energy: the huge tidal range of the Severn estuary – the second highest in the world. Building an 18-kilometre barrage between Brean in England and Lavernock Point in Wales would be one of the world's largest privately funded global engineering projects.

The barrage would produce clean, secure and predictable energy. It would generate as much electricity as three to four nuclear reactors or 3,000 wind turbines – around 5 per cent of UK demand. It would offset 7.1 million tonnes of CO_2 a year with a carbon payback – the time required for the power station to offset as much carbon as was required for its production – of around two years.

Most importantly, after the normal renewable price support period – at a low and very competitive 'strike price' – the Severn Barrage would produce the cheapest electricity in the UK: half the cost of alternative sources such as gas, nuclear and coal as well as other renewables. After a period of consumer subsidy lasting less than 25 per cent of its life – very small compared with other renewables –

the barrage would generate electricity at £20/MWh for at least a century, less than half the current wholesale market price.

Although the enormous scale of the barrage proposal has attracted criticism from wildlife groups, their concerns could be accommodated by innovative design and joint consultation – and it has considerable other benefits. The waters upstream of the barrage would be calmer and clearer and would encourage an increase in leisure and tourism, and make the Severn region a more appealing place in which to live and to locate businesses. The 1,026 turbines required (each the weight of a jumbo jet) would be built at two factories in the region, most probably in Port Talbot and Bristol. The planned caisson-casting yard at Port Talbot deep-water docks could be converted into a port for ultra-large container ships – making it the biggest such port in North West Europe. From there, Britain could also establish a global leadership in tidal technology. Unlike wind technology, where we are the world's largest importers, Britain could export its technology and expertise in tidal barrage construction around the world.

The barrage would also defend 90,000 properties and 500 square kilometres of Wales and the South West (including the Somerset levels) from tidal and coastal flooding, and prevent storm surges. In 2010 a storm surge that narrowly missed the Severn estuary caused €1.3 billion worth of damage when it made landfall in France. Scientists expect such events to occur more often in future.

Excluding the savings from storm surges, government and Environment Agency figures suggest that flood defence and damage savings from the barrage would be in the order of £2 billion to £15 billion. Land that would be protected from a rise in sea level and coastal flooding could be developed, encouraging local property values to rise and insurance premiums to fall. These considerable 'free' savings over the whole of its long life mean that the consumer price support subsidy the barrage would receive for much less than a quarter of its life is very good value for the nation.

Action on skills

There is another steep barrier to faster, sustainable growth in Britain. That is our reluctance to face up to fundamental problems, due in part to an allergy to active government. Perhaps the starkest such problem is the skills shortage that was first identified in the 1880s when newly industrialised Britain began to face serious competition from America and Europe. It has been holding the British economy back ever since, and we have never got to grips with it. In 1994 NIESR economists reckoned that even halving the skills gap between Britain and Germany would mean investing £40 billion extra per year every year for ten years. No one wanted even to acknowledge the size of the task, let alone tackle it. But the Commission on Social Justice – set up by the then Labour leader John Smith, chaired by Sir Gordon Borrie and served by its young secretary David Miliband – came closest.

The Commission reported in 1994. It recognised that in a market economy neoliberal economics could leave companies training too few staff for fear of losing them to poaching rivals, but that the most successful economies had overcome this failure of the market mechanism by setting minimum standards for *all* employers. They had not relied on market forces alone. In Singapore employers had to contribute 1 per cent of payroll to a national skills development fund. In Japan they were required to support a national employment insurance fund which provided training as well as unemployment insurance. In Germany employers contributed nearly 3.5 per cent of payroll towards training, employment and unemployment programmes. In France they were required to invest a minimum of 1 per cent of payroll in training or pay a training levy. While two thirds of UK employers invested *less* than 2 per cent of their payroll costs in training, three quarters of French employers invested *more* than 2 per cent of payroll in training. In 1994 the Social Justice Commission proposed a UK training levy set initially at 1 or 1.5 per cent of payroll, rising gradually to at least 2 per cent.[29]

But that same year Tony Blair and Gordon Brown succeeded John Smith and their New Labour approach was hypersensitive to new taxes on business. They hoped that peer pressure would encourage more employers to train, and pointed to role models like Rolls-Royce, renowned for the standard of its skills training, and British Gas, which somehow combined a poor reputation for customer service with a good one for training apprentices. Perhaps most pertinent of all was the training example set by inward investors like Nissan, Honda and Toyota and by EU competitors like Volkswagen and Ford Germany.

In government David Blunkett launched employer-led learning and skills councils and Charles Clarke promised a 'skills alliance' between the education sector, companies and unions. But by 2000 a minority of members of the UK National Skills Task Force had called for a stronger statutory framework for training, one which coupled obligations on firms to train with tax incentives to do so. New Labour's 'Big Conversation' consultation document of 2003 admitted that 'in skills policy the old voluntary and ad hoc measures did not work'. Chancellor Gordon Brown kept hinting about his frustrations with a voluntarist approach to training that had been tried and found wanting. Yet the Social Justice Commission call for a training levy went unanswered, just one more might-have-been where good intention triumphed over delivery.

New Labour had taken office at a time when one of the worst failings of the British education and training system was the proportion of mature people without even basic skills. The percentage of working people with only a basic education was 41 per cent in the UK, compared with only 14 per cent in Germany. In Britain we are rightly proud of our world-class universities and Nobel Prize-winning professors. But by steering resources towards an educational elite we have badly neglected more than half the population who never enter higher education. German school leavers enter an extensive training system designed to equip them with technical skills plus a grasp of law and business management. The Japanese spread their education and training efforts right across their society, making their workforce one of the most adaptable in the world. In both Germany and Japan active government and funding for training is the key ingredient, one which is missing in Britain.

The potential gains from improving human capital are enormous. The LSE Growth Commission estimated that improving UK school standards moderately, to German levels for instance, could put us on a growth path leading to a doubling of average incomes compared to current trends.[30] It would also tend to reduce wage inequality, welfare dependency and crime. However, the LSE study also found that Britain's education system suffers from a major systemic failure:

it lets down children from disadvantaged backgrounds. A fifth of children on free school meals do not reach the expected maths levels at age 7 and a third fall short by age 11.

Labour must tackle this failure to develop the talents of disadvantaged children. This can be done by focusing resources on underperforming schools serving disadvantaged children and by making 'outstanding' grades for schools depend on achieving improvements in the performance of disadvantaged pupils. Redesigning targets to reduce the emphasis on average pupil performance, which leads schools to steer resources towards children close to the threshold rather than those in greater need of support, would also help. So would focusing relentlessly upon excellent school leadership and demanding high standards regardless of school catchment deprivation indices; my own home education authority, Neath Port Talbot, demonstrated how vital that is by propelling what is a low income area containing high deprivation communities from mediocre to high levels of achievement.

The CBI began the 1990s calling for lifetime learning and claiming that business was spending £25 billion per year on training.[31] Two decades later the picture is worse, not better: the equivalent figure is £20 billion. Today, of total UK spending on adult learning of £55 billion, or nearly 4 per cent of GDP, £26 billion comes from the public purse and £9 billion from individuals (including the self-employed). Additionally, the public subsidy for vocational training through various forms of tax relief amounts to £3.7 billion.[32]

The challenge remains the same as it was in the 1990s: to upgrade the skills of the whole workforce, not just young entrants. And that means the state resourcing lifelong learning where nobody else will. Launching Labour's Agenda 2030 plan for long-term sustainable growth in March 2014, Shadow Business Secretary Chuka Umunna backed 'Catapult centres' (government-backed innovation and technology centres which aim to help turn new technology ideas into new businesses) and made a welcome call for them to train apprentices. Some 80 per cent of the workforce in ten years' time will be those who are today already in work or looking for a job, underlining the gravity of what amounts to a chronic UK under-skills back-log. Moreover, the least skilled workers are the ones with the lowest chance of receiving training and the ones most likely to lose their jobs. The people most in danger of receiving a redundancy notice are those most likely to have trouble reading it. And the workers who struggle most with numbers are the ones most likely to receive a P45.

Most people studying in further education do so part-time. They are the ones for whom post-school education never was free. Baroness Helena Kennedy once called them the Cinderellas of the education world. Most of the growth in student numbers in colleges and universities in recent decades has been among people studying part-time, and most of these have been women. They should be a priority for state support.

The skills gap separating Britain from our rivals is no narrower today than in the past. Despite persistent and wholly justified calls across the political spectrum for greater investment and focus upon skills; despite employers continuously complaining that the skills of new recruits are either inappropriate or well short of requirements; despite almost everyone worshipping at the same skills shrine, short-term self-interest keeps favouring poaching instead of coaching. Training places matter less than parking places to too many employers. It is time to make the poacher pay, first by requiring employers to invest the equivalent of up to 2 per cent of their pay bill in skills training or face a statutory levy, and second by enforcing training standards – much as safety standards or obligations to pay the national minimum wage are enforced today.

Adopting such a democratic socialist approach to skills upgrading would launch Britain into a rapid catch-up with our competitors. Understandably, business may complain at an 'extra cost'. But without it, business leaders and politicians would be more honest if they declared nothing could be done and Britain together with its businesses might as well continue to totter along, resigned to falling behind on growth and prosperity.

Whichever way it is examined, Britain's economic predicament – our low investment, meagre exports, weak infrastructure, limited skills and poor productivity – cannot be overcome without active government willing to defy neoliberal austerity and propel the country on a new path to both international competitiveness and domestic prosperity for all.

CHAPTER 12

A fairer, more equal society

Seventy years after Labour created the welfare state based on the Beveridge report, a fresh and complementary set of social priorities is needed, both to reduce the acute inequalities that are undermining social cohesion and to match social policy to the current and future requirements of contemporary society.

However, this is not only about creating a fairer society, it is also about building a more successful economy.

Taxation

Tony Crosland's focus was on promoting greater equality by taxing wealth more, and taxing income from work less. He specifically ruled out any further major redistribution of earned income by direct taxation, because the top rate of tax on earnings then stood at 83 per cent. Instead he envisaged using the proceeds from higher death duties to lighten the income tax load on earnings.

Crosland saw the distribution of wealth, especially inherited wealth, as flagrantly unfair and the primary cause of inequality in Britain, for two reasons.

First, because inherited wealth distorts the distribution of *investment income* in favour of those who are already well off – since capital gains, dividends and interest payments go disproportionately to people who own assets like company shares or property or who can afford to lend. To tackle that particular problem he called for a tax on capital gains, which Harold Wilson's Labour government introduced in 1965. By 2007 individuals were charged capital gains tax at their highest marginal income tax rate. That changed when

Alastair Darling's October 2007 budget announced a single rate of capital gains tax of 18 per cent from April 2008. Since June 2010 capital gains tax has been charged at either 18 per cent or 28 per cent depending on the individual's total taxable income, way below the 45 per cent top rate of income tax in 2014. By adjusting their affairs to receive rewards as capital gains instead of as income, some highly rewarded people can pay less tax.

Second, and much more important to Crosland, inherited wealth perpetuates privilege from one generation to the next. It does so by providing access to the best possible education, to contact networks and to career ladders, meaning that most of the best jobs stay in the hands of a favoured few – witness the composition of David Cameron's Conservative Cabinets (mostly millionaires, many Old Etonians), the top ranks of the judiciary, Britain's business boardrooms, our military and diplomatic services and the senior civil service. Income inequality therefore persists and inherited wealth is passed on.

Therefore Crosland also supported reforming death duties to make all gifts made during someone's lifetime subject to some form of inheritance tax, with appropriate exemptions and limits. The Labour government's 1975 capital transfer tax did so. It was highly progressive, with a top rate of tax for cumulative transfers over £2 million of 75 per cent. But it was fundamentally weakened by the Thatcher administration which quickly abandoned the whole idea of a 'cradle to grave' tax, slashed the tax rate, and renamed it inheritance tax.

New Labour said and did next to nothing about inequality due to inherited wealth, and until 2006 'paid little attention to inheritance tax'.[1] In his October 2007 Pre-Budget Report, Alistair Darling effectively doubled the threshold before inheritance tax became due for husbands and wives and civil partners to £600,000 and raised the threshold to £312,000 per person from April 2008. This followed the then Shadow Chancellor George Osborne's dramatic pledge to the 2007 Tory Party conference to lift the threshold to £1 million.

By 2013 the threshold was £325,000 and set to stay there until 2017. With plenty of homes worth far more than the average UK house price in 2013 of £240,000, many households and not just the elite appear potentially liable to inheritance tax. However, the high threshold, exemptions and a transferable allowance between married couples and civil partners meant that they in practice had an allowance of £650,000 against inheritance tax. As a result inheritance tax is actually paid in a tiny number of cases: fewer than 15,000 people, less than 3 per cent of those who die each year. So, no inheritance tax is paid on the estates of more than 97 per cent of people who die each year and the tax raises less than £3 billion in annual revenue. Inherited wealth continues to pass from generation to generation hardly touched by the taxman, and inequality endures. Under the Tory/Lib Dems it meant that, with only a modicum of so-called 'tax planning', millionaires could pass on their wealth more or less intact, untouched and untroubled by HM Revenue & Customs.

One exception remains: wealth in the form of residential property, which is subject both to stamp duty when bought and to council tax. But even here there are loopholes limiting the impact on the very wealthy. Some people with very high value homes who might otherwise have had to pay a relatively high rate of council tax each year on their property actually pay less, because rateable values for council tax purposes were frozen within eight bands based on their April 1991 values. Properties in the top band pay twice the standard rate of council tax however high their value soars (except in Wales where, since April 2006, properties have been allocated to bands based on April 2003 values, with a ninth band requiring council tax at 2.33 times the standard rate). Freezing council tax was a priority for the Tory/Lib Dem government, further favouring the very well off and ensuring that council tax remains a regressive tax which weighs more heavily on those with low or modest incomes than those at the top of the income ladder.

If no significant progress has been made since the 1970s in promoting greater equality of wealth by taxing it more heavily, what has happened to the distribution of income? Among the developed economies, according to Wilkinson and Pickett, the UK ranks close to Singapore, the US and Portugal as the most unequal, with the richest 20 per cent of households getting about *seven* times as much as the poorest 20 per cent, after taxes and benefits.[2] Comparable multiples for France and Germany are below *six*, and for the Scandinavian countries and Japan below *four*.

This evidence is given added resonance by Wilkinson and Pickett's other finding that a clear link exists between inequality and the incidence of a wide range of health and social problems like obesity, crime, poor educational performance, addiction, teenage births and low levels of trust, all of which add to the pressures on the public finances. In unequal societies everyone loses, the winners too. Social stability requires government to promote a fair society. That is clear from the evidence linking social problems to levels of income inequality.

Since Tony Crosland's day income inequality has soared in Britain. The big change came when the neoliberal era took a real grip in the 1980s when there was a rise that was unparalleled in recent UK history and unmatched by changes elsewhere in the developed world, save for the US. Incomes grew far faster among the very highest income groups and kept on doing so in subsequent decades, especially the 2000s, most notably in the finance sector and among chief executives across the private sector. In 2008 income inequality reached its highest level since at least 1961.[3] By 2014 the UK had become the only G7 member where wealth inequality had increased since 2000, according to Credit Suisse's *Global Wealth Report 2014*.

After taking account of inflation and changes in household structures over time, the average disposable income of all households in 2011–12 was 2.24 times higher than in 1977, with the average income of the poorest 20 per cent of households only 1.93 times higher while that of the richest 20 per cent of households was 2.49 times higher.[4] People on low and average incomes have seen their share of national income shrink for decades due to the rise in inequality that New Labour was so relaxed about, adding to the burden borne by what Deborah Mattinson began calling 'the squeezed middle' in 2005.[5]

People on low and middle incomes in Britain have been squeezed on two fronts. First, their share of total UK income shrank as the share enjoyed by people on very high incomes expanded. They lost out as inequality increased. Second, their incomes also suffered as recession led to slack in the economy, an output gap. They worked fewer hours and prices rose faster than pay. Their loss of income due to the first may well have exceeded that from the second, especially if the Office for Budget Responsibility's low estimate of the UK output gap is to be believed. This would mean that increasing inequality had done more than the recession to squeeze middle-class incomes,[6] making inequality a major issue rather than the minor one that New Labour treated it as.

In Britain three things have happened since the 1970s: incomes have grown fastest among those at the very top end of the scale; taxation has shifted from taxing income to taxing spending, especially by value added tax which hits the poorest the hardest; and the top rate of income tax has been cut much more than the basic rate. Between 1979 and 1988 the Tories cut the top rate of income tax from 83 to 40 per cent, and the basic rate from 35 to 25 per cent, while raising VAT from 8 to 15 per cent (and to 17.5 per cent in 1991 and 20 per cent in January 2011).

New Labour stuck to its pledge not to raise the top rate of income tax until the financial crisis compelled it to announce a new temporary top rate of 50 per cent from April 2010. It cut the basic rate progressively and finally to 20 per cent in April 2007 in Gordon Brown's last flourish as Chancellor of the Exchequer. Although this may have appeared to favour those on middle or low incomes, there was a more complex picture when national insurance contribution rates on earned income are taken into account. They did rise over the years to 11 per cent in 2009–10: in practice, a tax in all but label. But an upper earnings limit beyond which only a 1 per cent contribution was required meant that people on very high earnings saw their effective tax rate drop below that facing people on more modest earnings.

The upshot is plain. The common belief that the UK tax system is progressive, redistributing resources from the rich to the poor by taxing the well off at a higher rate than those on low and modest incomes, is false. UK taxes are broadly proportional, with progressive direct taxes like income tax being offset by regressive indirect taxes like VAT and duties on alcohol and tobacco. In 2011–12 the richest 20 per cent of households paid 35.5 per cent of their gross income in taxes (both direct and indirect, and including national insurance contributions). The poorest 20 per cent of households paid 36.6 per cent.[7] It is cash benefits like the state pension and benefits in kind from public services, especially the NHS and education, which genuinely redistribute in the UK – precisely the benefits and services neoliberals in general and the Tory/Lib Dems in particular have been assaulting through their cuts programme.

Which is why their threats to squeeze welfare benefits even further and to cut government consumption as a proportion of GDP (ie spending incurred providing public services like education and health rather than transfers like the state pension or child benefit) to what would be its lowest level since 1948 are so horrific. They would redistribute resources, both in cash and kind, away from those in greatest need, creating a less fair, a less healthy and a less stable society in the process, with incalculable consequences for all of us.

Meanwhile they made great play of declaring Britain 'open for business' by cutting corporation tax. But some of the world's greatest international companies doing big business in the UK pay little or no tax at all on the profits they make here. We know the reason why. Tax loopholes and tax havens have allowed illegal tax evasion to pose as legal tax avoidance for too long. Tax Research UK has estimated that a massive £47 billion annually is lost from tax avoidance and tax planning by companies like Amazon, Starbucks, Vodafone and Goldman Sachs, and super-wealthy individuals, some of whom base themselves in places like Monaco to avoid spending too many days at their homes in the UK to qualify for UK taxes.

The British government could take a real bite out of the budget deficit if it cracked down on tax avoidance, tightened loopholes and reformed tax relief. For instance, by stopping blatant abuses such as the exploitation of residency rules by City high-fliers who commute by jet between Monaco and London on Mondays and Thursdays. Or by restricting tax reliefs that benefit top-rate income taxpayers, following the example set by Alastair Darling in 2009 when he limited the tax benefit from private pension contributions by higher rate income taxpayers to the basic rate of tax. Or by taxing back from the big banks the billions of extra profit they make from the implicit subsidy represented by the guarantee of a state bailout – estimated to have been worth £50 billion per year to the big five UK banks over the period 2007 to 2009.

Seven-point programme of tax reform

Labour should encourage greater equality by raising tax on wealth, especially inherited wealth, and by shifting towards a progressive system of tax on income and spending through a seven-point programme.

First, by reforming inheritance tax, adjusting thresholds, reliefs, allowances and rates so that it once again becomes as progressive as capital transfer tax was 40 years ago.

Second, by introducing a 'mansion tax' through new council tax bands on the highest value residential properties, those worth more than £2 million. Ed Balls has made clear that a banded system would not require annual valuation of properties, that residents on modest incomes who happen to live in an area where property prices have shot up could be protected, and that a relief scheme could allow those on modest incomes to defer payment until the property is sold, to ensure that a mansion tax is fair to those who are asset rich but cash poor.

Third, by backing a financial transactions tax (or 'Robin Hood' tax) on share sales and currency transactions. Such a tax, agreed initially at EU level, would begin to create a communal benefit from the huge volume of foreign exchange trading that occurs in the world's largest financial market. The grand coalition government that took office in Germany in December 2013 included a financial transactions tax in its agreed programme. Levied at up to 0.5 per cent on currency deals, it could raise a phenomenal £20 billion annually in the UK.

Fourth, by scrapping the reduced rate at which employees on high earnings pay national insurance contributions (2 per cent in 2014), so that they pay at the standard rate (12 per cent in 2014) on *all* their earnings. Contributions paid by employers are already charged at a standard rate (13.8 per cent in 2014) all the way up the earnings scale. Why should people on high earnings pay standard rate national insurance contributions on only *part* of their earnings when lower paid people must pay contributions on *all* their earnings? Scrapping the reduced rate may make it possible to lower the standard rate so that only people on very high earnings pay more, or to raise the lower earnings limit (£111 per week/£5,772 per year in 2014) at which people start to pay national insurance contributions, to help the low paid.

The effect of scrapping the upper earnings limit would be to raise the top rate of income tax and national insurance combined from 47 per cent (45 per cent top rate of income tax plus the 2 per cent reduced rate of national insurance contributions in 2014) to 62 per cent (Labour's promised 50 per cent top rate of income tax plus the 12 per cent standard national insurance contribution rate). HM Treasury estimates the extra revenue from scrapping the upper earnings limit would range between £6 billion and £11 billion, depending on how top earners adjust to the new rates, with most of the extra revenue coming from the national insurance reform rather than from the income tax change.[8] An earlier estimate by the Institute for Fiscal Studies, in 2003, put the extra revenue from scrapping the national insurance upper earnings limit at around £8 billion.[9] Whatever the final figure, these are substantial additional revenues to help secure a much fairer and more civilised society and more efficient economy.

Although a combined top rate of tax and national insurance of 62 per cent on the highest earnings falls well short of Thomas Piketty's dramatic call for an 80 per cent top rate of income tax, it is well within the realm of practical politics, especially given the grotesque and widening inequality in modern Britain. By contrast, Piketty's proposal has no prospect of winning popular and political backing – something he acknowledges, in a masterpiece of understatement: 'It seems quite unlikely that any such policy will be adopted anytime soon.'[10]

The *fifth* tax change would be to reinstate Denis Healey's higher rate of VAT on high-value luxury goods such as those regularly promoted in colour supplements like *FT Wealth* and *How To Spend It*, and extending VAT to private fees for education.

Sixth, by learning from the single most successful tax innovation during the life of the last Labour government, the central London congestion charge. It was effective and it has been accepted. The congestion problems on our major roadways are a growing problem that is crying out for an appropriate road-pricing solution. The starting point should be our crowded motorways and congested city centres.

Seventh, by extending stamp duty to football transfer fees and by taxing the proceeds from sales of broadcasting rights by monopolistic sports organisations and using the money for grassroots football support which might also help build high-quality national football teams in the UK instead of the uncompetitive ones we have now. The Premier League sold its domestic live TV broadcast rights in 2012 in a three-year £3 billion deal and could soon see sales to overseas broadcasters push total revenue above £5 billion.

Cuts in the top rate of income tax were supposed to boost economic growth by encouraging entrepreneurial activity through incentives to save more and work harder – but they had no such result. The UK growth rate slowed after the 1960s rather than accelerated. Increased inequality has been bad for growth. Restoring fairness to the tax system would help promote growth and the greater social cohesion and shared purpose that lie at the heart of Labour's values.

Financing students and universities

Another example where reform is needed to promote fairness is student finance, which in Britain is an utter shambles. Students are emerging from universities with mountainous debts. Universities are increasingly short of funds, driving down Britain's position in the absolutely crucial global league of higher education. Fees were first introduced by New Labour at £1,000 annually and increased to £3,000. But they were trebled by the Tory/Lib Dems to £9,000 and are a disincentive for some to go into higher education, with clear indications that mature students and working-class male applicants are worst affected.[11] And on top of all that, the Treasury is facing rising defaults from fees and loans that will never be repaid, increasing borrowing and debt – the very consequence which excessively high fees were intended to avoid when the Tory/Lib Dems effectively privatised university teaching with an 80 per cent budget cut that transferred the cost from taxpayers to students and their families.

Government answers to parliamentary questions revealed in March 2014 that write-off costs had reached 45 per cent of the total £10 billion in loans to students each year. And indeed that if the default level crept up a bit to 48.6 per cent, the government would be losing more money than it would have saved before it trebled annual student fees from £3,000 to £9,000. Given that the loans would be repaid over a long period by those earning over £21,000, it has been estimated that around the midpoint of this century when the 30-year rule kicks in and the debt is written off, fully £90 billion of the £200 billion would remain unpaid.[12] That is a colossal waste of the very public expenditure that neoliberal architects of the policy are ideologically fixated with cutting, and which could have been directed at vital public projects like social housing, schools, hospitals and railways – or, for that matter, universities.

According to research undertaken by my former Cabinet Minister colleague John Denham MP, taxpayers now spend £7.50 on debt cancellation for every £1 they spend on teaching students.

> The system runs so hot that a small misjudgement about student numbers creates a huge hole in the [government departmental] budget. So we have ministers arguing about whether to cut research or support for poorer students. The National Audit Office have highlighted the black hole of unrecoverable loans, including those to EU students. The cost of debt cancellation – the so-called Resource Account Budgeting or RAB charge – is rising steadily … Half of all today's students will pay 9 per cent of all their income above the repayment threshold for the next 30 years and they still won't clear their debts. And that takes no account of bank loans, credit cards and any other debts that mount up while studying.

Meanwhile university capital spending has been severely cut and in consequence more universities have been plunged into greater debt to finance the investment they require. The science budget will have fallen by 20 per cent in real terms by 2016, reversing most of what had been achieved during Labour's significant ten-year investment in science.[13]

John Denham added:

A high-fee, high-debt cancellation policy forces up everyone's fees and institutionalises waste. If more were spent on teaching, fees would fall, as would the level of loans, the amount the Government had to borrow, the level and rate of debt cancellation, and the liability on the taxpayer. As a result of fees being lower, we would enjoy the virtuous outcome whereby all graduates would pay back less on their loans and more graduates would fully repay what they had borrowed.

The system is not only unfair and discriminatory, it is also unsustainable and damaging to both Britain's long-term economic prospects and our social well-being.

So could the system of repaying university fees and maintenance loans with a tax paid by new graduates (that is, those who go through higher education *after* a new system has been introduced) be fairer and better? A graduate tax might well offer a more sustainable stream of revenue for the Treasury than the current system and thus be more fiscally responsible. To examine this alternative let's assume that there is no alteration in the real value of money received by higher education institutions from the Treasury, and there are no changes in student numbers.

The only detailed studies currently available come from the Million+ higher education think tank. Its 2010 study estimated that a graduate tax of 1 per cent could be adequate,[14] but figures have risen sharply with the increase in fees, as a more recent Million+ study shows.[15] It looked at replacing the current funding system (including the repayment of both fees and maintenance loans), giving two options for 30- and 40-year repayment periods. It made calculations on the basis of abolishing the current fees system in the future, and also repaying maintenance loans. Graduates would make a contribution based on their salary, with the rate of tax rising across bands in much the same way that income tax already does. Nothing would have to be paid on earnings up to £10,000 per year. Earnings between £10,000 and £25,000 would attract an extra tax rate of 2 per cent, then 2.75 per cent applied to earnings between £25,000 and £42,000. Earnings above that would be taxed at 3.5 per cent.

It would be perfectly practical to implement such a system, and the economic costs to government would be the same.[16] It would be much, much simpler and undoubtedly fairer. It seems certain that graduates would prefer a graduate tax over the current system which involves them in a greater cost, saddles them with debts affecting mortgage credibility and is highly regressive. The clincher surely is that the new tax rates involved will all feel very much lower than what is paid now, and thus have less of a disincentive effect on entering university.

With a graduate tax, those earning between around £10,000 and £21,000 annually would pay extra tax at 2 per cent, whereas under the present system such graduates pay no extra tax at all until their pay exceeds £21,000, when they face a jump to an extra 9 per cent. Compare even the highest graduate tax rate of 3.5 per cent which would be paid on earnings greater than £42,000 with the high 9 per cent now paid by former students earning over £21,000 (in England). A graduate tax would also favour citizenship and community over the privatisation favoured by neoliberals: exactly where a democratic socialist Britain should be.

Welfare reform

When Secretary of State for Work and Pensions from 2007, I pursued policies and introduced reforms to support people getting into work and off benefits. And before the banking crisis, Labour had considerable success with its programme to do so, making a start on bringing down the welfare benefits bill bequeathed by the Thatcher and Major Tory governments in the 1980s and 1990s. Contrary to Tory claims, Britain did not have an over-generous welfare state whose costs 'were spiralling out of control under Labour': in 2007 the UK spent 4.5 per cent of GDP on income support to the working-age population compared to 5.6 per cent by Sweden, 6 per cent by Finland, 7 per cent by Denmark and 7.2 per cent by Belgium.[17]

In the 1980s and 1990s millions of redundant workers such as miners and others in traditional industries like clothing and textiles and heavy engineering were expressly encouraged to go onto incapacity benefit (then termed 'invalidity benefit') – not taxable and more generously funded than allowances paid to jobseekers – to conceal the true level of unemployment. Most never worked again, and that legacy was to last at least a generation – often passed on to their children – condemned to a life of worklessness and the ill-health which accompanies that lifestyle.

But Labour's programmes to tackle this problem were costly. What is insensitively termed in the jargon *the flow* (the people moving in and out of work and reliant upon benefits temporarily) are relatively cheap to support. But it is very costly to retrain and equip *the stock* (those who have been off work for years), in order to give them both the confidence and the ability to succeed in a job interview. I witnessed moving examples of people who had been able to come off years on benefit and take on jobs. But the support that they required was both very intensive and very expensive. As I saw for myself, the same experience is evident in New York City's tough work programmes: they do not save the local state any money, but are judged a success by getting people into work with all its benefits to the local economy as well as to their lifestyle, self-esteem and health.

Yet the Tory/Lib Dems swept in with fierce cuts to funding for work programmes and punitive procedures to cut the number of claimants for disability benefits. If Britain's working poor were cast as so many Oliver Twists condemned to the workhouse, then the government was surely Mr Bumble, looking aghast at a starving child and exclaiming 'More? You want more?' Ministers seemed not to have the faintest idea of the devastating impact of their welfare reforms on the most genuinely vulnerable and needy. One of my Neath constituents told me she felt 'terrorised'.

The impact was indeed terrifying in communities like those in South Wales which, for historical reasons, had lower than average wages, higher unemployment, more industrial injuries, more disability, more illness, and therefore more benefit claimants. Many forced to work part-time in low-paid, often insecure jobs were competing with the thousands more unemployed in their local labour market, with six people or even more chasing every vacancy. Like the peloton in the Tour de France, everyone on their bike in hot pursuit of a job but with only one yellow jersey to be won. Far from conquering poverty and making it pay to work, as ministers constantly professed, their policies had the very reverse effect.

Government suggestions that people shore up their income by taking on more hours simply ignored local realities. '*Under*employment' also became a trend. Across Britain the number of people working part-time who wanted to work full-time soared to a record level. In Wales, before the recession in 2005–08 there were on average 86,000 underemployed workers. By early 2014 there were more than 149,000, a jump of over 73 per cent. It meant more than one in ten Welsh workers were thwarted from working as much as they wished – indeed often thwarted from bringing themselves above the working benefits threshold. They were also supposed to compete locally against hundreds of youngsters between the ages of 16 and 24, including graduates demoralised by being rejected as both 'overqualified and underexperienced'.

There was no practical support, either, for carers having to balance work with other duties, and trying to make extra hours fit into already unmanageable timetables. Being in work should always be preferable to relying on welfare, but this will only be the case if the government helps to create jobs and guarantees a living wage across the public and private sectors. As long as full-time work is so badly paid in so many parts of Britain that it falls beneath certain welfare thresholds, then the case for removing those benefits cannot be made in good faith.

An impact study undertaken at Sheffield Hallam University in 2012 showed Neath to be one of the worst affected constituencies.[18] An old industrial area dominated in the past by coal and steel, it had around 6,000 people in receipt of incapacity benefits, one of the highest counts in the country. Under the Tory/Lib Dems, official estimates showed over a third of them were assessed 'fit for work', stripped of their incapacity benefit and arbitrarily forced to seek jobs which either didn't exist or, if they did, were likely to be low-paid, part-time, temporary – or a combination of all three. Often in their late fifties or early sixties, they experienced stigmatisation by local Job Centre workers forced to administer oppressive regulations and procedures designed solely to cut the welfare bill, not to increase job opportunities.

People with serious health problems, including cerebral palsy, hemiplegia and a speech impediment, previously worked in sheltered employment in the local Remploy factory. But that was closed. One constituent taking over 20 tablets a day and in and out of hospital was found fit for work. Meanwhile, hard-working people were made to feel tawdry and ashamed by the government.

Added to this chaotic and upsetting process was the payment of housing benefit to tenants rather than landlords, ostensibly to teach a semblance of 'responsibility', but loudly denounced by addiction and mental health charities as fundamentally misunderstanding the predicament of vulnerable citizens.

Government ministers deliberately presented the choice as between 'scroungers and strivers', or between 'workers and shirkers' – encouraging a frenzy of bile in largely compliant newspapers. This demonstrated wilful ignorance about the realities of poverty, unemployment, lack of jobs and welfare reliance, and their highly complex causes. Far from promoting a sense of pride and opportunity, government 'reforms' humiliated through dehumanising assessment tests performed by quota-ticking private companies like Atos and Capita, preoccupied with meeting government cost-cutting targets come what may. In Neath, appeals by the local Welfare Rights Unit against test results that forced people with serious disabilities onto the jobs market had an 80 per cent success rate – proof not simply of the grief involved but also of a chronic waste of money in the system.

A zealous drive to cut the budget deficit no matter what was predicted to make 500,000 people with disabilities worse off under the new Universal Credit system, on top of big cuts to child disability payments. Single parents with disabilities would lose twice over. Overall, the think tank Demos revealed in March 2013 that up to 3.7 million disabled people were set to lose £28.3 billion in support by 2018 – with thousands simultaneously hit by as many as six different welfare cuts, some losing out multiple times.

The notorious 'bedroom tax' meant people with disabilities no longer had a spare room for relatives to come and stay to take care of them. The bedroom tax hit over 400,000 people with disabilities and 60,000 carers. One of my constituents affected was a carer for his severely disabled, bedridden wife who hardly slept at night and so had the TV on constantly – yet the government aimed to deprive him of his second bedroom, in an area where there were no local one-bedroom homes available. Meanwhile young families were unable to have a relative to stay to ease soaring childcare costs, forcing people out of work and onto benefits in order to look after their young children.

In Neath there were bedroom tax cases when separated parents who did not have full care of the children were unable to have them on weekends because they were not considered eligible to have a 'spare room'. Under the Tory/Lib Dems, Neath became one of 69 areas in Wales where half or more of all children were living in poverty, with a household income totalling less than 60 per cent of the average. These official figures are shocking enough without taking into consideration the rising cost of living, with utility bills and food prices spiralling. Or indeed the Tory/Lib Dem cap on benefits, which was estimated to push a further 200,000 children across Britain into poverty.

Local food banks saw soaring numbers needing help, half of them in work but desperate – some 'Big Society'. Across Britain the number of food banks run by the Trussell Trust rose from 80 in January 2011 to 400 by December 2013, with a further 100 run by others. In the UK a third of a million people received at least three days' emergency food from Trussell Trust food banks in 2012–13.[19] Viewed from Neath, the prospect of returning the country to a Victorian state of dependency on charitable handouts was all too real, the image of the government as a Dickensian cabal rang only too true. Partly Bleak House, partly Clique House, with 10 Downing Street run by a small elite of hard-hearted, out-of-touch Old Etonians. Neoliberalism had reached its apotheosis.

It also failed even on its own terms by adding billions to the cost of social security by failing to control those costs. The government was on course to spend £15 billion more than budgeted in 2010 on social security and tax credits,[20] despite imposing cuts on working families. The total cost to the Exchequer of the record number of people working part-time who wanted full-time jobs was £4.7 billion a year, with £1.8 billion of those costs in housing benefit alone.[21] The housing benefit bill was on track to increase over the Parliament, and the amount of housing benefit alone paid to those who were either in work or short-term sick was expected to rise by over £1 billion between 2013–14 and 2016–17.[22] And forcing poor people caught by the bedroom tax into homelessness was set to add to local council costs. Total spending on in-work benefits such as housing benefit and tax credits was set to rise in real terms beyond 2015, despite signs of economic recovery at last in 2013 and real-term cuts to individual entitlements.

The Tory/Lib Dem focus upon punishing benefit claimants rather than encouraging decently paid jobs also backfired. Lower than expected increases in wages between March and December 2013 meant higher compensating state subsidies which alone were expected to add £100 million to the tax credit bill in 2015–16, and £200 million in 2016–17 and 2017–18.[23] Cumulatively these cost increases represented a failure to curb public expenditure on a grand scale as well as misery for human casualties along the way.

The best way to get the social security bill down for the long term remains for government to invest in growth by getting people into jobs, ensuring those jobs are secure and well-paid, and to build more homes. Labour's commitment to a jobs guarantee illustrated the role for active rather than neoliberal government. Young people aged 18–24 and out of work for 12 months or more would be offered a six-month job paid at the national minimum wage, with training and development included; those failing to take up those job opportunities risking losing their benefits. Similarly there would be a compulsory jobs guarantee for the long-term unemployed, with the assurance of a six-month job paid at the national minimum wage for all those claiming jobseeker's allowance for two years or over; again those failing to take up those jobs risking losing their benefits.

This is not only a fairer, more just policy, it is also firm: people who can work should do so. It is no part of a socialist society to have low-income taxpayers providing a subsidy for neighbours choosing not to work when jobs are available. But a willingness to invest in supporting the unemployed to get into work is much more likely to bear fruit, by bringing down joblessness and saving public money, than the right-wing programme of cost cutting and punishing claimants. Welfare policy throws into sharp relief the stark choice facing Britain.

Ageing society

So most certainly does our ageing society, which did not feature as a major problem in the mid-1950s when Tony Crosland wrote. Baroness Joan Bakewell, who acted as a Voice for Older People for the last Labour government between 2008 and 2010, explained the reality of modern Britain and its threadbare elderly care in a Fabian Society study:

> No outright cruelty is being inflicted. Instead there is a steady erosion of care, and with it human dignity, that sees people spiral downhill in health and wellbeing. This is what awaits each of us and each of those we love unless something is done. Things must change soon and radically.

In the same study, it was reported that the UK population aged over 65 is set to triple to nearly 16 million by three quarters of the way through this century, with dementia rife. Already, as former Labour Secretary of State for Health Andy Burnham pointed out, 'Stories of older people neglected or abused in care homes, isolated in their own homes or lost in acute hospitals – disorientated and dehydrated – recur with ever greater frequency.'[24] The Nuffield Trust and the Health Foundation jointly reported in March 2014 that four years of cuts to local authority funding had already forced councils to ration social care services tightly.[25] A quarter of a million older people had lost their state-funded help for carrying out everyday activities such as bathing, climbing the stairs, taking medicine, using the toilet, dressing and eating. Although *fully a third* of women and a fifth of men over the age of 65 needed help with such basic daily living activities, they were unable to get it, putting huge pressures on friends and family carers, and leading to unnecessary hospital admissions. And without radical changes, things can only get radically worse.

Labour's 2010 manifesto promised a 'National Care Service' – for England at least, since devolution has left Wales, Scotland and Northern Ireland responsible for policy and delivery. Although, should a universally funded scheme be implemented, the devolved governments may wish to (and probably should) become part of it to attract UK funding, rather as the NHS does, even if it is delivered in different ways.

Because it was to be partly funded by a retrospective claim on estates, Labour's policy was luridly attacked by the *Daily Mail* as a 'death tax' and seized upon by the Tories in the run-up to the 2010 election. After which – and amidst the Tory/Lib Dem austerity orthodoxy – Labour seemed more nervous, though Ed Miliband, Andy Burnham and Liz Kendall were very clear that in the century of the ageing society, social care has to be part of the NHS settlement. They proposed the full integration of physical, mental health and social care into a single-budget, single-service looking after a person's complete health and care needs. But that 'whole person care' applies as much to the child with complex needs and the working-age adult with disabilities as it does to the older person.

The Treasury has resisted biting the bullet of an ageing society by refusing to sanction sufficient public spending that, coupled with a contribution from the individual, could fund full care in dignity and decency. Yet there is no alternative solution – indeed the consequences of an ageing society have left neoliberals and their 'stand on your own two feet' dogma with no answers. Only a collective solution will meet the sheer scale of the challenge.

In March 2014 the charity Age UK's annual review of the state of social care reported a 'catastrophic' situation developing in England, with growing numbers of vulnerable elderly people being denied care: the proportion of over-65s getting help had fallen by a third since 2005–06. In 2013, under 900,000 of vulnerable over-65s got help – just 10 per cent of people in that group – compared with 15 per cent seven years before. The report estimated that at least 800,000 older people were going without vital help, including local council-funded help in the home for daily tasks such as washing, dressing and eating as well as care home places.

Age UK explained that Tory/Lib Dem government cuts in funding had forced councils to reduce budgets by 15 per cent in real terms since 2010. The result was that councils increasingly rationed services, and that a paltry 13 per cent of local authorities were providing help to people with moderate needs compared with nearly half in 2005–06.

There are ever greater numbers of very frail people in their eighties and nineties, with intensive physical, mental and social care needs. In fact there are over 1.4 million people aged 85 or over and this figure is rising year on year. Yet hospitals have hardly changed to reflect this new reality, with nurses struggling to cope with it, as Andy Burnham heard from a senior nurse: hospitals 'were still operating on a 20th century production-line model, with a tendency to see the immediate problem – the broken hip, the stroke – but not the whole-person behind it'. As he argued in a speech to the Kings Fund in January 2013:

> They are geared up to meet physical needs, but not to provide the mental or social care that we will all need in the later stages of life. Our hospitals, designed for the last century, are in danger of being overwhelmed by the demographic challenges of this century. And that is the crux of our problem ... deep in the DNA of the NHS is the notion that the home, the place where so much happens to affect health, is not its responsibility. It doesn't pay for grab rails or walk-in showers, even if it is accepted that they can keep people safer and healthy. The exclusion of the social side of care from the NHS settlement explains why it has never been able to break out of a 'treatment service' mentality and truly embrace prevention. It is a medical model; patient-centred, not person-centred.

Since the inception of the NHS in 1948 there have been three entirely separate services looking after an individual's needs. 'Medical' problems have been dealt with through hospitals and GPs in the overwhelmingly free NHS. Mental problems are allocated to an underfunded fringe of the NHS, and social care to barely adequate means-tested and charged-for local council services which vary hugely across the country and face cuts under the Tory/Lib Dems to a point where they will be completely swamped. Councils are warning that, if nothing changes, within a decade their budgets will be overwhelmed by the costs of care at the expense of every other service.

But as we have lived longer, physical, mental and social needs have increasingly merged while the services have remained freestanding. The mental and social needs of patients in acute hospital wards are often badly neglected, which is why older people tend to deteriorate rapidly on admission to hospitals focused upon their physical needs alone. Similarly patients in mental institutions frequently have their physical health overlooked, dying on average 15 years younger than the rest of the population. And in too many areas there is such a poor standard of social care provision, both at home and in residential care, that few needs are properly met.

This is not only grossly unfair, it is also economically inefficient. Instead of spending the equivalent of a few hundred pounds in the home, we are spending thousands on hospital bills, while the basic problem becomes uncontrollable. This is failure on a grand scale, both socially and in cost to the taxpayer. Around 30 to 40 per cent of general hospital beds are occupied by older people who, if better provision were available at home, would not need to be there.

Instead of separate budgets of £104 billion for the NHS and £15 billion for social care, there should be full integration of health and social care providing whole-person care.

And the relentless march of health markets and private provision with no limits is undermining not just the NHS but any ability to meet the challenges of our ageing society. Right across the world, market-based health systems cost more per person, not less, than Britain's NHS. Instead of encouraging the NHS model to be gradually eroded, we should be protecting it and extending it as the most efficient way of meeting this century's pressures. The ageing society demands integration whereas markets deliver fragmentation. Open tendering for services brings ever-increasing numbers of providers at the expense of an overall co-ordinating approach.

In a complex public service such as health, competition is not the same thing as choice – something the 1997–2010 Labour government didn't get right and the Tory/Lib Dems got abysmally wrong. Greater choice in the ageing society comes from giving people and families what they want – as much control as possible, so that patients have more choice over their care, whether that is choosing to have dialysis treatment in the home or choosing to die at home rather than in a hospital. Which means an NHS providing all care – physical, mental and social – supported by new and powerful patient rights.

The question then is how can this be funded? Beyond the current limit of £23,000, care charges are unlimited. As Andy Burnham described it:

> These are 'dementia taxes': the more vulnerable you are, the more you pay. As cruel as pre-NHS or US healthcare. No other part of our welfare state works in this way and, in the century of the ageing society, failure to resolve how we pay for care could undermine the NHS, the contributory principle and incentives to save.

What is the point of saving for retirement when this is increasingly likely to be gobbled up by care costs? As the years go on, for more and more people old age will be a lottery, with everything they have worked for – their home, savings, and pension – at risk.

The Dilnot Commission advocated setting a cap of £35,000 on the cost of care to elderly people, after which the state would pick up the bill. That is a cap that would have made sense combined with means-tested help and an individual contribution of up to £10,000 to cover general living costs. But the Tory/Lib Dem government responded with setting a cap of £72,000, which is far too high – at £144,000 for couples, and at more than *twice the amount proposed by Dilnot*, it is for the vast majority a huge amount of money. This might offer some protection to those in the South, with its high house prices, but little for those elsewhere in average-priced houses. By failing to address the chronically looming collapse in council budgets it leaves people exposed to ever-increasing care charges and more likely to have to pay up to the level of the cap. Local authorities currently help with care costs but the cap is so high that it will do little to ease the pressure on councils who have been struggling with swingeing budget cuts.

Furthermore, those without access to £72,000 in savings would have to rely on the private insurance industry stepping in with new products to help insure against the sum and deliver their social care – likely to be far more expensive than state provision, just as it is has been for healthcare.

There were other problems in the Tory/Lib Dem government's approach. The 'cap' was computed on the standard rate that local authorities paid for a bed in a care home, not the amount most people actually had to pay, which is much higher. Because of this Labour's Shadow Minister Liz Kendall predicted that pensioners would actually be confronted with bills of £150,000 for their residential care before the government stepped in to help. Also, it transpired that, on top of the care costs, there would be so-called 'hotel and accommodation' costs for a room, bed, food and heating – the government was expecting on average £230 a week contributions outside their 'cap' on costs.

The only fair solution remains for all people, whatever their savings and however severe their needs, to be able to protect most of what they have worked for. Assuming the imperative is a fully merged health and social care system, then it can be funded by either a voluntary or an all-in approach.

The Dilnot Commission's proposed cap and means test would mean people only paid as much as they needed to but, in the worst-case scenario, could still stand to lose a significant chunk of their savings. This voluntary approach is also based upon maintaining the complexity, unsustainability and unfairness of the two care worlds we currently have – one which is charged for, the other free at the point of use.

However, moving to an all-in system – that is extending the NHS principle to all care – would mean requiring everyone to contribute, rather than just the most vulnerable. Everyone would pay, everyone would be protected, but obviously not everyone would end up using the service. Yet that is the very principle upon which all universally provided public services, notably the NHS, work. Without an all-in system we won't be able to tackle the crisis of ageing in a way that is fair and equitable.

An individual's contributions could be made through general taxation. Or through using existing benefit payments differently, to pay towards social care provision (both working-age benefits for adults with disabilities and those received by the older population). Or people could be asked to pay, after death, a deferred payment percentage of their estates towards social care. Or there could be a combination of these.

Despite previously damning it a 'death tax', the Tory/Lib Dems, even through their watered-down version of Dilnot, accepted the deferred payment principle – by allowing people to borrow for their care needs from their council and pay the amount back (with interest) after death. What people want is fairness and clarity – what is provided 'free' and what they will have to pay for.

Whichever funding model proves most equitable, we need to assert the case for a properly resourced, government-backed system of elderly care now – and just as resolutely as those who founded the NHS out of the lottery of unfairness and misery had to do 70 years ago.

Yet fully funding elderly care is not the only critical financial challenge. The total gap between NHS resources and needs could reach almost £30 billion annually – nearly a third of the total NHS budget – by 2020, according to NHS England Chief Executive Simon Stevens. Without closing that gap the NHS faced a mortal crisis, he stated in October 2014. But his call for just £8 billion extra public spending annually rested on heroically optimistic assumptions about improvements in NHS productivity delivering the rest. In truth, the gap can only be completely closed by government, supported by taxpayers, delivering a fully funded health service.

Universal, affordable childcare

When Tony Crosland was writing in the mid-1950s, the typical family unit had the father at work and the mother at home looking after the children. Crosland could therefore readily be excused for not addressing the contemporary public policy imperative for childcare.

But imperative it certainly is, to ensure both parents have the choice to work and for two other pressing reasons. First, because it has become increasingly the case that, in order to maintain acceptable living standards, lower and middle income parents *both* have to work. Second, because all the evidence shows that pre-school care and education is a vital springboard to subsequent achievement. Although the state ensures free, compulsory schooling for all children aged from five to sixteen, children arrive into reception year at age five in the state education sector with already noticeable inequalities, including between those who benefited from early years' education and those who did not. These inequalities remain evident throughout a child's schooling. According to the Family and Childcare Trust, 30,000 of the UK's poorest two-year-olds miss out on nursery education, which, with a few tightly controlled exceptions, only three- to four-year-olds are entitled to receive free of charge. Yet early education is crucial for a child's social and cognitive development, and the poorest are the very children in most immediate need. The inequalities gap has not and will not be bridged by relying upon private provision.

The cost of privatising childcare costs by forcing parents to fund it themselves is prohibitive and reinforces existing inequalities. In March 2014 the Family and Childcare Trust calculated that the cost of having one child in part-time nursery care and another in an after-school club was £7,549 a year – more than the average UK mortgage payment, plainly unaffordable for most families and exacerbated by childcare costs rising faster than wages. The only solution is for government to fund free childcare for children under five.

New Labour significantly expanded both pre-school education and childcare, much of which was dismantled by the Tory/Lib Dem government with its emphasis on private sector providers, deregulation, closures of 'Sure Start' projects and early years funding cuts. An entitlement to 15 hours a week free early education and care for three- and four-year-olds was an admirable Labour achievement from 2001. But this needs to be significantly upgraded; for example, extending this by ten hours to 25 hours a week, equivalent to five hours daily, would allow parents to share the remaining time between them, and enable either both of them to work part-time or at least one to go full-time.

More than *three quarters of part-time workers* feel trapped on low pay without any chance of promotion because of the lack of affordable childcare. Not only is existing childcare provision very expensive, it is in short supply. Only 49 per cent of local authorities have enough availability for working parents, and even fewer local authorities provide sufficient childcare for school-aged children during working hours. Furthermore only a quarter of local authorities are able to properly cater for families with children with disabilities.

But childcare needs to be available up the age scale to include pre- and post-school clubs in secondary education. Britain needs wrap-around services for children with parents who work early in the morning and late into the evening. A well-designed programme to cover these extra hours for children up to the age of 16 would help undo some of the damage done by the Tory/Lib Dem cuts. Free children's clubs would also help to fill gaps in sport, art and music caused by recent narrowing of the curriculum. At the moment these types of services, outside of the independent sector, are limited to the better-funded schools in more affluent areas or to the free schools and academies that have enjoyed central government patronage in England.

Of course there are public spending consequences of such a programme of universal childcare. But those have to be balanced against greater tax revenues from parents working and contributing to economic well-being, living standards and growth. Universal childcare would be an investment in the future of the country because, by helping an estimated 250,000 parents back to work, £1.5 billion would be injected into the economy, according to the Institute for Public Policy Research – a benefit which *exceeds* the cost of such care to taxpayers. It is yet another example which confounds neoliberal orthodoxy on small government and low public spending. A combination of the lowest possible level of public funding and unreliable and patchy private provision dependent upon parental income is no answer, either to the needs of families or those of society.

British governments have to make up their minds on whether to support and invest in key social policies to build both a fairer society and a stronger economy, or to withdraw, hands held up pronouncing 'not me guv', leaving people to fend for themselves.[26]

From student finance to welfare, from childcare to ageing, none of these key features of a just and economically efficient society can be secured without both government intervention and funding. That is the elephant in the room which even the most eloquent neoliberal advocates of a small state refuse to acknowledge.[27] In labelling *big* government the enemy, they are in denial over the fact that *smart* government – which provides generous albeit efficient public spending and investment – is the only route to both economic success and the social cohesion and support necessary to underpin that success.

CHAPTER 13

A future for Labour

To fulfil its historic mission, Labour must get into power. And to achieve that it has to win over sufficient layers of 'middle Britain' as well as maintain its core – though shrinking – support from both progressive middle-class and working-class voters. Under New Labour an absolute priority was given to winning the 'middle' on the assumption that the 'core' had nowhere else to go. A mistake, because actually, it did go elsewhere – either to another party or to stay at home.

Half of those saying in 2010 that they had voted Labour in the 2005 general election also said that they did not do so again five years later. They split almost equally in 2010 between not voting at all (23 per cent) and voting either Liberal Democrat (13 per cent), Tory (9 per cent) or other (4 per cent).[1] In 2010 the other major parties held onto many more of their 2005 voters than Labour did: the Tories 76 per cent, the Liberal Democrats 58 per cent.

But the big winner in 2010 was the Why Bother? Party: 48 per cent of electors who had been too young to vote in 2005 said they did not vote at all in 2010. Staying at home is always an option. There is no comfort for Labour in learning that we had a big lead in each of the last four general elections among non-voters.[2]

Thus it was that by 2010 under Gordon Brown New Labour had lost 5 million votes from its 1997 high, 4 million of these under Tony Blair, who in 2005 achieved a paltry 35.2 per cent (the lowest percentage for a winning party since 1918), nevertheless securing a comfortable Parliamentary majority, partly because first Iain Duncan Smith's, then Michael Howard's leadership made the Tories unelectable.

Therefore simply reincarnating New Labour, turning the Parliamentary Labour Party into Björn Again Blairites, is no formula for future success, no elixir for electoral victory – quite apart from its studied indifference to rising inequality, lofty disdain for working-class concerns and ideological incapacity to confront the systemic problems of the new capitalism.

Equally, however, neither a caricature 'Old Labour' recipe of extensive renationalisation and state control, nor a 'Romantic Labour' prospectus of profligate public spending, could be delivered in a world of globally mobile capital and footloose finance – and in any case would be even more unelectable.

A future for socialism

Today only a different Labour programme can offer 'A future for socialism' for coming generations, both in Britain and in similar advanced industrial economies. It denies that we face an all-or-nothing-at-all choice between either cut-throat competition coupled with a threadbare social safety net – the kind of society favoured by Tea Party Republicans, Thatcherite Tories and Orange Book Liberal Democrats – or big state dominance with no scope for individual initiative, the kind of nightmare world that left-leaning fundamentalists on the fringe are accused of fantasising about. There is plenty of political space between the cold wind of unrestrained market forces and the icy grip of total state control, though that is not to pretend that the ground on which to make our stand is either uncontroversial or unproblematic territory.

Building a better-off, fairer and safer society means shifting today's boundary between market forces and state intervention, redefining the roles of competition and cooperation, and changing the rules about privilege, poverty and shares in prosperity. It means striking a new balance between rivalry and fraternity, between entitlement and obligation, and between continuity and change. It means shaking up the status quo, in both the private and the public sectors. It means having the courage of our convictions.

Despite its huge achievements – from landslide victories and massive public investment to record economic performance (pre-banking crisis) – New Labour too often turned into Nervous Labour, settling too easily for the status quo. For instance refusing to raise the top rate of income tax to 50 per cent until the financial crisis forced fairness back onto the budget agenda in 2009. Even then that tax change only took effect one month before we lost office in 2010.

On some really big issues New Labour waited until the coast was clear, only undertaking to restore the link between the basic state pension and average earnings, for instance, after David Cameron had already promised to do so. Where New Labour did act, it habitually took half-measures – for instance, by dumping the question of the charitable status of public schools in the lap of the Charities Commission rather than scrapping that status. Nervousness is infectious. Even the Fabian Society waited until six months after the 2010 general election before floating the idea of levying VAT on private school fees.[3] Caution not conviction was New Labour's driving force, and spin not soul was its watchword. That has to change for Labour to regain respect among the millions of voters whose backing it lost between 1997 and 2010.

The alternative means a programme that is both purposeful and practical. It means encouraging competition in markets that have been rigged, like the energy businesses and parts of the finance sector; regulating it where the herd instinct periodically threatens to stall the entire economic system, as in investment banking; supplementing it where state intervention can help to foster innovation and growth, as in support for small and medium-sized enterprise; and replacing it where collaboration works better than competition, as in most health services.

This alternative offers a policy agenda rooted in a strong set of values – social justice and individual freedom, equality and social mobility, community and full employment, democracy and human rights – the values distilled by Tony Crosland. The values that have united Labour supporters throughout generations of social change. And an agenda which proves that Labour has rediscovered its soul.

Winning on such a more radical Labour agenda is eminently achievable. Even when the party was at a modern nadir in May 2010, the overall election result suggested a core 'progressive' support at 49 per cent, according to Polly Toynbee and David Walker in their convincing verdict on New Labour's record.[4] They split and reallocated the Liberal Democrat vote, and added Green and Nationalist support: 'what the voting demonstrated was potential for progressive policy, even at Labour's lowest ebb,' they argued. The respected US Democrat pollster Stan Greenberg echoed this by demonstrating that British voters in 2010 strongly favoured more, not less, financial regulation, more government not more free markets, and modest tax rises instead of savage public investment cuts. It was a British public more in tune with Labour's core values than those of any rival political party, provided – and this is a big proviso – that the party can win their *trust*. The Tory failure to break through with a clear majority in 2010 was proof of that. Even in the most unpromising of *electoral* circumstances for the party, Labour's *ideology* was nearer to what the public supported.

Growth again

Reflecting on 60 years' study of economic growth in 2013, Robert Solow argued that the question of equitable growth is the central economic issue of our time and that there was no good evidence of a trade-off between equity and growth.[5] Joseph Stiglitz found that inequality undermines the American economy by contributing to economic instability.[6] Both were backed up by an IMF staff study of inequality and economic growth which also found no evidence of a trade-off between redistribution and growth. Rather it is inequality that acts as a drag on growth, with greater equality robustly linked with faster and more durable growth.[7] We can pursue greater equality and faster economic growth at the same time: indeed they are linked, despite neoliberal protestations to the contrary.

In January 2014 a further IMF staff paper confirmed that in the mid-2000s tax changes did far less than cash transfers like the state pension and family benefits or in-kind services like spending on health and education to reduce inequality in the UK. This is consistent with the point noted earlier that the UK tax system is proportional, not progressive, and that we rely on transfers in cash and kind to redistribute income, which is why cuts in welfare benefits and in public services are so unfair. The IMF paper acknowledged that for one group of countries – including the UK, the US, Canada, China and India – the share of gross income going to the top 1 per cent fell through much of the 1950s and 1960s but had now risen back to levels like the 1920s and 1930s. However, in another group – France, Germany, Japan and Sweden – the share going to the top 1 per cent had first declined and then flattened out.[8]

Oxfam's 2014 report 'A tale of two Britains' found that the five richest families in the UK were wealthier than the bottom 20 per cent of the entire population and that since 2003 the vast majority of the British public (95 per cent) had experienced a 12 per cent real-terms drop in their disposable income while the richest 5 per cent of the population had seen their incomes increase.[9]

The Oxfam report confirmed that Britain faces a similar 'inequality crisis' to the one that New York City Mayor Bill de Blasio identified in his successful 2013 election campaign when he pledged to take aim at New York's 'Tale of Two Cities' – the grotesque inequality between the top 1 per cent and the rest. De Blasio promised to turn his city into 'a place where everyday people can afford to live, work and raise a family'. His starting point was a promise to raise tax on the very wealthy to pay for universal pre-kindergarten programmes, so that those earning between $500,000 and $1 million per year (£330,000 to £660,000) would pay $973 more per year (£650).[10] He also set a target of building 200,000 affordable homes over the next ten years. These are the kinds of priorities that Labour needs to pursue.

Greater equality our mission

Ed Miliband sent a clear signal of the new place that tackling inequality should occupy among Labour's priorities under his leadership in his Hugo Young lecture in February 2014:

> For decades, inequality was off the political agenda. But there is growing recognition across every walk of life in Britain that large inequalities of income and wealth scar our society ... it holds our economies back when the wages of the majority are squeezed and it weakens our societies when the gaps between the rungs on the

ladder of opportunity get wider and wider. And that our nations are less likely to succeed when they lack that vital sense of common life, as they always must when the very richest live in one world and everyone else a very different one.[11]

A month later he developed his case that inequality was not only socially unjust but also bad for economic performance. Denouncing David Cameron's 'global race to the bottom', he said:

> The Tories think the way to succeed is through insecure work, zero-hours contracts, and fewer rights in the workplace. A recovery for the few is not an accident of this government's economic policy – this *is* its economic policy ... Unless we use the talents of all and see rising prosperity for all, our productivity risks remaining low, personal debt will remain high and our economy will be more exposed.[12]

In the same article, he added to his attack on inequality by pointing out that

> the average wages for young people getting into work have fallen back to the same level in real terms as they were in 1998. It means that, for the first time since the Second World War, wages paid to young people risk being below those once paid to their parents.

This, Ed Miliband insisted, was destroying the 'promise of Britain': that successive generations were better off than their predecessors. Supporting his case in October 2014, a report by the government's social mobility adviser, Alan Milburn, said that young people were on the wrong side of a divide opening up in society. Home ownership among 25-year-olds had halved in just two decades. Young people's wages were falling and, relative to a decade before, their job prospects diminishing. There was a real risk, he argued, that the current generation – from low-income families especially – would simply not have the same opportunities to progress as their parents' generation.

By contrast, New Labour had occupied reserved seating on the equality fence for years. It is time to come down unambiguously on the side of both greater equality, and of the faster growth needed to get the economy back on track. That is the way to deliver results that revive the spirits of Labour supporters and win back those whose votes we lost between 1997 and 2010. Otherwise Labour risks becoming the butt of something similar to the best joke of the 1992 American presidential election, told surprisingly by George Bush senior. He complained about Bill Clinton facing both ways and sitting on the fence on issue after issue. As Bush put it: 'he's been riding that fence for so long now, he's straddle sore.'

Labour's unique role remains what it has always been: to reach out to the neglected and rejected sections of society. Our historic mission still stands: to care for the whole community, not just to cosset the comfortable classes and those who aspire to join them. We want a more equal, fairer society and we see economic growth, not further austerity, as helping to get us to our desired destination.

We are not interested in 'targeting' or 'punishing' the rich out of some sort of envy. We want people to be well rewarded for risk taking, entrepreneurship and hard work. But we expect those who do well to contribute fairly to the society which has both nourished them and underpins their success.

We see the state, reformed as discussed in Chapters 5 and 7, as the key instrument for driving society forwards. Journalist Polly Toynbee chose New Year's Eve 2011 to remind us what 'reclaiming the state' really means:

> it is not a threatening monolith but a motor for economic growth, with regulators to keep capitalism straight. 'The state' is not a faceless threat: it is doctors, nurses, teachers, park keepers, police, tax collectors and apprentice trainers, all precious assets. Reclaim Blair's best heritage, when Labour's state improved life for most people, from lower crime to no waiting lists, better schools and public places,

with better chances for more children. No apology needed.[13]

That means a sharp change of direction from where the Tory/Lib Dem coalition took the country. For Britain has been pursuing a course that offers our young people a future which is debt-laden, pensions-lite, home ownership-less, and in which their living standards will be nowhere near as high as those of their parents or grandparents – reversing history.

The conundrum the right needs to answer is this. When the economy is fully recovered from recession, Britain will be a richer society than ever before, better off even than at the height of the pre-crisis boom in 2008. Yet those on the political right say that we will somehow not be a society that can afford even the standards of public service and social infrastructure of 2000, let alone what these should be to remain both socially fair and economically competitive in 2020. Why? The answer surely is that the requirements for a civilised society and an efficient economy come down to a choice: private greed or public good, individual self-indulgence for a few or collective responsibility for all? Which is why the country cries out for a democratic socialist alternative.

Overview

Tony Crosland's 1956 restatement of what socialism meant, and what the Labour Party should stand for, has been oversimplified as amounting only to greater equality. In fact this was only one among a set of aims that Crosland believed the Labour Party should pursue, alongside cutting poverty, countering social distress, encouraging fraternity and cooperation, and achieving full employment.

On these criteria, for 20 years many things turned out much as Tony Crosland had hoped and expected. Successive governments accepted responsibility for promoting full employment, for alleviating poverty and social distress, even for reducing inequality. From 1945 to the mid-1970s Britain grew quickly by pre-war standards, due in part to Keynesian economic policies, and everyone shared in the greater material prosperity to some degree, with real incomes growing as

GDP grew. A political consensus saw cross-party support for a welfare state inspired by Beveridge, and acceptance of steps, both in cash and in kind, that produced greater equality and fewer class differences. These included tackling dimensions of inequality that *The Future of Socialism* hardly addressed, like discrimination on grounds of gender, race, sexual orientation and disability.

But the advent of Margaret Thatcher as Tory Party leader in 1975 saw the start of a neoliberal challenge to the hegemony of social democratic ideas. In the following four decades even the concept of society was called into question, and the role of the state acting on behalf of society to promote the common good was belittled by the Tory Party. The ties that bind us together as members of the same society were put under unparalleled strain. Mining communities were destroyed and trade unionists labelled as traitors. Public services were derided and privatised, state-owned industries denationalised, and Britain's social infrastructure starved of funds. Top rates of income tax paid by the few were halved as taxes on spending paid by the many were doubled. Financial institutions were deregulated, 'free' markets lionised, and a 'greed is good' mentality applauded.

Seeds were sown in the 1980s and 1990s that bore fateful fruit with the 2008 financial crisis, bringing the entire economic system to the very brink of complete collapse. A crisis whose impact was all the greater for being so unexpected. Indeed a crisis that 'could not happen', according to neoliberal theory. A private sector crisis that only government intervention could overcome, and a rescue package that saved the financial system from itself but also put the public finances under great strain.

The priority for socialism today: is *faster fairer greener growth*. *Growth* because only an expanding economy can provide the resources needed to tackle the problems that confront society, like homelessness, a decaying social infrastructure, inadequate educational opportunities especially for the disadvantaged coupled with high student debt, a shortage of vocational skills, a mismatch between health and social care, lack of childcare, and poor provision for the elderly. *Faster growth* because that holds the key to bringing the public finances back into balance, and to generating the work that 900,000 unemployed young people want and millions more unemployed, insecure or underemployed people need. *Fairer growth* because unequal societies are unhealthy societies in which everyone loses out as all forms of social ills rise and economic growth rates slow. *Greener growth* because without vigorous action to meet the threat posed by climate change, such as by backing a low-carbon economy and actively promoting renewable energy, environmental disasters can only become more frequent and more intense.

And, contrary to the stifling grip of neoliberal orthodoxy on the 'Westminster bubble', *faster fairer greener growth* is eminently feasible. The scope for fiscal action to boost public investment in housing, in the social infrastructure, in training and skills, and in green growth is substantial. It would mean the government borrowing more today in order to borrow less tomorrow, by raising Britain's economic growth rate above the pedestrian pace expected by the Office for Budget Responsibility. A £30 billion per year for two years increase in annual public investment as part of a ten-year programme to renew Britain's failing social infrastructure would give a boost to growth at a time when the OBR expects the economy to slow down. By contributing to a higher plateau of ongoing public infrastructure investment it would also provide a spur to industrial innovation and faster future growth, as well as full employment. Higher current public spending paid for from a mix of higher, fairer taxation, extra charges and greater efficiency would allow Labour to protect public services from the worst of planned Tory spending cuts, and even to reinstate some services already scrapped due to past cuts.

What makes faster growth feasible in the short term is the margin of spare capacity in the economy that could be brought back into operation, yielding extra 'catch-up' growth for three or four years, just as it did as Britain recovered from depression in the 1930s. What makes faster growth feasible and sustainable over the medium to long term is the more active role that this book envisages for government. A reformist role, especially in respect of the financial system, to guard against any repeat of the financial crisis that killed off the steady growth that the UK economy had enjoyed for 15 years before the 2008 crisis. An interventionist role, like that played by governments in other successful market-based economies, where the state encourages innovation and obliges industry to take responsibility for the social and environmental consequences of its actions.

Bold ambitions

Back to the Future of Socialism argues that an initial (and if necessary sustained) budget boost is affordable. It rejects the hair-shirt austerity so in vogue after the banking crisis, just as it was in the 1930s before the Second World War forced a turn to Keynesian economics of growth and public investment as the only route to a successful and just society. It insists that the state has vital new roles to play in keeping expansion going, in meeting needs and providing opportunities that market forces alone cannot supply, in countering capitalism's corrupting influences on civilisation, and in ensuring that the benefits that economic growth brings are shared fairly throughout society.

The cramped circumstances likely to face government up to and beyond 2020 do not dictate that public services be scrapped wholesale and the social fabric torn down in a frenzied attempt to reduce national debt. We owe most of it to ourselves because the vast bulk of the national debt is not owed to foreigners: over two thirds is money borrowed from UK investors and savers, mainly through insurance companies and pension funds, or from the Bank of England, and such debt can be brought down anyway with a buoyant economy.

There remains significant scope for state action well beyond the rudimentary social safety net that the Conservatives regard as sufficient for their 'Big Society'. It lies within our power as a people to eradicate poverty, to promote social welfare and tackle disadvantage, to strike a fresh and healthy balance between competition and cooperation, to provide jobs for all, and to deliver greater equality.

These are bold ambitions worthy of wide support. They hold appeal both to traditional Labour supporters and to people of no fixed political abode, whichever rung of the social ladder they stand on, and however aspirational they may be. Since 2008, in particular, both these sectors of our society have seen what kind of threat market forces, left to their own devices, can pose to material living standards and to the foundations of mutual dependence on which social stability is built. Reforming the market system and modernising state institutions are essential for Britain to pull free from the economic and social quagmire that has been holding us all back.

Labour must revive the momentum for radical reform. There is plenty more for us to do to realise our aims. We must not be dismayed by the unending grind of politics, nor despair if the slog of daily endeavour sometimes leads our supporters to wonder whether we have lost our way. All progress is gradual and much good can come from compromise and collective decisions. 'If political change was easy, it would have been achieved a long time ago. Stick there for the long haul,' my father, Walter Hain, told me when I was a teenager living in apartheid South Africa in the mid-1960s.

Labour's fight goes on. Our journey has always been a Pilgrim's Progress, always looking beyond the last blue mountain, always impatient for progress. The brilliant *Daily Mirror* journalist, the late Geoffrey Goodman, summed it up well in 2009: 'A revived, reblooded Labour Party is still capable of proving the Jeremiahs wrong: still capable of lifting people's hopes and dreams towards a decent, more equal and just society. And that, as both Nye Bevan and Tony Crosland always agreed, is the real point of the socialist idea.'[14]

Notes

Introduction: Back to the future of socialism

[1] Sidney Webb, 'The new constitution of the Labour Party', Labour Party leaflet no. 1 (new series), 1918.

[2] Anthony Crosland, *The future of socialism* (Jonathan Cape, 1956; abridged and revised paperback edn 1964), ch 3.

[3] Roy Hattersley, 'A lot to be modest about', *Guardian*, 31 July 2010.

[4] Deborah Mattinson, *Talking to a brick wall* (Biteback, 2010), p 326.

[5] Eric Shaw, *Losing Labour's soul?* (Routledge, 2007), p 42.

[6] Thomas Piketty, *Capital in the twenty-first century*, trans. Arthur Goldhammer (Belknap Press, 2014).

1 The Crosland agenda

[1] Ben Pimlott, 'Über-Tony', *London Review of Books*, 3 September 1998.

[2] David Sainsbury, 'Progressive capitalism', 20 May 2013 (www.progressonline.org.uk).

[3] David Sainsbury, *Progressive capitalism: How to achieve economic growth, liberty and social justice* (Biteback, 2013), p 101.

[4] David Lipsey, *In the corridors of power* (Biteback, 2012), p 43.

[5] Bryan Gould, *A future for socialism* (Cape, 1989), pp 2–3, 6–7.

[6] John Gray, 'Ralph Miliband and sons', *Guardian*, 4 September 2010.

[7] Ralph Miliband, 'The future of socialism in England', in *Socialist Register 1977*, p 40.

[8] Ralph Miliband, *The state in capitalist society* (Weidenfeld & Nicolson, 1973), p 99.

[9] John Silkin, 'Parliament, government and socialism', in Gerald Kaufman (ed), *Renewal: Labour's Britain in the 1980s* (Penguin, 1983).

[10] See the comparison of GDP per capita in 24 countries before the fall of the Iron Curtain in matched samples – one Eastern block, one Western block – in J. Bradford DeLong, 'Lecture notes for economics 2', 29 January 2014, University of California at Berkeley.

[11] Anthony Crosland, *Socialism now* (Cape, 1974).

[12] Lipsey, *In the corridors of power*, p 44.

[13] Roy Hattersley and Kevin Hickson, 'In praise of social democracy', *Political Quarterly*, 83(1) (January–March 2012): 5–12.

[14] David Miliband, 'Time to rethink, not reassure', *New Statesman*, 2 February 2012.

[15] Roy Hattersley, 'Why Labour chose Ed not David Miliband', 3 February 2012 (www.guardian.co.uk/commentisfree).

[16] Kevin Hickson, 'In defence of social democracy', 3 February 2012 (http://labourlist.org).

2 New Labour, Crosland and the crisis

[1] *'Fiscal adjustment in an uncertain world'*, IMF Fiscal Monitor, April 2013, statistical tables 4 and 12a.

[2] National Audit Office estimate, December 2010.

[3] *'Fiscal adjustment in an uncertain world'*, table 5, p 14.

[4] Leadership unacknowledged by former US Treasury Secretary Timothy Geithner in his reflections on financial crises, *Stress test* (Random House Business Books, 2014).

[5] Gordon Brown, *Beyond the crash* (Simon & Schuster, 2010), p 129.

[6] Edmund Dell, *A hard pounding: Politics and economic crisis 1974–76* (Oxford University Press, 1991), p 66.

[7] HM Treasury, 'Budget 2010: Securing the recovery', HC 451, March 2010, table C17.

[8] Tony Blair, *A journey* (Hutchinson, 2010), pp 665, 666, 668.

[9] Robert Joyce and Luke Sibieta, 'Labour's record on poverty and equality', Institute for Fiscal Studies, June 2013 (www.ifs.org.uk/publications/6738).

[10] Institute for Fiscal Studies briefing note updated by James Browne and Andrew Hood, 'A survey of the UK benefit system', November 2012.

[11] Allyson Pollock, 'How PFI is crippling the NHS', 29 June 2012 (theguardian.com).

[12] John Edmonds, 'New Labour is damaging our people', *Guardian*, 6 September 2002.

[13] See Peter Hain, *Outside in* (Biteback, 2012).

[14] James Plunkett, 'Growth without gain?', Resolution Foundation, May 2011.

[15] From the benediction prayer given by Methodist minister Kirbyjon Caldwell at the 55th American presidential inauguration.

3 Finance and the new capitalism

[1] Simon Johnson, 'The quiet coup', *The Atlantic*, May 2009.

[2] Robert E. Lucas, Jr, 'Macroeconomic priorities', *American Economic Review* (March 2003).

[3] Thomas Piketty, *Capital in the twenty-first century*, trans. Arthur Goldhammer (Belknap Press, 2014).

[4] Report of the Radcliffe Committee on the Working of the Monetary System, August 1959, Cmnd 827 (HMSO).

[5] Carmen M. Reinhart and Kenneth S. Rogoff, *This time is different: Eight centuries of financial folly* (Princeton University Press, 2009), pp 150–2 and 205.

[6] Gary B. Gorton, *Misunderstanding financial crises: Why we don't see them coming* (Oxford University Press, 2012), p 29, and Reinhart and Rogoff, *This time is different*, pp 387–8.

[7] Milton Friedman and Anna Jacobson Schwartz, *A monetary history of the United States 1867–1960* (Princeton University Press, 1963), pp 434–40.

[8] Adair Turner, 'What do banks do? Why do credit booms and busts occur? What can public policy do about it?', in *The future of finance: The LSE report* (London School of Economics and Political Science, 2010), ch 1.

[9] Andrew Haldane, Simon Brennan and Vasileios Madouros, 'What is the contribution of the financial sector: Miracle or mirage?', in *The future of finance*, ch 2.

[10] Alan S. Blinder, *After the music stopped: The financial crisis, the response, and the work ahead* (Penguin Press, 2013), pp 66–8.

[11] Maurice Obstfeld, 'On keeping your powder dry: Fiscal foundations of financial and price stability', June 2013, figure 2, p 18 (http://eml.berkeley.edu/~obstfeld/fiscalfoundations.pdf).

[12] *'Fiscal adjustment in an uncertain world'*, *IMF Fiscal Monitor*, April 2013, table 5, p 14 (6.7% of UK GDP is about £100 billion).

[13] *'The state of public finances cross-country'*, *IMF Fiscal Monitor*, November 2009, p 37.

[14] Comptroller and Auditor General's Report to the House of Commons, National Audit Office, HC 46, July 2012.

[15] Andrew Haldane, 'The $100 billion question', Bank of England, March 2010.

[16] *IMF global financial stability report*, April 2014.

[17] *'Fiscal adjustment in an uncertain world'*, statistical table 4, p 62.

[18] Peter Boone and Simon Johnson, 'Will the politics of global moral hazard sink us again?', in *The future of finance*, ch 10.

[19] Reinhart and Rogoff, *This time is different*, p 151.

[20] Martin Wolf, *Fixing global finance* (Yale University Press, 2009), p 31.

[21] Charles Morris, *The two trillion dollar meltdown*, paperback edn (PublicAffairs, 2008), p xiv.

[22] Blinder, *After the music stopped*, pp 200–3.

[23] Luc Laeven and Fabian Valencia, 'Resolution of banking crises: The good, the bad and the ugly', working paper, IMF, August 2012, table A.3.

[24] Reinhart and Rogoff, *This time is different*, p 232.

[25] Office for Budget Responsibility, 'Economic and fiscal outlook', December 2013, Cm 8748, table 1.4, p 17.

[26] Jonathan Portes, 'Recessions and recoveries: A historical perspective', NIESR blog, 9 April 2013.

[27] 'Davos 2014: World Economic Forum – Day Two as it happened' (http://www.theguardian.com/business/2014/jan/23/davos-2014-world-economic-forum-day-two-live).

[28] David Clark and Duncan Weldon, 'The foreign policy of responsible capitalism', in Marcus Roberts and Ulrich Storck (eds), *One nation in the world* (Fabian Society and Friedrich Ebert Stiftung, 2013), pp 67–8.

[29] Richard Wilkinson and Kate Pickett, *The spirit level: Why more equal societies almost always do better* (Allen Lane, 2009).

4 Growth not cuts

[1] Between 2009 and 2012 the structural or cyclically adjusted fiscal balance as a proportion of potential GDP was cut by 4.3 per cent in the UK, 1.7 per cent in the US and 2.2 per cent in the eurozone: 'Fiscal adjustment in an uncertain world', IMF Fiscal Monitor, April 2013, statistical table 2.

[2] Martin Wolf, 'Austerity in the eurozone and the UK: Kill or cure?', Financial Times, 23 May 2013.

[3] Office for Budget Responsibility, 'Economic and fiscal outlook', December 2013, Cm 8748, table 1.2.

[4] Maurice Obstfeld, 'On keeping your powder dry: Fiscal foundations of financial and price stability', June 2013, p 11 (http://eml.berkeley.edu/~obstfeld/fiscalfoundations.pdf).

[5] Report of the Radcliffe Committee on the Working of the Monetary System, Cmnd 827 (HMSO, August 1959), table 25, p 193.

[6] Tom Clark and Andrew Dilnot, 'Measuring the UK fiscal stance since the Second World War', Institute for Fiscal Studies, 2002.

[7] Professor Dennis Leech, University of Warwick, letter to the Guardian, 23 December 2013.

[8] Mark Carney's opening remarks, inflation report press conference, Bank of England, 12 February 2014.

[9] Their projections were: International Monetary Fund (2.4 per cent), NIESR and Lombard Street (4.3 per cent), Oxford Economics (revised down from 5.1 per cent in December 2013 to 4.3 per cent in February 2014), and Capital Economics (6.0 per cent). Paul Krugman and Cambridge University's Bill Martin and Bob Rowthorn share these criticisms.

[10] Alistair Darling, Back from the brink (Atlantic Books, 2011), pp 227–8.

[11] Nicholas Crafts, 'Escaping liquidity traps: Lessons from the UK's 1930s escape', VoxEU.org, 12 May 2013.

[12] Alan S. Blinder, After the music stopped: The financial crisis, the response, and the work ahead (Penguin Press, 2013), p 22.

[13] Simon Wren-Lewis, 'Confusing levels and rates of growth', mainly macro blog, 5 August 2013.

[14] Institute for Fiscal Studies, 'Green budget', February 2014, p 89.

[15] Institute for Fiscal Studies, 'IFS green budget press release', 5 February 2014.

[16] William Keegan, 'Keynes versus household economics', in Roy Hattersley and Kevin Hickson (eds), The socialist way: Social democracy in contemporary Britain (I.B. Tauris, 2013), ch 1.

[17] James Brown and Andrew Hood, 'A survey of the UK benefit system', Institute for Fiscal Studies, November 2012, appendix A.

5 Growth by active government

[1] Rowena Crawford and Paul Johnson, 'The changing composition of public spending', Institute for Fiscal Studies, 2011.

[2] See Peter Hain, Outside in (Biteback, 2012), pp 274–85

[3] Alan S. Blinder, *After the music stopped: The financial crisis, the response, and the work ahead* (Penguin Press, 2013), pp 182–3.

[4] Alistair Darling, *Back from the brink* (Atlantic Books, 2011), pp 1, 154.

[5] *Financial Times* interview, 10 October 2013.

[6] Paul Seabright, *The company of strangers: A natural history of economic life*, rev. edn (Princeton University Press, 2010).

[7] Gregory Clark, *A farewell to alms* (Princeton University Press, 2007), p 5.

[8] Robert Solow, 'A contribution to the theory of economic growth', *Quarterly Journal of Economics* (February 1956): 65–94 and Robert Solow, 'Technical change and the Aggregate Production Function', *Review of Economics and Statistics*, 1957, 39(3), pp 312–20.

[9] J. Bradford DeLong, Econ 1 lectures, spring 2012, 'Growth economics', University of California at Berkeley, 25 April 2012.

[10] Paul Romer, series of papers including 'Endogenous technological change', *Journal of Political Economy* (October 1990). See also Charles I. Jones, *Introduction to economic growth* (W.W. Norton, 2002), pp 97–106.

[11] Adair Turner, 'What do banks do? Why do credit booms and busts occur? What can public policy do about it?', in *The future of finance: The LSE report* (London School of Economics and Political Science, 2010).

[12] Jones, *Introduction to economic growth*, pp 143–7, citing a study published jointly with Robert Hall in 1999.

[13] HM Treasury, 'National infrastructure plan 2013', December 2013, p 3.

[14] 'KPMG: "Government playing catch-up" on infrastructure', BBC Today programme, 4 December 2013 (http://www.bbc.co.uk/news/business-25212872).

[15] As reported by Gill Plimmer and Jim Pickard, *Financial Times*, 20 March 2014, p 17.

[16] World Economic Forum, 'The global competitiveness report 2013–14', p 381.

[17] Ofgem, 'Electricity capacity assessment report 2013', 27 June 2013.

[18] Royal Academy of Engineering, 'GB electricity capacity margin', October 2013, p 7.

[19] 'The Armitt review: An independent review of long term infrastructure planning commissioned for Labour's policy review', September 2013, p 10.

[20] Lord Heseltine of Thenford, *No stone unturned in pursuit of growth* (Department for Business, Innovation and Skills, October 2012), para 4.121.

[21] HM Treasury, *Investing in Britain's future*, June 2013, Cm 8669, para 1.8.

[22] HM Treasury, 'Budget 2010: Securing the recovery', HC 451, March 2010, table C18, p 222.

[23] 'UK government's infrastructure spending plan unveiled', BBC report, 4 December 2013 (bbc.co.uk/news).

[24] Office for National Statistics, 'Construction output, September and Q3 2013', Statistical bulletin, 8 November 2013.

[25] Office for Budget Responsibility, 'Economic and fiscal outlook', Cm 8748, December 2013, table 4.35, p 152.

[26] David Sainsbury, *Progressive capitalism: How to achieve economic growth, liberty and social justice* (Biteback, 2013), p ix.

[27] International Monetary Fund, 'Reassessing the role and modalities of fiscal policy in advanced economies', policy paper, September 2013, figure 10.

[28] Philip Stephens, *Financial Times*, 12 April 2011.

[29] David Miles, Jing Yang and Gilberto Marcheggiano, 'Optimal bank capital', Discussion Paper 31, Bank of England External MPC Unit, April 2011.

[30] Andrew Haldane and Robert May, *Financial Times*, 21 February 2011.

[31] Yalman Onaran, 'US weighs doubling leverage standard for biggest banks', Bloomberg.com, 21 June 2013.

[32] Adair Turner, Chairman of the UK Financial Services Authority, see *Financial Times*, 8 December 2010.

[33] Andrew Smithers, *The road to recovery* (Wiley, 2013).

[34] Phil Thornton, 'A gateway to better lending: Learning from the German model', www.financialdirector.co.uk, 25 February 2014.

[35] Nicholas Tott, 'The case for a British investment bank', Labour Party, 2012.

[36] Jonathan Portes 'The Chancellor accepts the logic of more government-financed investment', niesr.ac.uk/blog, 15 June 2012; Martin Wolf, 'Cameron is consigning the UK to stagnation', FT.com, 17 May 2012 and 'Promoting UK growth through the balance sheet', 18 June 2012.

[37] Alasdair Smith, 'The OBR should speak out on public investment', Financial Times Economists' Forum, 12 July 2012.

[38] Andrew Sheng, 'What was the real cost of the Great Recession?', Institute for New Economic Thinking blog, 19 August 2013.

[39] Stephen Wright, 'Labour's record on financial regulation', Birkbeck, University of London, 26 September 2012, p 31.

[40] Simon Wren-Lewis, 'The "official" cost of austerity', mainly macro blog, 28 October 2013.

[41] Geoff Hodgson, *Conceptualizing capitalism* (University of Chicago Press, 2015), p 245.

[42] Peter Boone and Simon Johnson, 'Will the politics of global moral hazard sink us again?', in *The future of finance*, p 272.

[43] Hugh Williamson, 'Decay in Stoiber's backyard threatens election campaign', *Financial Times*, 14 June 2002.

[44] My first task after the 2001 general election had been to agree to such a directive, following the collapse of the Anglo-German veto once Chancellor Gerhard Schröder withdrew his support for Britain's opposition. It began to take effect in the UK in 2005 by which time neither New Labour nor the TUC were comfortable preaching partnership at work. My own union, the GMB, soon dropped it from its own statement of purpose.

[45] Department of Trade and Industry, 'Prosperity for all: The strategy: Analysis', September 2003, pp 7, 18–21.

[46] William H. Janeway, *Doing capitalism in the innovation economy* (Cambridge University Press, 2012), pp 231–2.

[47] D.C. Mowery, 'Military R&D and innovation', in B.H. Hall and N. Rosenberg (eds), *Handbook of the economics of innovation* (North-Holland, 2010), pp 1222–3, quoted in Janeway, *Doing capitalism in the innovation economy*, p 231.

[48] Global Letter, *Formula 1: A case study in incentives* (www.llewellyn-consulting. com), reported by Larry Elliott, 'When nudge comes to shove, innovation can result', *Guardian*, 24 March 2014.

[49] Paul Stevens, 'Fracking has conquered America ... Here's why it can't happen in Britain', *Observer*, 19 January 2014, p 34.

[50] John Reed, 'The Israeli take on start-up risk', *Financial Times*, 19 February 2014.

[51] Mariana Mazzucato, *The entrepreneurial state* (Anthem Press, 2013) and 'Let's rethink the idea of the state: It must be a catalyst for big, bold ideas', *Observer*, 15 December 2013.

[52] Janeway, *Doing capitalism in the innovation economy*, p 87.

[53] John Edmonds, 'International competition: Sounding a retreat?' *Financial Times*, 16 March 1990.

[54] Ha-Joon Chang, 'Decent wages or a breadline economy: It's a no-brainer', *Guardian*, 8 November 2013.

6 Fraternity, cooperation, trade unionism

[1] *Workers' playtime* was the BBC radio variety programme broadcast three times a week live from factory canteens between 1941 and 1964, and not to be confused with *Music while you work*, the non-stop light music programme broadcast twice daily by BBC radio on workdays between 1940 and 1967 to help keep up the pace of production.

[2] David Metcalf, 'Transformation of British industrial relations? Institutions, conduct and outcomes 1980–1990', LSE Centre for Economic Performance, March 1993.

[3] Larry Elliott, 'Britain needs its trade unions more than ever', *Guardian*, 23 June 2014.

[4] See Peter Hain, *Political strikes* (Penguin, 1986).

[5] Anne Collins, 'Song', in Louise Bernikow (ed), *The world split open: Women poets 1552–1950* (Women's Press, 1979), p 65.

[6] David Metcalf, 'British unions: Resurgence or perdition?', Work Foundation, January 2005.

[7] Anne Perkins, 'Collective failure', *Guardian*, 22 April 2006.

[8] See Hain, *Political strikes*.

[9] Michael Kumhof and Romain Rancière, 'Inequality, leverage and crises', IMF working paper, 2010 (https://www.imf.org/external/pubs/ft/wp/2010/wp10268.pdf).

[10] Elliott, 'Britain needs its trade unions more than ever'; Ian Aitken, 'Captain fails to score so a bigger boost must go in hard', *Tribune*, 27 June 2014.

[11] TUC, 'A perfect union? What workers want from unions', August 2003.

[12] GMB, 'Your collective voice at work', special report to the GMB Congress, 2003.

[13] Hetan Shah and Sue Goss (eds), *Democracy and the public realm* (Compass and Lawrence & Wishart, 2007), p 72.

[14] Brian Groom and Gill Plimmer, 'G4S fiasco puts business in dock', *Financial Times*, 20 July 2012.

[15] Brian Groom,'Nestlé move on living wage hailed as "significant milestone"', *Financial Times*, 30 June 2014.

[16] 'Workplace representation' (http://www.worker-participation.eu/National-Industrial-Relations).

7 But what *sort* of socialist state?

[1] See http://www.bluelabour.org/.

[2] John Harris, *Guardian*, 6 January 2014.

[3] Jesse Norman, *The big society* (University of Buckingham Press, 2010).

[4] Noam Chomsky, *For reasons of state* (Fontana, 1973).

[5] Fenner Brockway, *Britain's first socialists* (Quartet, 1980).

[6] Geoff Hodgson, *Conceptualizing capitalism* (University of Chicago Press, 2015).

[7] See Barbara Taylor, *Eve and the New Jerusalem* (Virago, 1983).

[8] Although it was replaced in 1995 because it was felt to be an old fashioned charter for mass nationalisation, the text of Clause IV was actually capable of a more libertarian interpretation: 'To secure for the workers by hand or by brain the dual fruits of their industry and the most equitable distribution thereon that may be possible upon the basis of the common ownership of the means of production, distribution and exchange, and the best obtainable system of *popular administration and control* of each industry or service' (emphasis added).

[9] John Gyford, *The politics of local socialism* (Allen & Unwin, 1985).

[10] G.D.H. Cole, *Self government in industry* (G. Bell, 1917).

[11] Anthony Wright, *G.D.H. Cole and socialist democracy* (Clarendon Press, 1976).

[12] Aneurin Bevan, *In place of fear* (Quartet, 1990 edn).

[13] Sheila Rowbotham, Lynne Segal and Hilary Wainwright, *Beyond the fragments* (Merlin Press, 1979).

[14] Lynne Segal, *Is the future female?* (Virago, 1987).

[15] Provided that their decentralising case is not interpreted merely as a mechanism for coping with constrained public spending levels – a sort of New Labour-lite version of the Tory 'Big Society' – then for some interesting policy examples see Kayte Lawton, Graeme Cooke and Nick Pearce, *The condition of Britain* (Institute of Public Policy Research, 2014), pp 39–52.

[16] Hugo Young memorial lecture, *Guardian*, 10 February 2014.

[17] Labour Party, 'Devolution and regional government in England: A discussion document for the labour movement', September 1975. Under Jim Callaghan's leadership the Labour Party also issued 'Regional authorities and local government reform: A consultation document for the labour movement' in July 1977.

[18] Gordon Brown, *My Scotland, our Britain: A future worth sharing* (Simon & Schuster, 2014).

[19] Independent Commission on Funding and Finance for Wales, *Fairness and accountability: A new funding settlement for Wales* (http://wales.gov.uk/funding/financereform/report/?lang=en).

[20] Royal Commission on the Constitution, Cmnd 5460 (HMSO, 1973), para 531.

[21] For a short summary of the main options for achieving that see Brown, *My Scotland, our Britain*, p 253.

[22] Brown, *My Scotland, our Britain*, p 262.

[23] The term libertarianism has also been appropriated by some on the New Right, and in America it is almost always associated with extreme individualist and pro-market views. For instance, Ron Paul called himself a libertarian and was the Libertarian Party nominee for US President in 1988. He ran in the Republican Party primaries in 2008 and 2012, was a Republican Member of Congress from Texas until 2013, and is regarded as the 'intellectual godfather' of the Tea Party movement.

[24] Ed Miliband, 'The future is local – if Labour is elected' (http://www.theguardian.com/commentisfree/2014/jul/06/future-is-local-labour-reverse-centralisation-ed-miliband).

[25] Stephen Ball, 'Free schools: Our education system has been dismembered in pursuit of choice', *Guardian*, 23 October 2013.

[26] Despite these exemplary sentiments, however, he also held British parliamentary democracy in fair contempt. See Ralph Miliband, *Parliamentary socialism*, 2nd edn (Merlin Press, 1973).

[27] Ralph Miliband, *Socialism for a sceptical age* (Polity, 1994).

[28] Geoff Hodgson, *The democratic economy* (Penguin, 1984).

[29] See Hodgson, *Conceptualizing capitalism*.

[30] Will Hutton, *The state we're in* (Cape, 1995).

[31] Bryan Gould, *A future for socialism* (Cape, 1989).

[32] Michael Meacher, *Diffusing power* (Pluto, 1992).

[33] See Matthew Goodwin and Robert Ford, *Revolt on the right* (Routledge, 2014).

8 A new internationalism

[1] Mark Leonard, 'Making Britain China-proof', in Douglas Alexander and Ian Kearns (eds), *Influencing tomorrow* (Guardian Books, 2013), p 39.

[2] Paul Collier, *The bottom billion: Why the poorest countries are failing and what can be done about it* (Oxford University Press, 2008).

[3] Reported by John Vidal, *Guardian*, 3 July 2014.

[4] See Peter Hain, *The end of foreign policy?* (Fabian Society, Green Alliance and Royal Institute of International Affairs, January 2001).

[5] G. John Ikenberry and Anne-Marie Slaughter, *Forging a world of liberty under law: U.S. national security in the 21st century* (Princeton University Press, 2006).

[6] Alexander and Kearns, *Influencing tomorrow*, pp 286–7.

[7] Lawrence Korb and Max Hoffman, 'What is power in the 21st century?' in Alexander and Kearns, *Influencing tomorrow*, p 245.

[8] Reported by Larry Elliott, *Guardian*, 20 January 2014.

[9] See my lecture at the University of South Wales, 20 March 2014 (http://caspp.southwales.ac.uk/peter-hain/).

[10] Nicholas Stern, *A blueprint for a safer planet* (Bodley Head, 2009).
[11] Reported in the *Observer*, 23 March 2014.
[12] See Jeffrey Mazo, 'Climate conflict: How will global warming threaten our world?', in Alexander and Kearns, *Influencing tomorrow*, pp 182–201.
[13] Paul G. Harris, *What's wrong with climate politics and how to fix it* (Polity, 2013).

9 Britain in Europe

[1] Douglas Alexander and Ian Kearns (eds), *Influencing tomorrow* (Guardian Books, 2013), pp 129–30.
[2] Mark Leonard and Hans Kundnani, 'Think again: European decline', *Foreign Policy*, 29 April 2013.
[3] See Paul Mason, *Why it's kicking off everywhere* (Verso, 2012).
[4] Ha-Joon Chang, 'We need to focus on the quality of our life at work', *Guardian*, 23 December 2013.
[5] Figures, rounded, taken from House of Commons Library note 1309-174.
[6] The story is brilliantly catalogued by Hugo Young, *This blessed plot* (Macmillan, 1998). See also Roger Liddle, *The Europe dilemma* (I.B. Tauris, 2014) for an insightful analysis of Britain's mercurial European relationship.
[7] In Steven Blockmans (ed), *Differentiated integration in the EU: From the inside looking out* (http://www.ceps.eu/book/differentiated-integration-eu-%E2%80%93-inside-looking-out).
[8] Richard Corbett, 'A Labour view on Europe', 17 September 2013 (http://labourmovement.eu/2013/09/a-labour-view-on-europe/).
[9] See Charles Grant, *How to build a modern European Union* (Centre for European Reform, 2013).
[10] See Corbett, 'A Labour view on Europe'.
[11] Haroon Siddique, 'Figures show extent of NHS reliance on foreign nationals', *Guardian*, 26 January 2014.
[12] Liddle, *The Europe dilemma*, p 234.

10 Refounding Labour

[1] Peter Mair, *Ruling the void: The hollowing of Western democracy* (Verso, 2013), pp 34, 42.
[2] Mair, *Ruling the void*, pp 73, 98.
[3] See 'Case studies', Labour Values (http://labourvalues.org.uk/category/case-studies/) for more information on the how, who, what and why of these campaigns.
[4] Electoral Commission, 'Great Britain's electoral registers 2011', news release, 14 December 2011.
[5] For more on how to counter Conservative efforts to drive down turnout see 'How to deal with the challenge of voter registration changes', LabourList, 17 December 2013 (http://labourlist.org/2013/12/how-to-deal-with-the-challenge-of-voter-registration-changes/).

[6] 'Ed Miliband launches voter registration drive', 5 December 2012 (http://www.huffingtonpost.co.uk/2012/05/12/ed-miliband-launches-voter-registration-drive_n_1511612.html).

[7] 'Hung Parliaments look set to stay', 14 September 2010 (www.hansardsociety.org.uk/hung-parliaments-look-set-to-stay/).

[8] See Andrew Adonis, *5 days in May: The coalition and beyond* (Biteback, 2013).

[9] For a contemporary though critical analysis see Peter Hain (ed), *Community politics* (John Calder, 1976).

[10] For more on the statistical proof of this approach see 'Lessons from recent GOTV [get out the vote] experiments', Institution for Social and Policy Studies, Yale University (http://gotv.research.yale.edu/?q=node/10).

11 Faster, sustainable growth

[1] David Laws, 'Cuts: Our best decision', *Guardian*, 18 January 2011.

[2] Cited by Jonathan Portes, 'What Osborne won't admit: Growth has increased because of slower cuts', *New Statesman*, 10 September 2013.

[3] Simon Wren-Lewis, 'The left and economic policy', mainly macro blog, 31 March 2014.

[4] Simon Wren-Lewis, 'Osborne's plan B', mainly macro blog, 17 December 2013.

[5] 'Economic strategy - The IMF', memorandum to Cabinet by the Secretary of State for Foreign and Commonwealth Affairs, CP(76) 118, 29 November 1976 (http://filestore.nationalarchives.gov.uk/pdfs/small/cab-129-193-cp-76-118-8.pdf).

[6] Cash limits put ceilings on how much government departments could spend in the coming year, meaning they would run out of funds before year-end if they overspent. The effect was for them to hold something back and finish the year underspending their budget. George Osborne began to anticipate such underspends in his annual budgets, adding to the downward pressure on public spending.

[7] Ha-Joon Chang, 'Think welfare spending is spiralling out of control? You're wrong', *Guardian*, 28 March 2014.

[8] Martin Wolf, 'Britain's needlessly slow recovery', *Financial Times*, 6 December 2013.

[9] HM Treasury, 'Budget 2014', HC 1104, March 2014, para B.29, chart B.4.

[10] '2030 vision', final report of the Fabian Commission on Future Spending Choices, October 2013, pp 7–10.

[11] Nicolas Crafts, 'Escaping liquidity traps: Lessons from the UK's 1930s escape', VoxEU.org, 12 May 2013.

[12] Stephanie Flanders, 'Cheer up Britain, things really are going to get better', *Financial Times*, 7 December 2013.

[13] Martin Wolf, 'How the financial crisis changed our world', 2013 Wincott memorial lecture (http://www.wincott.co.uk/lectures/2013.html).

[14] John Van Reenen, 'The man from the IMF, he says: "Increase public spending on investment and follow the LSE Growth Commission"', 22 May 2013 (http://blogs.lse.ac.uk/politicsandpolicy/archives/33667).

[15] Jonathan Portes, 'The pasty tax could pay for a £30 billion infrastructure programme: Four charts show why history will judge us harshly', 12 May 2012 (http://niesr.ac.uk).

[16] TUC, '£30bn infrastructure spend could boost growth and reduce long-term debt levels', 10 May 2013 (www.tuc.org.uk/economic-issues).

[17] Paul Krugman, 'What it would have taken', 25 March 2014 (http://krugman.blogs.nytimes.com/2014/03/25/what-it-would-have-taken/).

[18] Labour's 1976 Development Land Tax Act put a charge on the development value realised from land. It applied from August 1976 until scrapped by the Tories in March 1985.

[19] John Muellbauer, 'It is time for the state to jump on the property bandwagon', *Financial Times*, 3 April 2014.

[20] 'The Armitt review: An independent review of long term infrastructure planning commissioned for Labour's policy review', September 2013, p 13.

[21] Martin Wolf, 'Promoting UK growth through the balance sheet', Martin Wolf's Exchange blog, FT.com, 18 June 2012.

[22] Professor Alasdair Smith, 'The OBR should speak out on public investment', FT Economists' Forum blog, FT.com, 12 July 2012.

[23] 'Forget our AAA rating, £10bn more borrowing could deliver growth', 12 February 2013 (http://www.telegraph.co.uk/finance/comment/9866283/Forget-our-AAA-rating-10bn-more-borrowing-could-deliver-growth.html).

[24] *The Economist*, 7 December 2013, p 16.

[25] Aditya Chakrabortty, 'London's economic boom leaves rest of Britain behind', *Guardian*, 23 October 2013.

[26] Ed Cox and Bill Davies, *Still on the wrong track: An updated analysis of transport infrastructure spending* (IPPR North, June 2013), figure 1.3.

[27] James Pickford, '"Dark Star" sucks more wealth away from the rest', *Financial Times*, 20 January 2014.

[28] Gill Plimmer and Jim Pickard, 'Industry rails at infrastructure "damp squib"', *Financial Times*, 20 March 2014.

[29] Commission on Social Justice, *Social justice: Strategies for national renewal* (IPPR/Vintage, 1994), p 135.

[30] 'Investing for prosperity', LSE Growth Commission report, 2013, p 16.

[31] Howard Davies, 'A social market for training', Social Market Foundation, 1993, cited in Commission on Social Justice, *Social justice*, p 134.

[32] Mick Fletcher, Visiting Research Fellow at the Institute of Education, in *FE Week*, 8 November 2013.

12 A fairer, more equal society

[1] IFS, *Taxation of wealth and wealth transfers*, Appendices by Robin Boadway, Emma Chamberlain and Carl Emmerson, p 2.

[2] Richard Wilkinson and Kate Pickett, *The spirit level: Why more equal societies almost always do better* (Allen Lane, 2009), p 17.

[3] Jonathan Cribb, Andrew Hood, Robert Joyce and David Phillips, 'Living standards, poverty and inequality in the UK: 2013', Institute for Fiscal Studies, 2013, pp 3 and 34–5.

[4] Office for National Statistics, 'The effects of taxes and benefits on household income 2011–12', 10 July 2013.

[5] Deborah Mattinson, *Talking to a brick wall* (Biteback, 2010), pp 19, 76.

[6] Paul Krugman makes this point in respect of the US in his *New York Times* blog 'The conscience of a liberal', see his 'Inequality as a defining challenge', 14 December 2013 (http://krugman.blogs.nytimes.com).

[7] Office for National Statistics, 'The effects of taxes and benefits on household income 2011–12'.

[8] See replies to questions in the House of Lords, *Lords Hansard*, HC Deb, 12 July 2010: cWA107 and HC Deb, 5 Feb 2014: cWA68-69.

[9] Institute for Fiscal Studies, 'UK Budget 2003', p 61.

[10] Thomas Piketty, *Capital in the twenty-first century* (Belknap Press, 2014), p 513.

[11] Independent Commission on Fees, '18,000 fewer mature students apply to university since fees increase', September 2013, and 'Working class gender gap widens in first year of £9000 tuition fees' (http://www.independentcommissionfees.org.uk/wordpress/?page_id=47).

[12] 'Tuition fees: Teetering on the brink', editorial, *Guardian*, 22 March 2014.

[13] John Denham MP, 'The cost of higher education', Royal Society of Arts lecture, 16 January 2014 (http://www.thersa.org/__data/assets/pdf_file/0003/1538229/RSA-lecture-Higher-Education-Finance.pdf).

[14] 'A graduate tax: Would it work?', Million+, 2010, p 2 (http://www.millionplus.ac.uk/documents/reports/GRAD_TAX_REPORT_FINAL.pdf).

[15] 'Higher education funding in England: Do the alternatives add up?', Million+, 2013 (http://www.millionplus.ac.uk/documents/reports/HE_Funding_in_England_-_Do_the_alternatives_add_up.pdf).

[16] House of Commons Library 2013/11/161-SGS.

[17] Ha-Joon Chang, 'Think welfare spending is spiralling out of control? You're wrong', *Guardian*, 28 March 2014.

[18] Christina Beatty and Steve Fothergill, 'Hitting the poorest places hardest: The local and regional impact of welfare reform', Sheffield Hallam University, 2013 (http://www.shu.ac.uk/research/cresr/sites/shu.ac.uk/files/hitting-poorest-places-hardest_0.pdf).

[19] Simon Wren-Lewis, 'Inequality and the media', mainly macro blog, 9 March 2014.

[20] Office for Budget Responsibility, 'Economic and fiscal outlook – December 2013'.

[21] House of Commons Library figures.

[22] Department for Work and Pensions, 'Benefit expenditure and caseload tables', December 2013.

[23] Office for Budget Responsibility, 'Economic and fiscal outlook – December 2013'.

[24] Andy Burnham (ed), *A vision of whole person care for a 21st century health and care service* (Fabian Society, 2013), pp x, 8, xiii.

[25] Sharif Ismail, Ruth Thorlby and Holly Holder, 'Social care for older people', QualityWatch, 2014 (http://www.qualitywatch.org.uk/focus-on/social-care-older-people).

[26] For an excellent overview see Kayte Lawton, Graeme Cooke and Nick Pearce, *The condition of Britain* (Institute for Public Policy Research, 2014).

[27] Although profoundly flawed, an eloquent example of this neoliberal perspective is John Micklethwait and Adrian Wooldridge, *The fourth revolution: The global race to reinvent the state* (Allen Lane, 2014)

13 A future for Labour

[1] David Denver, 'The results: How Britain voted', in Andrew Geddes and Jonathan Tonge (eds), *Britain votes 2010* (Oxford University Press and Hansard Society, 2010), p 12, table 3.

[2] David Denver, Christopher Carman and Robert Johns, *Elections and voters in Britain* (Palgrave Macmillan, 2012), p 50, table 2.7.

[3] Sunder Kadwala, 'Why VAT on private school fees would be a fair way to fund the pupil premium', Next Left, Fabian Society blog, 22 December 2010.

[4] Polly Toynbee and David Walker, *The verdict* (Granta, 2010).

[5] Interview with Robert Solow, Washington Center for Equitable Growth, 20 November 2013 (www.youtube.com/watch?v=jLzY6Bc1UYM).

[6] Joseph Stiglitz, *The price of inequality* (W.W. Norton, 2013).

[7] Jonathan D. Ostry, Andrew Berg and Charalambos G. Tsangarides, 'Redistribution, inequality, and growth', IMF Staff Discussion Note, February 2014.

[8] IMF, 'Fiscal policy and income inequality', policy paper, 23 January 2014.

[9] Oxfam GB, 'A tale of two Britains: Inequality in the UK', 17 March 2014.

[10] Ed Pilkington, *Guardian*, 2 January 2014.

[11] Ed Miliband, Hugo Young lecture, 10 February 2014 (http://labourlist.org/2014/02/ed-milibands-hugo-young-lecture-full-text/).

[12] *Guardian*, 18 March 2014.

[13] Polly Toynbee, 'As the cuts bleed harder, the cruel Tory truth will emerge', *Guardian*, 31 December 2011.

[14] Geoffrey Goodman, *Tribune*, 4 September 2009, reviewing Roger Liddle and Patrick Diamond (eds), *Beyond New Labour: The future of social democracy in Britain* (Politico's, August 2009).

Index

Page references for notes are followed by n